The Lecherous Professor

The Lecherous Professor

Sexual Harassment on Campus *Second Edition*

BILLIE WRIGHT DZIECH

LINDA WEINER

UNIVERSITY OF ILLINOIS PRESS
Urbana and Chicago

Grateful acknowledgment is made for permission to reprint the following: student letter to Marlyn Lewis, assistant dean of Harvard College, and letter to student from Marlyn Lewis, as reprinted in the 1982 Commencement Issue of *The Harvard Crimson,* by permission of *The Harvard Crimson;* six lines from "When We Dead Awaken," from *Poems, Selected and New, 1950-74,* by Adrienne Rich, reprinted by permission of the author and W. W. Norton & Co., Inc., © 1975, 1973, 1971, 1969, 1966 by W. W. Norton & Co., Inc.; "Statement on Sexual Harassment, American Council on Education," April 1989, by permission of Sheldon Elliott Steinbach, vice president and general counsel, American Council of Education; "Presidential Statement and Policy on Sexual Harassment, University of Minnesota," 20 January 1989, by permission of the President's Office and the University General Counsel, University of Minnesota; "Institutional Committee Statement and Policy on Sexual Harassment, Gettysburg College," 24 February 1986, by permission of Robert Nordvall, associate provost, Gettysburg College; "Sexual Harassment Survey, University of Illinois at Urbana-Champaign," by permission of Deborah Allen.

Except in the discussions of well-publicized cases, the names of students, professors, departments, colleges, universities, and other identifying features have been changed.

Illini Books edition, 1990

© 1984 by Billie Wright Dziech and Linda Weiner
Second edition ©1990 by the Board of Trustees of the University of Illinois
Manufactured in the United States of America
P 5 4 3 2 1

Reprinted by arrangement with Beacon Press

This book is printed on acid-free paper.

Library of Congress Cataloging-in-Publication Data

Dziech, Billie Wright, 1941–
    The lecherous professor : sexual harassment on campus / Billie
Wright Dziech, Linda Weiner. — 2nd ed.
      p.   cm.
    Includes bibliographical references.
    ISBN 0-252-06118-7 (alk. paper)
    1. Sexual harassment in universities and colleges—United States.
2. Women college students—United States. 3. Sexual harassment of
women—Law and legislation—United States. 4. College teachers—
United States. I. Weiner, Linda. II. Title.
LC212.862.D95 1990
370.19′345—dc20   90-10898
                                                       CIP

for Robbie, Erica, Katie, Jeff, and Daniel,
who deserve better

CONTENTS

ACKNOWLEDGMENTS

We would like to acknowledge those whose activities, assistance, and support have contributed to this work. Our collaboration as coauthors has been enriched by the broader collaboration among all those who devoted their attention and intelligence to the problem of sexual harassment of women students in higher education.

We are indebted to the individuals and organizations that have made sexual harassment on campus a public concern: the Working Woman's Institute, the National Advisory Council on Women's Educational Programs, Bernice Sandler and the staff of the Project on the Status and Education of Women of the American Association of Colleges, Donna Shavlik and the staff of the Office of Women in Higher Education of the American Council on Education, Catharine MacKinnon, Lin Farley, the Modern Language Association's Commission on the Status of Women in the Profession, Phyllis Crocker, the American Council on Education Leadership Seminars on Sexual Harassment, and the National Association of Women Deans and Counselors and its *Journal.* These people and their publications have fostered information and awareness that is realistic without being cynical and that aided our efforts enormously.

We benefited from many who freely shared their expertise, perspectives, and professional experiences: Regina Sofer, Claire Guthrie, Linda Lorimer, Ed Hammond, Bea Larsen, Claudia Geraci, Mary Ellen Ashley, Dee Graham, Marty Davis, Kitty Uetz, and Donna Carroll.

We are deeply grateful for the patient and generous assistance given by Susan Novik, Tom Wagner, David Hartleb, Bill Vilter, and John McCall. Their expertise and support gave greater meaning to the words "professional" and "colleague."

Kathy Wright Schear, Sharon Snow, Lynnette White, Mary Ellen Stegman, Alice Suhr, Bonnie Thomas, and Judy Morgan provided invaluable assistance with the manuscript.

Our editor for the first edition, Joanne Wyckoff of Beacon Press, nurtured and encouraged us with insight, humor, and concern. Carole Appel, our editor for this second edition by the University of Illinois Press, lent her expertise and enthusiasm to this new phase of the project.

We owe a unique debt to the women whose stories provide the lifeblood of this book. We learned from their experiences, their insights, and their courage. We hope we have conveyed their messages with the integrity and trust they deserve.

We are especially grateful to C. Michael Curtis, who believed in the book, and more than anyone, encouraged us to see it through.

And, of course, our personal thanks:

To Mike Curtis, whose encouragement and friendship have turned my books into realities; to Linda Yeager and Mabel Gilliam, who keep me organized and laughing; to my sister, Kathy, to my father and to Carol, Kate, Jeffrey, Daniel, and Neal, whose love and loyalty are part of all I do; to my husband and son, who share my days and are all I ever wished for; and in memory of my mother, whose strength and sacrifice made my career possible.

Billie Dziech

To the memory of my parents; to Phil, Martha, Susan, Linda, Carol, and Chuck, who provide kinship and caring; to Erica, who is proud of mom's work; and, always, to Ted, with love.

Linda Weiner

PREFACE TO THE SECOND EDITION

When *The Lecherous Professor* was researched and written almost ten years ago, sexual harassment was just emerging as an issue in higher education. The questions were basic: how should it be defined, who were its victims, who was responsible, what priority did it deserve, and—sometimes—was it really a problem? The worries ranged from fears of encouraging false complaints to how to protect complainants from retaliation. With only a handful of public cases, new federal guidelines, and limited legal precedents, the fundamental need on most campuses was for information and sound policies and procedures.

In these past ten years there has been progress, but the discussion in *The Lecherous Professor* is still relevant and necessary. This second edition includes an updated selected bibliography and new materials in the appendixes. In this preface, we briefly note major areas of progress and developments in sexual harassment. We also take the opportunity, in separate notes, to reflect individually on our experiences and perceptions concerning sexual harassment since we wrote the first edition.

- Most colleges and universities probably now have established policies prohibiting sexual harassment and have developed procedures for formal complaints. Many also have informal systems that include advising and mediation for addressing sexual harassment. Because the number of formal and informal complaints remains minuscule compared to the total incidence of sexual harassment, the issue for many has become how to get victims to come forward and use the systems. Some believe there may never be a dramatic increase in actual complaints and that success in confronting sexual harassment may reside in educating and training administrators, faculty, and students to be more aware and assertive in dealing with the problem.

• Higher education has had more experience with sexual harassment; many more campuses have had their first formal cases, dealt with victims and harassers, and imposed disciplinary sanctions. Theoretical discussions have been transformed into educational programs; excellent pamphlets, workshop designs, and videotapes are available as models and resources. Because more people are more knowledgeable, it is now easier to secure informed guidance from colleagues, external consultants, other institutions, professional networks, and national organizations.

• Although campus harassment cases have not often resulted in legal action, educators have closely analyzed litigation originating in the workplace. A survey of Fortune 500 companies found that 90 percent had received sexual harassment complaints; more than 30 percent of these companies have been sued, 25 percent more than once. Detailed discussion of legal issues was and is beyond the scope of *The Lecherous Professor,* but it is worth noting that *Broderick* v. *Ruder* and *Meritor Savings Bank, FSB,* v. *Vinson* have alerted higher education to the dangers of sexually hostile work environments. Higher education associations and campus sexual harassment programs are evaluating the implications for the educational environment.

• In the past there were sporadic publications on sexual harassment, but now articles of varying types and quality appear regularly. Theoretical and empirical scholarship on sexual harassment is expanding. In psychology, philosophy, education, and law, these efforts are further refining our understanding of the dynamics of sexual harassment and its relationships to broader social issues.

• *Peer harassment* has emerged as a term that groups student-to-student problems such as sexist language, date rape, hostile living or social environments, and sexual harassment. *Peer harassment* is a useful concept that efficiently draws attention to serious problems. At the same time, it should not be used to overlook or forget the serious problem of sexual harassment of students by nonpeers.

• Student-faculty dating continues to be a thorny and controversial issue, and institutional approaches and policies are extremely varied. The University of Minnesota policy, included among the revised appendixes, offers a constructive model that addresses conflict-of-interest principles, student-faculty role differentials, and the "mutual consent" defense.

We wrote *The Lecherous Professor* because we hoped to answer questions, increase awareness, and encourage constructive remedies. As the following authors' notes indicate, we do not always share a common approach to the issue. Nevertheless, we are in agreement on the most crucial points. One of these is that sexual harassment has not disappeared from our campuses and that development of policies and programs has not eliminated the problem—and perhaps never will. But at least the issue is out of the closet and in the public consciousness, so we can discuss it, confront it, and, we hope, reduce its harmful effects on students.

Billie Wright Dziech
Linda Weiner

AUTHOR'S NOTE: BILLIE WRIGHT DZIECH

When *The Lecherous Professor* was published in 1984, no one anticipated the media response. The book undeniably had its hour upon the stage. Sexually harassed collegians were the focus of publications as diverse as *The Chronicle of Higher Education* and *People* magazines and of local and national interviewers like Oprah Winfrey, Bryant Gumbel, and Phil Donahue. Given the book's heady reception, I was naive enough to assume that the public would rise in indignation, descend upon America's colleges and universities, and demand dignity and justice for female students.

That didn't happen. Parents, public officials, and students themselves raised little clamor. Since the book had reproached academicians for their "irresponsibility" and "irresolution" in dealing with sexual harassment, one might logically assume that if consumers of higher education were unwilling or unable to contend with the issue, it was destined for oblivion, consigned to become simply another lost crusade by impractical academicians. But that assumption also proved inaccurate. Today the topic of harassment is as recurring and sometimes controversial as it was six years ago. Some institutions still struggle with denial, with refusal to admit the existence of the problem or of their legal and ethical responsibilities to deal with it. On the other hand, the most progressive have risked contention and acrimony to discuss and frequently enact policies inconceivable in 1984. The majority are somewhere in between. Their presidents have made statements defining and disavowing sexual harassment: they also have established rarely used grievance procedures and initiated sincere but inconsistent attempts at education and communication.

Probably none of these scenarios is gratifying to zealots or to those unfamiliar with academe; but for me, they are nothing short of miraculous. Having once compared progress in academe to the movements of "a paralytic snail," I'm grateful now that our editor convinced me to delete the phrase from the original manuscript. And I'm amazed and gratified that my profession, though far from perfect, has had the courage to struggle with this issue that extends to the very essence of our individual and collective attitudes toward gender, social decorum, and pedagogy.

I like to think that this book has contributed to changes in the academic climate and that it will be instrumental in helping to move backward institutions into the mainstream, but I suspect that the latter will be accomplished more by pressure from enlightened faculty and administrators responding to the leadership of other institutions, professional associations, and organizations like the American Council on Education. Nevertheless, I'm proud of the contribution *The Lecherous Professor* has made. There are, of course, alterations or additions I would make if it were possible. Some are more crucial than others, but all of the following reveal something about my personal experiences and the progress of academe and society over the last decade.

- *The title* I might change it. Too many assume that it's a sweeping indictment of all males in the profession instead of an attempt to differentiate the offenders—or, as we originally called them, the "outlaws"—from the vast majority of male academicians, who are anything but "lecherous." My own experiences at the University of Cincinnati and other institutions around the country confirm this assertion. There were innumerable times when I considered abandoning the writing project, but three male academicians—Tom Wagner, the university's senior vice provost; David Hartleb, my dean; and Bill Vilter, my department head—

were always there to support and encourage me. By now I have traveled thousands of miles and spoken at more colleges and universities than I can remember, and everywhere there are male faculty and administrators just as concerned about sexual harassment as I. They have helped me to retain my original conviction that genuine change can occur only when this problem is approached as a professional rather than a gender issue. Men have both the right and the responsibility to participate in the process of eliminating harassment on the nation's campuses and I believe that many have and will make a difference.

● *Discussion of "the mutual consent" or "consenting adult" myth* I wish that in 1984 we had been able to report the experiences of institutions like the Universities of Minnesota and Illinois, which have developed strong statements discouraging faculty-student relationships. For all the uproar discussions of "consent" have evoked on some campuses, it appears to me an absurdly vacuous issue. Choosing to become a member of a profession means committing oneself to adherence to its ethics. Physical intimacy with students is not now and never has been acceptable behavior for academicians. It cannot be defended or explained away by evoking fantasies of devoted professors and sophisticated students being denied the right to "true love." Where power differentials exist, there can be no "mutual consent." The infinitesimal number of cases in which professors/teaching assistants and students do develop genuine and seemingly abiding attractions can, as the book suggests, be treated on individual bases without denying students protection from the campus lotharios who claim "consent" every time they seek to bed a confused or intimidated victim.

● *Differentiation of "sexual harassment and sexual hassle"* The latter is a term we invented to describe the converse of sexual harassment. We needed a way to acknowledge the existence of seductive female students and yet to distinguish their limited power and numbers from the enormous authority and threat of sexual harassers. If I had it to do again, I would expand this section of the book and insist that it be printed in italics. By now I have lost track of the times I have responded to interviewers and individuals in audiences that there *are* seductive students but that they pose, in both efficacy and quantity, insignificant threats to the professoriate. "Even if a young woman rips off her clothes, throws herself naked across a professor's desk, and begs him to 'take' her in exchange for an 'A,' " I have said, "it is his professional responsibility to reject her advance, to encourage her to seek psychological help, and to advise her about appropriate procedures for attaining meritorious grades in his class." I don't think those words have made a modicum of difference to individuals who choose to believe the worst of both women and men, and I fully expect that, despite the insignificance of the problem, a best-seller on the misfortunes of sexually "harassed" professors is near at hand.

- *The attention devoted to verbal or "gender harassment"* So much interest, perhaps including ours, has centered on the high visibility, physically motivated forms of harassment that people are tempted to overlook or minimize the other, equally insidious and damaging forms of imposition. The woman who has been degraded by an undesired touch or kiss has the consolation of apprehending her problem and its cause, yet there may be equal or greater peril in the plight of a woman who, day after day, endures references to her inadequacies and inferiority. I wish we had made this point more emphatically, as does "The Classroom Climate: A Chilly One for Women?" a paper published by the Project on the Status and Education of Woman of the Association of American Colleges.

- *The emphasis on victimization of female students by male professors* On the one hand, our decision to concentrate on the epidemic form of sexual harassment appears wise. Gay and peer harassment involve very complex and dissimilar dynamics and deserve thorough discussion in works devoted solely to each. Sexual harassment of male students by female professors is, while still quantitatively insignificant, so similar to that upon which we concentrated that the discussion in the original manuscript is comprehensive enough to cover it.

  On the other hand, male students are harmed by sexual harassment in ways that we did not consider in 1984, and such victimization has been of increasing concern to me—partially because the problem has received so little attention and, equally important, because my own son is now a college student. Lack of interest in the plight of males not only suggests additional transgression by academe but also contributes to the lukewarm reception that the issue of sexual harassment has had among students. Singling women out as almost the exclusive victims of the offense eliminates approximately half the student population. The numbers are further depleted by the reluctance of many females to respond vigorously to a cause that is identified with only their gender. If sexual harassment is not gripping business on the nation's campuses, the reason is, in part, that few people recognize its damage to indirectly affected third parties, who may be either male or female. Female students may be made to feel intimidated, inferior, or impotent when confronted with a harasser's behavior toward a victim (whether the victim "consents" or not).

Nevertheless, male students, the "forgotten" victims of sexual harassment, also experience feelings of frustration and powerlessness. Protesting lewd remarks by a male authority figure is extremely forbidding for women and may be doubly so for males who find the classroom environment threatening and hostile. Yet another difficulty that may emerge for males is that they may misinterpret victims' fear and passivity as assent and encouragement. A subtle lesson the classroom experience may teach them is disrespect and even animosity for females, who appear to enjoy advantages and privileges males lack. Male students who admire and identify with a college professor may also be adversely affected if the object of respect happens to be a sexual harasser and the student assumes that his behavior is appropriate and perhaps worthy of imitation. One of our objectives in eliminating sexual harassment on campus is to provide students with a standard for conduct in the workplace and their personal lives. That lesson is as imperative for males as it is for females, and the struggle to overcome this social ill cannot be genuinely successful until we recognize its damage to male as well as female students.

● *Addition of discussion on improving reportage of sexual harassment* When the issue first attracted national attention, predictions of calamity on the campus were everywhere. According to the prognosticators, attention to sexual harassment would create a national epidemic of capricious complaints. Those prophecies were totally erroneous. Most institutions do not attempt to quantify the number of informal complaints they receive, but there is general agreement that even those with five-figure enrollments hear fewer than five formal complaints a year.

Students' reluctance to report sexual harassment has been variously interpreted. Some regard the low reportage rate as proof that the statistics are exaggerated or that the victims of sexual harassment are not sufficiently disturbed to feel the need to complain. Others naively assume that low grievance rates imply low incidence of sexual harassment. But surveys and anecdotal evidence are by now decisive enough to prove that low reportage does not suggest that "all is well"; rather, low reportage demonstrates that the majority of victims deliberately avoid institutional remedies.

A 1987 survey by the University of Illinois at Urbana-Champaign offers perhaps the clearest insight to date into factors that would increase the rate of reportage. Respondents indicated that they would be more likely to report harassment to a university office or official if they had "assurance that [their] complaints [would] be taken seriously and thoroughly investigated" (98.3 percent); "assurance of confidentiality" (98.2 percent); "protection from retaliation" (97.4 percent); knowledge that "the person [they] report[ed] the incident to [would have] the authority to take action" (96.1 percent); and assurance of "clear and uniform consequences for specific behaviors [of harassers], with severity of the punishment increasing with the severity of the incident" (88.9 percent).

Women do not report sexual harassment because they sense that, depending upon the individual campus environment and its personnel, such guarantees are at best tentative. No one, not even a university president, can unequivocally ensure protection from retaliation; confidentiality extends only so far as the accused's constitutional rights begin. As this book points out, the diffused authority system of academe encourages few definitive solutions to problems; thus, it is difficult, perhaps impossible, to feel completely assured that complaints will be thoroughly investigated or that the person hearing the complaint has absolute power to effect a solution. If there are academicians anywhere who are willing to establish and publish "clear and uniform consequences for specific behaviors," I have yet to meet them. This is not to suggest that institutions should accept defeat and ignore students' entreaties for more sensitive institutional responses to sexual harassment. All of the items mentioned in the Illinois survey are crucial to creating environments in which victims will feel comfortable enough to report harassment, but there is an additional method of encouraging reportage and keeping the issue before the campus community.

Fraught with ambiguity and complexity, the concept of institutional disclosure seems to me a "cutting edge" for subsequent action on sexual harassment. The term *disclosure* is not, as employed here, applicable to concerns about whether or not the identities of complainants should be divulged. Controversy around this issue has been diffused somewhat—at least on campuses with established procedures, which tend to differentiate informal from formal grievance processes and, if the complainant desires, guarantee anonymity in the former, though not the latter, case.

The other kind of disclosure, which few institutions are currently likely to consider, may be crucial to stimulating reportage and seriously discouraging harassment. Many colleges and universities do attempt to fulfill students' demands for thorough investigations and for definitive responses to sexual harassment, but their efforts go unrecognized because their obsessions with preserving privacy and maintaining their images lead them to behave surreptitiously when grievances arise. The results are devastating. In the absence of awareness and candid discussion of sexual harassment, people can be lulled into the complacent assumption that it is nonexistent. Victims erroneously assume that theirs are isolated circumstances and that their complaints will be unwelcome. Institutions that discipline professors for inappropriate behaviors and do not bother to inform victims create skepticism and mistrust among students.

The argument for disclosure does not require that institutions publish names and details of grievances, nor that they jeopardize recruitment and public image. It suggests simply that faculty, administrators, staff, and, most of all, students would benefit from straightforward communication about sexual harassment on their campuses. As they have designed individualized policies and procedures, institutions can and should establish disclosure mechanisms fitted to their particular needs and circumstances. Grievants whose complaints are judged credible deserve information about the discipline administered; otherwise, supposition and rumor triumph and the victim's risk appears worthless. The entire campus community has the right and the obligation to be notified about the number and types of grievances heard and the penalties allocated.

Such information does not have to be distributed in a manner that encourages identification of victims or perpetrators or that creates an impression that sexual harassment is rampant on campus. It can instead be a conscientious documentation of the institution's attempt to recognize, resist, and eradicate unacceptable behavior by academicians. Students are far more secure in an environment that admits its problems than in one that cloaks them in secrecy, and institutions that reduce sexual harassment to a professional discipline issue rather than allowing the media to magnify it into titillating scandal maintain control over their public images.

Any recapitulation of my experience should not overlook one final point. When we began *The Lecherous Professor,* I did not anticipate the mail we would receive. Most of the letters were pleas for help and were so numerous and disturbing that after a while I, at least, stopped trying to answer them. Some were more curious—one from a self-proclaimed reformed harasser who reported affairs with as many as nine students in a quarter; another that was, even for a literature professor who reads a lot of contemporary fiction, shockingly obscene. The most disturbing of all was a long diatribe from an engineering professor in Arizona. With the exception of harassers themselves, he seems to me an example of the most dangerous person in higher education because his arrogance and self-deception prevent him from recognizing that we owe students more than instruction in the fundamentals of electricity. In the course of his letter he denounced the humanities as "service organizations," subordinate to engineering, law, medicine, and science; described attempts by his institutions's president to emphasize "good teaching" as "bleeps"; and discounted sexual harassment as "insignificant . . . trivia."

I have given considerable thought, not to this professor's comments on harassment, which were too absurd to take seriously, but to his closing remarks, which demonstrated how far even the supposedly educated will go to explain away immoralities they do not wish to admit. In this case, the engineering professor was able to delude himself about sexual harassment by viewing it as a figment of the imagination of an ambitious English professor: "The successful faculty member in English who actually writes a book that becomes popular is treated like a prostitute and finally goes off to live at the beach in California. One of our women faculty members commented that writers who took up the RIGHT CAUSES did very well out of it in terms of money, tenure, and reputation. It is a bit like the missionaries that went to Hawaii to 'do good.' They did very well indeed and ended up taking the whole island away from the natives."

If I ever have the opportunity, I would like to tell this "colleague" that the book didn't make us rich; that I was a tenured professor when I wrote it; and that if I did gain a "reputation" because of it, depending upon the reader, the book worked as much to my disadvantage as to my advantage. Perhaps I would explain to him that research indicates prostitutes are treated poorly, not well; and that I still live in Ohio, not on the beaches of sunny California. Most of all, I would like for him and all academicians who doubt the existence of harassment and the motives of those who write about it to know that after six years I *am* sure of two things: (1) ours *was* a right cause, and (2) ours was an attempt to *keep* "the island" in the hands of people who know best what it is and what it should become.

AUTHOR'S NOTE: LINDA WEINER

Sexual harassment has been a whetstone for my feminism, giving it a keener, more radical edge. Before *The Lecherous Professor,* I encountered the issue as an advocate for women faculty, students, and staff in a series of cases. These were abrading experiences that rubbed away several layers of my trust in institutional systems; they also sharpened my insights about those systems. The incidents themselves were crude and abusive. So were the ways they were handled. I heard speculations about the women's sexual histories and sexual orientation, and how they might have provoked the harasser. I watched powerful alliances form to protect the harassers and discredit the victims. I had to listen to discussions about the seriousness of hurting the careers and reputations of the harassers. And, I was told, how could a decision be made when it was just her word against his?

Those of us who worked with these cases did our best, but it wasn't good enough. We had been successful with other kinds of problems, but this was different. We had discovered sexual harassment, and I began to see what made it different. Sexual harassment is not about sex, it's about sexism. It is a particularly nasty form of sexism because it interferes with a woman's ability to get an education or perform at work. Making sexual harassment illegal is the closest we come to making sexism illegal, and that is threatening.

When *The Lecherous Professor* was first published, the general mood on campuses was one of discovery. The most pressing issue for administrators was which policies were legally required. Since then I have lectured and consulted on a variety of campuses and have found real progress in many places. Good policies, fair procedures, educational programs, and committed presidents now exist. They are absolutely necessary. But they aren't enough. We need to look more closely at the connections between sexual harassment and sexism if we hope to do more than just respond to the few cases that come forward.

Talking about sexual harassment is easy for me. I can describe it, define it, and make it real with the stories women victims have shared with me. Talking about sexism is very difficult, because I'm told it's a thing of the past. But if it is, then why are we still asked the question, "Don't women sexually harass men, too?" The answer is simple: it is logically possible, actually rare, and insignificant compared to the magnitude of sexual harassment of women by men. But the persistence of the question is sexist; it grants equal status to unequal problems and trivializes what happens to women.

If sexism is no longer a serious problem, how do I explain:

- A male student telling his brilliant female peer, "You don't have to worry about a job, you're a woman."

- Faculty being terribly intrigued with the question of student-faculty dating, even though it has little to do with the great majority of sexual harassment incidents.

- Professors splitting hairs over how physically to give a pat on the back, but not believing that assault and rape occur as part of sexual harassment.

Dealing with sexual harassment means dealing with sexism. I know that it begins by asking, What part of the problem do I personally own? What do I do at my job that contributes to sexism? What do I observe and give silent consent to? What responsibility do I have? Only after we admit that we may personally contribute to the sexism of our society and campuses can we begin to change ourselves and our institutions.

Dealing with sexual harassment on campus means changing our institutions. It's rude to point, but men have the lion's share of power on most campuses. They are the chancellors, presidents, and vice presidents. They are also the deans, the full professors, the grievance chair, not to mention the student affairs officer, student body president, and the important alumni. And there is both personal and institutional resistance to changing the distribution of power.

The Lecherous Professsor points out that higher education already has long-standing principles that prohibit sexual harassment on campus. In these conservative times, this should be an appealing point. It says, "You already have the right views; you don't have to change to deal with sexual harassment—just recognize and include it." But sexual harassment takes what has long been within the range of normal male behavior—if not practiced by a man himself, then tolerated in others—and makes it illegal. For many, that puts the personal and the professional in disturbing conflict. Institutional change always comes slowly; in the case of sexual harassment, resistance to change runs particularly deep.

To make things worse, there is currently a backlash concerning sexism and racism that affects personal and institutional interest in addressing sexual harassment. People are, to my ear, more comfortable making sexist, racist, and ethnocentric statements than they were a decade ago. White males, and many white females, feel entitled to express their hostility, ridicule, and feelings of superiority about those different from themselves. They don't even fear being "politically incorrect." Not only does this make moving forward on sexual harassment problematic, it may also mean that more sexual harassment will occur as part of a renewed male entitlement.

Despite the resistance to change, despite the backlash, and despite the odds, there is more we can do.

When sexual harassment combines with racism, classism, or homophobia—sometimes by the harasser himself, sometimes by the helping officers, sometimes by the institutional climate—the damage compounds geometrically. We seldom hear of these incidents, but they do exist. Minority, lesbian, and poor women are painfully aware of how marginal they are to the campus, and they have little reason to trust most institutions to hear their concerns. Sexual harassment is just one more isolating experience. Most of the people who work with sexual harassment are white and middle-class. For this and many other reasons, more nonmajority faculty and staff need to be available to assist these students. And while we are working to make that happen, the rest of us need to make visible efforts to establish our credibility, to become trustworthy resources to all sexual harassment victims.

The individual women who come to us as victims of sexual harassment deserve advice and support in the context of these deeper issues. I believe that the most honest and responsible statement we can make to a victim of sexual harassment is to take care of herself. This may mean pursuing a formal complaint, or getting counseling, or confronting the harasser, or doing nothing. The victims of sexual harassment are not responsible for solving the institution's problems. If we appeal to them to pursue complaints to help the institution or us, we are asking for a loyalty that isn't deserved.

If a women decides that taking care of herself includes pursuing a complaint, she deserves support and complete candor about what to expect. Policies, with their elegant language about due process and fair hearings, promise not only resolution but also justice; in most instances they deliver neither one. The outcomes of most sexual harassment proceedings are a compromise and even in dismissal cases the complexities of the procedures obscure a feeling of resolution for most victims. A woman who brings a formal complaint against a sexual harasser is a whistleblower and may be treated accordingly. Her motives are questioned, her experience is suspect, and there may be no recognition that she has brought forward a legitimate problem. Often, she becomes the problem. First and last, our concern should be: How damaged is the victim as a result of the harassment and how much more damaged will she be by the process?

Sexism on campus creates a second order of sexual harassment victims, those who advise, support, and rule in favor of the primary victims. These are the affirmative action officers, ombudspersons, counselors, assistant deans — the people assigned, and usually committed, to helping sexual harassment victims. Like their clients, they are overwhelmingly women. And this is simultaneously the source of their competence and their vulnerability in a campus system. I have never heard of anyone getting a merit raise for handling a sexual harassment case well, nor being thanked for solving a problem for the institution. Not only is their good work *not* valued, but they are *de*valued—as colleagues, as professionals, and as people. Their motives are questioned, their long-established professionalism challenged, and their credibility diminished or lost. Obviously these women deserve better treatment; in its absence, they deserve more of our involvement and support.

We should not be ashamed to call sexual harassment a women's issue. We should abandon strategies that hope to gain more support by casting sexual harassment as a men-and-women's issue, or worse, as gender-free. Not only does this concede the argument that women's issues are marginal, but it discredits the women who work on them. It *is* a women's issue, and declaring it androgynous only disguises its true nature. Nor should we describe sexual harassment as a ghetto issue just because it is handled by women. They are the most competent people around to work with victims, to design and monitor policies, and to conduct educational programs.

We should be cautious about the common wisdom that more men should be enlisted to help deal with sexual harassment. This strategy usually goes hand in hand with wanting the president or the chancellor to issue a statement on the importance of sexual harassment. The thinking is that sexual harassment needs support and attention from those who have the power to make decisions and influence others. It certainly does, and when that support and attention is genuine and informed, it can be invaluable in setting a tone for the campus environment. But involving men just for the sake of involving men begs an important question. The white male power structure has been—and in many cases still is—part of the problem. Alliances should be carefully considered, credentials and motives carefully scrutinized. If you hand over leadership to men who don't have genuine conviction or insight, you're inviting the fox into the chicken coop. But when a man in a position of authority is truly committed and willing to speak from his own insights and convictions, he should be welcomed to use all the power he has both to help women and to confront other men.

Campuses currently do next to nothing to educate students about sexual harassment—or other forms of discrimination—in the workplace. Even in the field of business ethics, these issues are rarely addressed. Men and women students should be taught about sexual harassment and their own responsibilities in the workplace: it's as important to their success as any single class and deserves time and attention in the curriculum. We may not be able to prevent sexual harassment—policies and procedures are remedial, not deterrent—but we can diminish its effects by educating women. If women know what sexual harassment is and how it works, they will recognize and confront it sooner. Women students deserve to be taught the facts: that sexual harassment exists and that it can happen to them. While women may still have to experience sexual harassment, with more knowledge they may avoid being victimized by it.

On most campuses today, talk about institutional sexism (or worse, educational patriarchy) is condescendingly dismissed with, "That was then, this is now." We've got women engineers, women lawyers, women vice presidents. Institutional sexism is just one of those " '60s issues," used as an excuse when women can't cut the mustard. "This is, after all, the '90s." For feminists on the faculty and in the administration who think there is more to be done on sexual harassment, this kind of environment is unfriendly. It makes it difficult to identify effective strategies, and the theoretical links between sexual harassment and sexism don't offer much in the way of practical advice. Even talking in these terms may be political suicide. The positive changes that have already occurred didn't come easily. Men in authority didn't wake up one morning thinking, "I realize we discriminate against women and we should change that."

Our continuing efforts on campus require sophistication about institutional systems and resources; they also demand cleverness, tact, and energy. It is important to talk with others of your kind to keep in touch with the deeper issues, which are easily obscured or sidetracked by negotiating. We must keep the practical as close as possible to the truth about sexual harassment and sexism.

The issues are so deep and so much has to change to make a real difference. In the end, I only know that we must keep talking, as candidly as possible. Those of us who are committed to these changes need to talk more to students, to secretaries, and to faculty. We need to talk to the converted and to the unconcerned. We need to talk to both men and women. We need to engage our friends and colleagues. Out of these conversations will come the insights that will make a difference for women.

The Lecherous Professor

Introduction

Sexual harassment of college students by their professors is a fact of campus life that many educators learn to ignore and, in their silence, to accept. We wrote this book about sexual harassment because our experiences revealed that the silence is part of the problem, that ignoring the issue only makes it worse. Over the years, we gradually realized that we could no longer disregard the confusion and fear in the faces of women who asked us to explain and prevent something we ourselves did not understand.

If you are a teacher or an administrator, you meet students like Carol Z. She comes to you because she has heard you can help her. She tries to control her emotions and tell her story calmly. She explains how one of her professors has persisted in propositioning her despite her refusals, how he discusses her "prudishness" with other students, how she has had to grapple with him physically to prevent his "pawing" her. Explaining that she has made a formal complaint, she shows some anger but even more fear. You reassure her that she's following the right procedural steps. You sense her feelings of isolation and betrayal as she goes on, telling you about two classmates who have witnessed the professor's treatment of her and who have had similar trouble with him themselves. They at first encouraged Carol to make a complaint but are now frightened about their own grades and are worried about what might happen to the professor. You explain that their reactions are not unusual, but you empathize with Carol's feeling of betrayal.

She nervously shows you the official letters filled with impersonal statements from the Grievance Committee. She feels as if everyone is avoiding her. Friends have told her the professor is saying she tried to seduce him. She is angry and worries he might be believed.

Professional and personal ethics require that you be realistic. You explain that *you* believe her but the professor probably *will* accuse her of trying to seduce him and that her classmates might even begin to doubt what they say. With tears in her eyes she asks, "Why can he do this? *I* didn't want any of this! I didn't do anything to him; he keeps hurting *me!*" You can't reassure Carol it will be all right because you realize that the damage to her is not over and that there are already scars. In that moment you are ashamed of your profession, yourself, and all the others who have allowed this to happen.

If you are a woman in higher education, you overhear male colleagues' crude sexist jokes about twenty-year-olds. You listen and try to contain your own anger as young women seek you out to ask if you agree with the engineering or architecture or economics professors who tell them they don't belong in "male" disciplines. You hear their stories of being fondled, belittled, propositioned, threatened. Gradually you begin to understand that your bond with these women students is as important as those you share with professional colleagues. You recall experiences with your own teachers and recognize that behaviors that seemed so obscure in the 1960s have finally received labels that can explain them in the 1980s.

We decided to study sexual harassment because it is part of what it means to be a woman and a professional, and we wrote the book as much for ourselves as for the students and the institution we hope to help.

When we began discussing sexual harassment in 1977, we had more curiosity than information. We knew only what it felt like to watch women's agony. People were just beginning to think and talk about the issue then, and few took it seriously. Definitions and data were sparse; there was a curious complacency on the campus, a reluctance to regard rumblings from the workplace and government as anything but sound and fury.

At first we talked to each other. Then because we lived and worked in academia, we did what curious academics usually do and went to the library. We didn't find as much as we hoped because sexual harassment was still an unexplored topic in higher education. We did find Catharine MacKinnon's *Sexual Harassment*, a precise argument that provided a legal and intellectual framework within which to talk and think about the issue. Lin Farley's *Sexual Shakedown* offered another insight into sexual harassment in the workplace and touched on the problems students encounter. We also learned from the newsletters and publications of professionals in higher education struggling to make sense of the issue. Especially helpful was the work of the National Advisory Council on Women's Educational Programs, the Association of American Colleges' Project on the Status and Education of Women, the Modern Language Association's Commission on the Status of Women in the Profession, and the Office of Women for the American Council on Education. From the time of our initial interest in the subject to the final draft of *The Lecherous Professor*, there was an enormous change in the issue's visibility. Today people are writing and talking about it, institutions are aware of the need for policies to deal with it, and researchers are attempting to measure its frequency and effects.

From the outset, we were interested in learning about sexual harassment from those forced to live with it. Statistics offer some insight, but much harassment goes unreported and unacknowledged. We decided to gather material from women who had endured it and from people who had heard their stories. For two years, we collected information from approximately four hundred students, faculty, administrators, and alumni from across the country. We queried our own students and analyzed the results of surveys from other institutions. We benefited enormously from the support and information provided us by those who work with harassment victims. They were willing to share their experiences, frustrations, and insights, and we learned much from them. In the book, names and minor details have been altered to protect the identities of people and institutions; however, the incidents are recorded in exact detail. Since most harassment victims have chosen not to make their stories public, this was the only way they would tell their stories.

Early in our investigation, we decided to treat only the subject of sexual harassment of women students by male professors. This is not to deny that there are incidents of female professors harassing male students or homosexuals harassing collegians. The problem exists in several forms, and each demands separate analysis. We chose to focus on the harassment of women students by male professors because surveys, informal discussions, formal grievances, and litigation convinced us that this is the epidemic and most damaging form of sexual harassment on campus.

Even though the issue is now highly visible, we have only begun to understand it. Sexual harassment by college professors is complex. Most attention to the subject focuses on narrow procedural issues — how to define the behavior, how to comply with legal demands on institutions, how to react when harassment occurs. But there are so many questions that no one has asked.

Are there specific characteristics of the academic profession that contribute to the problem of sexual harassment in higher education? Do college women desire and invite sexual attention from their professors? How much is known about men who harass? Do they share identifiable traits that might serve as "give-aways" to potential victims? What causes them to act as they do? What are the moral and professional responsibilities of harassers' male and female colleagues? Does higher education have the will and ability to combat the problem?

Our reading, listening, and talking convinced us of the need to do more than describe sexual harassment on contemporary campuses. We wanted to write a book that would convince students, parents, and academicians that the problem is serious and that they can do something about it. But we also hoped to encourage people to think about it in new and possibly controversial ways. For example, our interest in understanding the motivations of harassers led us to suspect that conventional interpretations did not probe deeply enough. Sexual harassers are typically thought to be individuals who need to exercise power over the opposite sex. The intriguing questions are when, how, and why such need develops. We wanted to know if answers could be found in examining common characteristics of academic harassers. There is no research that applies directly to the subject. Interested in the evolution of sexual identity and roles, we studied literature on adolescent and adult development. It led us to speculation about the relationship between the academic environment and the psychological development of some male professors.

Chapters two, three, five, and six contain our best conjectures on complex issues relating to sexual harassment. We have suggested that the environment of higher education, myths about college women, the developmental patterns of male professors, and the professional dilemmas of female faculty contribute to the problem. We hope our theories will be analyzed, tested and refined through continued research and analysis so we might all acquire fuller understanding of sexual harassment.

There is no consensus in higher education that this is an important issue. One lesson we learned is that sexual harassment is an extremely sensitive subject. When we began talking about the project, we did not anticipate the intensity of reactions from some of our colleagues. We found very few men or women who are dispassionate about the topic. Everyone has an opinion; many have full-fledged theories and arguments. Some academics seem threatened, angry, and hostile to those who ask questions about it. These reactions convinced us that we had struck a nerve, and that experience made us take stock. It taught us firsthand why students hesitate to report the offense and why higher education will not easily resolve this problem.

A professor commented casually in the hall one day, "Hey, tell me about what you're doing. I heard you're collecting information on people so you can give it to the Provost and get them fired." Another approached a dean and contended that someone should "monitor" our work because it might "embarrass the University." Still another complained to an administrator that our work might "violate the University's protection of human subjects policies." (Apparently, it had not occurred to him that sexual harassment constitutes one of academe's most persistent and serious violations of human rights.) When a faculty member on another campus sued a woman who brought a sexual harassment complaint against him and the story was reported in *The Chronicle of Higher Education*, someone anonymously sent us the article.

We had also struck a nerve with students. A few weeks after we asked a small group of students about their experiences with sexual harassment, people we had never met began contacting us to offer information. Male students approached us with descriptions of incidents they had witnessed. Over the years, we had dealt with occasional harassment complaints; but until then, we lacked realistic perceptions of the magnitude of the problem or the secrecy with which it is cloaked in academe.

Our responses to our experiences were complex. We felt not only shock and disgust at what we found but also very real regret at being in possession of a kind of knowledge we didn't want to have. Initially, people respected our requests that they not identify professors with whom they had had encounters. But after a while, in the privacy of our offices, they seemed almost driven to tell names. Perhaps they needed to test their experiences on someone who could corroborate their perceptions or maybe even miraculously to alter them, to tell them that they were mistaken and that things really weren't so bad.

We couldn't do it. In almost every case, the student added a little authenticity and a lot of horror to what we already suspected. Each of us has about thirty more years to work with some of these people, and lately that seems like a very long time. There are days when we doubt that our profession will muster the objectivity and courage to make hard decisions about its own members, and even more distressing is the knowledge that we can never measure the damage that has been and is being done to students.

This book is a very belated gesture, that is by no means enough, to Yehuda Bacon, an Israeli artist who survived a concentration camp. He said something that summarizes what happened, on a much smaller scale, to us as we wrote this book and to the women from whom we learned: "As a boy I thought: 'I will tell them what I saw, in the hope that people will change for the better.' But people didn't change and didn't even want to know. It was much later that I really understood the meaning of suffering. It can have a meaning if it changes *you* for the better."

To write a book about sexual harassment on the campus is to begin with optimism and self-righteousness and to end in frustration and self-deprecation. Frustration because the problem is far more serious and solutions much less likely than most dare to admit. Self-deprecation because there is always the possibility that self-preservation might outweigh concern for students and that courage and commitment to the project will prove transitory.

To write a book about harassment is to discover with shock how easily individuals and institutions delude themselves. The process brought us face to face with our own irresponsibility and the irresolution of our colleagues. We began to wonder why we had ignored so much and taken so long to speak out about what we had seen and heard. To write a book about harassment is to realize that the morality of an entire profession can be tested by its response to a single issue. Most of all, it is to hope that the test proves successful and that our words, however belated, will somehow make a difference.

1 : *Sexual Harassment on Campus*

THE STATE OF THE ART

Every sin is the result of a collaboration.

Stephen Crane

Sexual harassment was a way of life. Field trips — a tradition for geographers — were abandoned because women were considered contaminants. One memorable instructor (whose course was required of all graduate students) regularly informed each new generation of graduate students that women are not good for much of anything but sexual exercises. He enjoyed going into graphic description of the trials and tribulations of a journey taken with a group of students during which one female experienced the onset of menstruation. "Blood all over the damn place," our professor told the class, "had to hike miles out of the canyon to find wadding to stuff in her crotch."[1]

• •

I had a typing teacher who used to come up and sit by me when I was typing and touch the side of my breast. He'd make rude comments about my behind and he usually made it a point to pinch me. He'd keep me after class to discuss a paper or show me areas where I needed help. I was an A student, but he always wanted me to stay. If I said no, he'd get very defensive. I was afraid he might not give me the A I deserved. The final straw was when I had gotten ink on my sweater from the typing ribbon and he offered to help me get it off. Well, he put his hands up my shirt, feeling me up, and I pushed him away and yelled. I told my parents, and they said I should go to the Dean. I had my boyfriend come and wait for me after class. I didn't want to start trouble, so I didn't say anything. I decided to change my program and not to have him for a teacher anymore. Even though I wanted to tell the Dean, I was afraid it would just mean more trouble.

• •

I knew that this prof chased his students so when he started flirting with me in class, I just ignored it. I didn't want anything to do with all that and it made me nervous. But one day after class he sort of cornered me as I was leaving. He backed me up against the wall and was touching me and telling me that he wanted me. He was almost shaking and very intense. I was trying to figure out how to get out of there without an awful scene. He started telling me how his wife didn't like oral sex and he felt frustrated because he had so much to give and wanted to give it to me. He was sweating and shaking and said, "I have a magic tongue. That used to be my nickname." I couldn't believe it. I was frightened by him and wanted to laugh at the same time. I pulled away and ran out of the classroom. It still seems a little funny, but he stalks me in the halls and it's still scary to me.

• •

Dr. _____ asked me to come to his office to help him rearrange his books. Maybe it was my fault for going in the first place. He has these high bookcases, and the only way you can reach them is to stand on this little stool. I remember I had on this blue tight skirt that made it hard for me to step off and on that stool, but the skirt was pretty long. After a while, he got up and walked over and started bumping the stool. At first I thought he was just kidding around, and I laughed. Then I got sort of scared because he almost knocked me over. I told him to be careful and that I didn't think he knew I was really scared. "I know you are, but the only way to keep from falling is for you to go about your business while I lay down on the floor here and watch you." I think that's exactly how he said it. I didn't know what else to do. I was afraid to leave, so I just kept on taking books down while he laid on the floor and looked up my dress at my underpants. Then I left, and he said thank you and never ever mentioned anything about it again. I guess I should have reported him to somebody, but I didn't know who. No one would have believed it anyway.

These are stories of American college women. There are thousands like them. Most of the stories are unknown because students rarely tell them, because higher education keeps skeletons in the closet, and because few except the victims understand the seriousness of the problem.

Sexual harassment of college students is not new. A familiar jest is "Where there has been a student body, there has always been a faculty for love." Women were not admitted to the college campus until 1837, when Oberlin became the first to open its doors to them, but it seems likely that sexual harassment has existed as long as there have been women students and male professors. Only in the last few years, however, have women raised their voices in protest. Even now their cries usually fall on curious but uncaring institutional and public ears. Parents worry about tuition increases and financial aid; students worry about grades and job interviews; deans worry about the number of faculty publications and declining enrollments; college presidents worry about budget cuts and collective bargaining; and trustees worry about public images and endowment funds. But until one of their daughters is harassed or news of a case appears in a campus headline or a lawsuit is filed, few are disturbed that women students are sexually intimidated, fondled, propositioned, and even assaulted by their professors.

The silence surrounding sexual harassment is incongruous in light of the last two noisy decades of higher education. The 1960s and '70s were characterized by activism about student representation in governance systems and grievance procedures. During those years, a variety of women's issues were addressed on the campus. Discriminatory policies in admissions, testing, scholarships, and athletics were prohibited. Women's hours were abolished; birth control was incorporated into student health services; abortion ads were placed in student newspapers; and women's centers were established. Women's studies courses, programs, and departments were integrated into academic units. Yet despite all the visibility and public discussion of students' rights and women's concerns on campus, sexual harassment remained in the closet. Women students whispered to roommates about sexual propositions from their professors or hinted of their distress to counselors, but there was little else they could do because until very recently sexual harassment was simultaneously denied, ignored, disputed, discounted, and disregarded.

As late as 1974, there was still no general consensus about sexual harassment. In that year, the American Council on Education published an anthology titled *Women in Higher Education* in which only one essay touched on the experiences of women students as "sex objects." In "Women's Right to Choose, or Men's Right to Dominate," Joan Roberts observed:

> In recent hearings conducted with women students, in research interviews with women students, in discussions with individual women and groups of women, and in their responses to questionnaires, they accused some male faculty members of subtle and even blatant sexism ranging from verbal to physical, sometimes with put-out or get-out connotations. Verbally, a professor aggresses, saying, "Your sweater looks big enough for both of us." Or he may invade the woman's personal space, by touching a pin on her blouse while commenting on its ostensible beauty. (I sometimes wonder what the male professor would do if the woman student made equally personal gestures in public.) Or he may, as in one case reported, make sexual overtures, which, when rebuffed, led him to fail the woman student on her doctoral examination. The same man was later overheard telling a colleague that he did not bother to read her exam. Fortunately, this kind of overt unprofessionalism is infrequently reported.[2]

The assumption at that point in time was that no news — or at least not much news — was good news. Scarcity of information is one key to the historical invisibility of the issue. Because there is no definitive statistical answer to the question "How great is the problem?" it is convenient to deny and ignore the issue. There has been no national study of the frequency of sexual harassment, no data that can set a "standard" against which a campus might measure itself. The National Advisory Council on Women's Educational Programs was established under the 1974 Women's Educational Equity Act. In 1979-1980 it followed its charge to make policy recommendations and circulated "a call for information on the sexual harassment of students." Its results, published in 1980, represented the first attempt to examine the problem on a large scale. The council's report stated firmly that its study was not definitive and that "estimates of frequency [of sexual harassment on the nation's campuses] are beyond the scope of this report."[3]

During the last few years, some organizations and institutions have surveyed themselves and produced statistical indicators of the scope of the problem. These efforts at measuring sexual harassment do not mean that these campuses or organizations have special or unusual problems with harassment; they *do* demonstrate that there is genuine concern about and interest in examining the issue.

- In 1980 at Arizona State University, a joint student/faculty/staff committee distributed a 50-item questionnaire to a random sample of women faculty, staff and students. With an 80% response rate, 13% of the students, 11% of the staff, and 13% of the faculty said they had been sexually harassed. The report pointed out that, lest the 13% student response be considered small, the percent translated to 2,300 women students. Closer scrutiny of the data made it apparent that the real numbers were even higher. Respondents who viewed themselves as victims of harassment were not confined to describing only their *current* situations. Further analysis of the respondents' status at the time of harassment revealed that 46% of the episodes occurred while women were undergraduates and 18% while they were graduate students.[4]

- In 1981, the Iowa State University Committee on Women conducted a detailed study of sexual harassment of college students by faculty members. The survey found that 7% of the women students said faculty had made physical advances toward them; 14% of the women had received invitations for dates; 17% reported receiving verbal sexual advances; 34% had experienced leering or other sexual body language; 43% reported flirtation or undue attention; and 65% said they had been the target of sexist comments. Thirteen percent of the women had avoided courses because the faculty were known sexual harassers. No woman who had experienced one of the three most serious forms of sexual harassment included in the survey reported it to a university official.[5]

- In 1979-80, in response to general discussion on campus and in the press, a campus committee at the University of Rhode Island surveyed students, faculty, and staff about experiences of sexual harassment on campus. The study made distinctions between sexual intimidation, sexual insult and assault as defined in Rhode Island law. Sexual intimidation was defined as "a threat or a bribe by a person in a position of authority to coerce sexual contact." Citing personal knowledge of such cases, respondents indicated that teachers were initiators in 53% of the cases, graduate assistants in 8%, staff or administrators in 6%, employers in 14%, and students in 14%. Grades or exams were involved in 58% of the cases.[6]

- In 1979, the Michigan State University Student Affairs Office commissioned a survey of women students. A stratified random sample of 998 was contacted, and 47% responded. Twenty-five percent reported that they had been sexually harassed within the last year. A validation study indicated that sexual harassment victims may have been *under*represented in the respondent groups.[7]

- A 1979 University of Florida survey found that 26% of women undergraduate respondents and 31% of graduate respondents said they had been sexually harassed by faculty. Of those who said they had been victims, 70% did not feel free to report it to anyone.[8]

- At the University of California at Berkeley, a 1979 survey of women graduate students found that 20% of the respondents experienced unwanted touches, propositions, or sexual remarks from professors. A 1980 survey of senior women at Berkeley, found that 30% of the 269 randomly sampled respondents had experienced "unwanted and objectionable sexual behavior" by at least one male instructor either at Berkeley or at a school from which they had transferred.[9]

- In a 1980 study conducted by the University of Cincinnati Office of Women's Programs and Services, 47% of the women students, faculty, and staff choosing to respond reported several forms of sexual harassment, ranging from leers to assault.[10]

- At East Carolina University, 20% of the 226 women students surveyed in 1979 reported that they had experienced verbal sexual harassment from male instructors.[11]

- A national survey of psychology educators in Division 29 (psychotherapy) of the American Psychological Association in 1979 found that, of a random sample of 481 women, 10% had had sexual contact with their professors. Of those who had received their degrees within the last seven years, 25% reported having sexual contact while they were students of psychology educators.[12]

These individual campus or organizational studies employed different research techniques and slightly different definitions of sexual harassment. Some used random sampling; others reported on self-selected respondents. There clearly is a need for a standardized survey instrument that individual campuses could use to measure frequency so a national profile can be drawn. Yet despite the variations in the surveys, the results are remarkably similar: again and again 20 to 30 percent of women students report they have been sexually harassed by male faculty during their college years. Campus administrators, student affairs staff, ombudsmen, and consultants who have done workshops on individual campuses affirm the pattern: 20 to 30 percent experience sexual harassment.

Measurement of the problem is elusive, local, and often anecdotal, but the numbers involved are significant. In the fall of 1982, in its annual report on college and university enrollments, the National Center for Educational Statistics reported that 6,374,005 women were enrolled in American colleges and universities.[13] If only *1 percent* of all college women experienced sexual harassment, there would be 63,740 women victims. Twenty percent equals 1,274,800 women. And every year a new group of women enrolls in college to become part of the problem. Higher education faces a problem of epidemic proportion.

Although the numbers are large and indicate the need for serious concern, a conversation between two deans at a meeting reviewing a proposed policy on sexual harassment is a reminder that pressure for change comes only from personal experience. A business administration dean wanted to set his priority by quantifying the problem in his college: "If it's an 80 to 90 percent problem, then we have to do something. But if it's, say, only a 7 percent problem, I would give it less priority." At the other end of the table, a liberal arts dean cited the yearlong struggle he had had with a sexual harassment complaint. He described the pain and confusion of the student victims, the conversations with parents, the disruption within the department, and the time he had spent in hearings and conferences as he tried to resolve the problem. His priority had been set through experience: "One case is enough."

Scarcity of survey information on individual campuses and the national scene is one reason for sexual harassment's invisibility. Equally important is the reluctance of women students to report their experiences. As with rape victims, sexual harassment victims are hesitant to add the pain of self-disclosure and the risk of interrogation to the distress caused by the harassment. Students have several compelling problems when they consider what to do. The National Advisory Council on Women's Educational Programs, after reviewing the information that was sent to them, summarized the complexity:

Why do victims keep silent or try to cope without involving the authority of the school administration or the courts? Our responses and the work of almost all researchers indicate that there are several primary causes: fear that they — as victims — are somehow responsible for the incident, fear that they will not be believed, shame at being involved in any form of sexual incident, fear that by protesting they will call attention to their sex rather than to their work, a belief that no action will be taken, and fear of reprisals by the initiator and his colleagues.[14]

Students are pragmatic; they know they are subordinate to faculty and administrators. Individually and collectively, they have much less power. Those who are sexually harassed recognize that the professor's role and authority are major reasons for their own victimization, and their experiences with authorities only confirm their powerlessness. A member of a university commission on the status of women expressed the cynicism typical of many students:

I know, if this is occurring, if there are overtures being made, it's usually from people right over you who control all the power; whether your master's proposal is going to be accepted, how well you are doing on your comprehensives. After all, they are the people who are reading them. These are the people that you have for the majority of your classes, they hold your career in their hands. So you can complain about sexual overtures but then because of their rank they can find some way to get rid of you for a million or more reasons; it can be as simple as just undermining your performance. It can just get all mixed together and it's no longer clear what's happening to you.[15]

Students also understand the traditional difference in sex roles and power. One of the earliest survival lessons women learn is that they must handle problems like sexual harassment. Social conditioning leads many to believe that this is the way things are and that there is no point in public protest: no one would believe them. Even if someone did believe them, women are expected — and expect themselves — to resolve such problems.

Diane K., after enduring a yearlong struggle with an English professor, told her parents about his attempts to lure her into an affair.

I didn't really want them to do anything about it. I was out of his class and was pretty sure I could avoid him on campus. But I felt like I had to explain how it wasn't my fault to Mom and Dad. I didn't want them to think that I wasn't grown-up enough to handle the situation. That's why I didn't tell them at the time it was all happening, even though it really got to me sometimes. I mean, that's the way things are in the real world. I'm going to graduate next year and I'm supposed to be able to deal with all that.

The self-imposed silence of student victims, which contributes to the continued invisibility of the problem, is reinforced by the cloud of confusion that exists — and is sometimes conveniently created — around what sexual harassment actually is. While both rape and sexual harassment are underreported, sexual harassment trades on its victims' uncertainty about how to label their experiences. A woman knows when she has been raped. But there are many forms of sexual harassment, and the term itself is new. Women differ dramatically in their willingness and ability to identify and acknowledge the behavior. A college ombudsman, reflecting on her frustration at hearing students describe blatant acts of sexual harassment and their own ambiguous reactions, commented, "I have to remind myself that the terms are new. Ten years ago, when I was a student, we had the same experiences — a lower grade because you didn't go out with a professor, dropping courses to avoid propositions from the graduate assistant, getting felt up by faculty in their offices. We knew we didn't like what went on, but we didn't have a name for it."

"Sexual harassment" became a commonly used phrase only a few years ago. But the very words "sexual harassment" are ominous to some college women; they seem too legalistic, too political, too combative. Women students resist language that makes them feel set apart from or adversaries of men. Many resist identification with what they consider a "feminist" issue because they aren't comfortable with that label either. Already confused about the uncertain boundaries of male-female and student-teacher relationships, a woman student usually prefaces description of a sexual harassment experience with, "I've never been sexually harassed, but . . ." Then she proceeds to give a classic example of the behavior.

Students aren't the only ones bewildered by discussions of sexual harassment. Men and women faculty and administrators assume, are led to believe, or find it convenient to make sexual harassment a confusing topic. Just as discussions of the ERA rapidly deteriorated into arguments about whether women would be drafted or required to share public restrooms with men, attention is quickly distracted from the fundamental issues surrounding sexual harassment to debatable, speculative, or trivial ground. Some people, especially men, worry that sexual harassment is so vague and ill defined that they personally will suffer if the problem is confronted vigilantly. In casual discussions, there is usually a man who asks, "But if we take this harassment stuff too seriously, won't it mean that men and women will never get along again? Won't I have to worry about every look and every gesture and every word I say to a woman?" And there is always another man who adds, "You know, women can really ruin a man with this kind of thing."

Sometimes the confusion is transparent pretense. In the hallway of an undergraduate Midwestern college, a male professor of English observed a scene and commented:

> A group of men faculty — from the math department — were standing in the hallway outside their offices. A fairly attractive girl went up to one of them, apparently her professor, and asked about an assignment. He put his arm around her shoulders, walked a few steps with her, and said, loudly, so everyone could hear, "Let's go in my office and talk about it — and you can take your clothes off." Everyone — except the girl — laughed. One professor asked sarcastically, "Is that harassment?" And someone wisecracked, "Not unless she thinks it is."

Actually, sexual harassment is not that difficult to recognize. Sexual harassment is a professor talking about "wadding in crotches" and about having a "magic tongue." It is grabbing a student's breast or lying on the floor and staring up her skirt. It is not, in the vast majority of cases, ambiguous behavior. It is not, as some imply, a figment of students' imaginations or a weapon women use to damage men's reputations. These worries are usually expressed by men and women who have had little experience dealing with harassment cases or who impose confusion on themselves.

Most of the confusion is attributable to the fact that sexual harassment has only recently been defined as a distinct pheno- menon. "Harassment" means to annoy persistently, but "sexual harassment" is a particular type of abuse. The need for a common understanding of the term became pressing in the 1970s as discussions about sexual discrimination and women's positions in the workplace accelerated. If sexual harassment was actionable, whether in the courtroom, the corporate personnel hearing, or the college grievance system, there was a need for precise definitions of what constituted sexual harassment.

As part of its research on the problem in the workplace, the Working Women United Institute in 1975 developed an early working definition. Others followed in rapid succession. Lin Farley's *Sexual Shakedown* and Catharine MacKinnon's *Sexual Harassment of Working Women*[16] treated sexual harassment as a type of sex discrimination and an abuse of power rather than a sexual issue. Court cases, publications, and policy-makers refined and maintained that position.

The legal guidelines for sexual harassment were set in 1980, when the Equal Employment Opportunity Commission (EEOC) issued Title VII Guidelines on Sexual Harassment in the Workplace. Title VII of the Civil Rights Act of 1964 established that sex discrimination was illegal as a condition of employment. The Guidelines state that sexual harassment is a violation of Title VII and that an employer is liable for any acts that it "knows or should have known [about, unless it can show that it took] immediate and appropriate corrective action." The Guidelines stipulate that investigations of complaints will examine "the record as a whole" and the "totality of circumstances." This terminology means that investigation of sexual harassment must consider previous complaints and institutional efforts to comply with the law and remedy problems (see Appendix I).

Title VII is relevant to sexual harassment on the campus because it applies to all employees, including student workers. Title IX of the 1972 Education Amendments, administered by the Office for Civil Rights (OCR), is the law that prohibits sex discrimination against all students. OCR's definition of sexual harassment was designed to guide compliance officers who evaluate complaints:

Sexual harassment consists of verbal or physical conduct of a sexual nature, imposed on the basis of sex, by an employee or agent of a recipient that denies, limits, provides different, or conditions the provision of aid, benefits, services or treatment protected under Title IX.[17]

Despite the urging of many organizations, including the National

Advisory Council on Women's Education Programs, no guidelines on sexual harassment have been issued for Title IX. The parallels between Title VII and Title IX, however, seem to secure sexual harassment of students as a form of sex discrimination.

Title VII has been interpreted by the courts in several cases, but Title IX has a limited enforcement history. Thus far the only Title IX ruling directly addressing sexual harassment of students is *Alexander* v. *Yale University*. The case was filed in 1977 when an undergraduate woman charged she received a lower grade on a paper and in a course because she refused a professor's sexual overtures. She was joined in her legal action by four other students and a male professor who alleged that Yale's tolerance of sexual pressures on students created an atmosphere unconducive to teaching and learning. As relief, the suit asked for an adequate grievance procedure at Yale. The subsequent claims were dismissed by the court on the grounds that the charges were "untenable," "moot," or "inadequate." In 1980 the original complaint was dismissed by the United States Court of Appeals, which held that the student had failed to prove her case and that Yale had addressed her main concern by establishing a sexual harassment grievance procedure.

The significance of *Alexander* v. *Yale University* is that the District Court decision maintained that if sexual harassment does occur, it may constitute sex discrimination prohibited under Title IX. The ruling stated:

> It is perfectly reasonable to maintain that academic advancement conditioned upon submission to sexual demands constitutes sex discrimination in education, just as questions of job retention or promotion tied to sexual demands from supervisors have become increasingly recognized as potential violations of Title VII's ban against sex discrimination in employment.[18]

In addition to providing mechanisms for the processing of sexual harassment complaints, Title VII and Title IX can affect monies coming to the campus from the outside. Colleges and universities receiving federal dollars — almost all because of the federal support of research and student financial aid — can lose federal monies if they are not in compliance with the requirements for policy and procedures. This threat is primarily used as a persuasive tool by enforcement agencies in conciliations with university administrations.

Although there is not a real fear on college campuses that the existence of sexual harassment endangers federal assistance, the existence of a forum in the federal courts for individuals who suffer sexual harassment creates great concern about legal expense and publicity. This is the real impact of the regulations of Title VII and Title IX.

In addition to the federal regulations, there are state laws, both civil and criminal, relevant to sexual harassment (see Appendix II). The current need is not for more laws but for ways to help students translate laws and definitions and abstract descriptions of sexual harassment into their own experiences. If sexual harassment is to be identified, reported, and confronted, students must understand when the label applies. They need to know that for behavior to be sexual harassment, it does not have to be repeated; one time can be enough. Students need to understand that harassment does not have to be of a particular type or intensity; sexual innuendoes in class are as inappropriate as invitations to bed. In order to recognize sexual harassment, students need to learn that there are fundamental differences in their relationships to peers and to faculty and that the two are not governed by the same rules. Behavior that may be perfectly acceptable from a classmate may be totally improper for a professor.

This is the heart of the issue. "Sexual harassment" implies misuse of power and role by a faculty member. Although institutions' statements and definitions of sexual harassment are written to accommodate individual circumstances and legal requirements, they should also address this central concept of the power imbalance between students and professors. A sound definition not only sets policy, it also informs and educates the community. It should affirm that sexual harassment is sex discrimination, is illegal, damaging to the academic community, refers to a broad range of behaviors, and may occur as single or repeated incidents.

There is no universally accepted model definition of sexual harassment. The most publicized is that of the National Advisory Council. It describes sexual harassment as:

> objectionable emphasis on the sexuality or sexual identity of a student by (or with the acquiescence of) an agent of an educational institution when (1) the objectionable acts are directed toward students of only one gender; and (2) the intent or effect of the objectionable acts is to limit or

deny full and equal participation in educational services, opportunities, or benefits on the basis of sex; or (3) the intent or effect of the objectionable acts is to create an intimidating, hostile, or offensive academic environment for the members of one sex . . .

Academic sexual harassment is the use of authority to emphasize the sexuality or sexual identity of a student in a manner which prevents or impairs that student's full enjoyment of educational benefits, climate, or opportunities . . .

[Sexual harassment may be described as] (1) generalized sexist remarks or behavior; (2) inappropriate and offensive, but essentially sanction-free sexual advances; (3) solicitation of sexual activity or other sex-linked behavior by promise of rewards; (4) coercion of sexual activity by threat of punishment; and (5) assaults.[19]

The Modern Language Association's Commission on the Status of Women in the Profession distinguished gender harassment as a specific type of sexual harassment:

Gender harassment is considerably less dramatic in its manifestations than sexual harassment, but because it is more widespread, it seems more pernicious. It consists of discriminatory behavior directed against individuals who belong to a gender group that the aggressor considers inferior . . . The forms are often verbal — statements and jokes that reveal stereotypical discriminatory attitudes.[20]

In 1978 the Association of American College's Project on the Status and Education of Women provided a descriptive list of specific actions that might constitute sexual harassment. The list was intended as a guide and identified a broad range of behaviors. Obviously, any single behavior must be evaluated in the context of an individual complaint, as suggested in the EEOC reference to the "totality of circumstances." The list included the following:

verbal harassment or abuse
subtle pressure for sexual activity
sexist remarks about a woman's clothing, body, or sexual activities
unnecessary touching, patting, or pinching, leering or ogling at a
    woman's body
constant brushing against a woman's body
demanding sexual favors accompanied by implied or overt threats
    concerning one's job, grades, letters of recommendation and so
    forth
physical assault[21]

Discussion of sexual harassment began in regard to the workplace, where people are unequal in power but more likely equal in age and experience and where professional codes of ethics are few. On the college campus the situation is quite different. Sexual harassment of students involves an individual's decision to violate his professional ethics. To its credit, higher education has always had either written or implied standards of conduct. Colleges, professional associations of academic disciplines, and campus governance groups have lengthy statements on faculty's responsibilities to students. The American Association of University Professors in 1966 adopted a policy statement on professional ethics that outlined professors' responsibilities not to exploit students. In 1983 increasing attention led the AAUP to propose guidelines on sexual harassment and its redress to the national membership.

Intimate relationships between professors and students are regarded with suspicion because they pose conflicts with faculty responsibilities and ethics. The prevailing view among academicians is that the faculty member's job is to teach students. Whenever he chooses to treat his women students differently from the men, to become more man than professor, he manipulates his role and endangers his professionalism. Men professors do not kiss, fondle, or comment on the appearances of male students, and most maintain that there is no reason to treat women differently.

In reality, however, different norms *do* apply for men and women students in everyday campus life. If a male student offers a professor money to alter a grade, all would agree that the professor is wrong if he takes it. But when faculty fantasize about a woman student promising sexual favors in exchange for a better grade, the standard changes. Professional ethics become less important when the issue is sex. It is wrong to take money from students, but sex is another matter.

Discussion of sexual harassment usually includes the "yes, but" view: "Yes, but some women invite ogling, touching, or sexual propositions." Every campus has its real or imaginary tales of beautiful coeds who show their professors nude photographs of themselves or promise they will "do anything" for a better grade. Many are second- or third-hand accounts, more fiction than fact. The implication is that the campus is hazardous for male faculty, that men too are victims of sexual harassment. The underlying message, of course, is that men have a right to harass women because women "ask for it."

The "yes, but" notion distorts the issue. There *are* women who flirt with male faculty and women who cause professors discomfort and embarrassment by pursuing them. Some women *do* get crushes on professors; they *do* engage in seduction. But this has nothing to do with sexual harassment of students by professors. These are two separate problems involving very different dynamics, consequences, and resolutions.

One way to distinguish them is to use clearer terminology. A student is more capable of causing "sexual hassle" than she is of sexually harassing. There is too much difference in role and status of male faculty and female students to make flirtation or even seduction by students harassment. "Harassment" suggests misuse of power, and students simply do not have enough power to harass.

Persistent, unwanted attention from a female student can be extremely disruptive to a male professor. It may embarrass, annoy, and anger him; it may cause turmoil in both his private and professional life. But it cannot destroy his self-esteem or endanger his intellectual self-confidence. Hassled professors do not worry about retaliation and punitive treatment; they do not fear bad grades or withheld recommendations from women students. They are not forced to suffer in silence because of fear of peer disapproval. In fact, many men are eager to discuss being sexually hassled. Their talk may be locker room bragging or a self-protective strategy to prevent gossip.

Even in the most extreme cases of sexual hassle, men faculty seldom suffer the complex psychological effects of sexual harassment victims. They may have to endure unpleasant scenes, disturbed domestic relations, and temporary unease, but they have the power to control the problem. They work in an environment they understand. They are at home in academe as students are not and know how to protect themselves and to discourage students causing them discomfort.

Sexual hassle is not an excuse for tolerating or ignoring sexual harassment. Students do not set the tone or the parameters of interactions with professors. They do not have that kind of authority. No behavior, however seductive, from a student ever legitimizes inappropriate, irresponsible behavior by faculty. Sexual hassle does not give college professors the right to violate responsibilities to students or the ethics of their profession.

When defensive faculty are not bemoaning the vulnerability of professors, they are advocating for openness and sexual health in the academic environment. They worry that prohibition of sexual harassment will become zealous and jeopardize positive interaction between the sexes and make all give-and-take between men and women unacceptable.

The dynamics of men and women working together on the campus and elsewhere is not yet truly understood. Until there is more systematic analysis, the most that can be said is that the presence of both men and women lends a certain excitement and energy to work. Sexual give-and-take — the friendly verbal interaction between colleagues, the acknowledged attraction between coworkers, the accepted physical gesturing of male and female — is a healthy behavior in which individuals of various ages and stations choose to engage.

"Choice" is the critical concept. Give-and-take implies mutual choice by people of equal status. The boundaries of the relationship are understood and accepted by both parties. There is no confusion, no doubt, no feeling of coercion or fear. The effects of jokes, comments, and gestures are that both feel good. The humor and affection in sexual give-and-take may be a way to reduce sexual tensions. It may relieve the monotony of routine work. It may even be preliminary courtship, a kind of testing before proceeding with a more serious relationship.

Whatever the intent, sexual give-and-take is based on mutual consent of equals. This is obviously not the case in sexual harassment. Normal sexual give-and-take is not possible in student-teacher relationships because the power imbalance and role disparity are too great. The legal, public, and institutional concern about sexual harassment is a concern about *unhealthy* sexual dynamics, about behaviors that are exploitive, abusive, and psychologically and academically damaging. In fact, if people become more aware of the sexual harassment problem, a healthier sexual environment for both men and women should result.

The obscurity surrounding sexual harassment is fading, and a public record is being compiled. The few cases that reach the courts are reported in detail in the press. Judicial readings and interpretations are instantly analyzed by policy-makers in business and public institutions. National conferences of business, industry, professional, and academic groups include special sessions to keep abreast of the latest rulings and mediation techniques. Corporations, colleges, and women's groups conduct surveys in an attempt to put numbers on the problem. Survey results, however sketchy, make headlines. On individual campuses where students have pursued complaints, there is grapevine discussion of the cases and paper trails and institutional memories are being created. The history of sexual harassment, anecdotal and fragmented, is being written daily.

For too long, the college campus either ignored sexual harassment, hoped it was nonexistent, or waited for it to disappear on its own. Today, however, faculty and administrators, encouraged by the law, realize that they share the same problems and responsibilities as business, industry, and government. Sexual harassment exists. Women's resistance is increasing, and procrastination and inaction by institutions pose grave risks.

Some campuses have already suffered the embarrassment that inevitably results when charges of sexual misconduct by professors become public. Almost every campus periodically experiences a full-blown sexual harassment scandal, but most of these are kept within institutions, usually within the small circle of people actually dealing with the case. Some of the discreetness is due to regard for confidentiality; some is because campuses are adept at avoiding unwanted publicity. When the news media do report a sexual harassment case, it is usually because a special-interest group has created public attention or the student or public press discovers a case and investigates. However it happens, institutions are understandably unhappy about such notoriety. The best they can hope in such situations is to demonstrate that the institution itself acted responsibly and resolutely.

Accounts in the *Los Angeles Times* and *San Jose News* suggested that San Jose State University acted resolutely after five women students accused Associate Professor of Philosophy Phillip D. Jacklin of persistently touching, embracing, kissing, fondling, and propositioning them. The incidents were reported to have occurred in his office or in telephone conversations. Following an investigation by Jacklin's department chairman and dean, the university advised him in writing that he was being charged with immoral and unprofessional conduct. President Gail Fullerton recommended his dismissal. Under university procedure, Jacklin had three choices: accept dismissal without admitting to the charges, resign, or request a hearing.

He originally opted for a public hearing before a three-member faculty committee. His attorney later requested that the hearing be closed to the public. Acting on the unanimous recommendation of the committee and President Fullerton, the Chancellor of the California State University and Colleges fired Jacklin on January 2, 1980. The action was upheld fifteen months later when Superior Court Judge James Wright handed down a ruling on an appeal by Jacklin.

Wright said, "The record is replete with a series of numerous incidents in which petitioner violated his professional responsibility over a period of years with his young female students. There was no abuse of discretion in [the university's] ordering the maximum penalty of dismissal." Denying that he had engaged in harassment, Jacklin commented on the students' charges, "Sometimes they initiated it; sometimes I did. Student-faculty relationships are very prevalent on campus."[22]

The case of Elbaki Hermassi, Assistant Professor of Sociology at the University of California, Berkeley, aroused great controversy on the Berkeley campus, in the University of California system, and in the news media in 1979. Hermassi, who had been at Berkeley nine years and was awaiting tenure, was accused by thirteen students of fondling and propositioning them, offering one a grade in exchange for sex, and writing an unfavorable recommendation for a student who refused his advances. The complaints against Hermassi surfaced after protests by a group called Women Organized Against Sexual Harassment (WOASH). Although he never was named by the University, the *Los Angeles Times* and other publications identified Hermassi as the accused. The women complainants were not publicly identified, and a controversy arose over whether Hermassi was denied the right to confront his accusers.

Hermassi, who denied all allegations of sexual harassment, first received an oral reprimand. Finally, the university appointed Professor Susan F. French of the University of California, Davis, Law School to conduct a confidential investigation. Her report was not made public but led Chancellor Albert H. Bowker to issue a statement that "misconduct warranting discipline" had occurred. Bowker's statement of January 7, 1980, said that in determining its sanction the administration considered that the behavior occurred during a "relatively short period of time" while the professor was "suffering personal emotional stress." Bowker made clear that, in accordance with campus procedures, the professor had been told of the administrative findings and proposed discipline. "Although the professor continues to deny the charges, he has agreed to accept the administration's proposed disposition of the case in order to avoid formal proceedings and set the matter at rest," said Bowker in his statement.

Hermassi was suspended without pay for one quarter, and a copy of the investigative report and administrative view of it was included in his personnel file. Students protested the sanction. WOASH called the action a "slap on the wrist" because Hermassi was scheduled to be on sabbatical during his suspension and contended his teaching status would not change. In the weeks prior to the administrative action, the Office of Student Advocate had accused the University of "stalling" in investigating complaints against the professor. In the general controversy, students staged a sit-in against sexual harassment in the sociology department, where slogans against the professor were printed on the walls. Hermassi, who ultimately resigned to accept a position in Tunisia, declared, "These people are looking for a cause, and I got in the way. I am not an American citizen, and because of my origins they regard me as easy to victimize."[23]

In December 1979, Martin L. Kilson, a Professor of Government at Harvard, was given a letter of reprimand by Dean Henry Rosovsky and warned that his tenure might be revoked if he was found guilty of further incidents of sexual harassment. As reported in the *Boston Globe*, Helene Sahadi York, a freshman, said Kilson patted her hair, kissed her on the top of the head, tried to kiss her on the lips, and made suggestive remarks to her during a visit to his office on November 15, 1979. She left his office after he told her "in a low, seductive voice," "I like you very much," and shortly afterward she filed a formal complaint.

York said that a university administrator asked her not to say anything about the incident but that she felt "other women have a right to know . . . In claiming I am a victim of sexual harassment, I am also saying that I am a victim of emotional rape." Kilson stated that the student's perception of his act as a sexual advance was "valid" and added that he did not intend to offend her. "I committed an act of impropriety . . . My general affectionate air could be misinterpreted," Kilson said.[24]

In 1982 Harvard again made newspaper headlines when a freshman woman accused visiting poet and professor Derek Walcott of sexual harassment. The incident became known largely through the persistence of the *Harvard Crimson*, which convinced the woman to make the case public. Her letter to Assistant Dean Marlyn M. Lewis was printed in the *Crimson* and contained a classic sexual harassment account:

To Dean Marlyn Lewis and whoever it may concern:
I,_____ , state that I was sexually harassed by Derek Walcott . . . on Monday night, November 2nd, 1981.

Before I recount our conversation together I would like to make two things clear: 1) that after class, Mr. Walcott would freely invite his students to have coffee with him to discuss aspects of poetry and the poet's life, and 2) that class and after-class discussions were frequently of a sexual nature.

Shortly after the end of class at five o'clock in Lehman Hall, Mr. Walcott asked his students if they would like to join him for a cup of coffee. I volunteered, expecting others to join me, but all the students had other things to do, and I alone remained with him. He asked me to recommend a place to go nearby, for he had a poetry reading to do later that night at the Faculty Club. I recommended the Science Center and we set off. When we arrived there we sat outside on the terrace because it was especially warm, and our conversation (reconstructed to the best of my abilities) went as follows:
Mr. Walcott: Do you have a boyfriend?
_____: Oh, I don't know . . . I wrote a poem.
W.: Don't talk about poetry. I don't want to talk about poetry.
_____: I wrote a poem about a guy I was with last Friday night.
W.: What did you do with this guy?
_____: What do you mean? . . . I made love with him.
W.: How did you make love?
_____: Why should I tell you? It's none of your business.
W.: Imagine me making love to you. What would I do?
_____: Huh? I guess you'd be sort of slow and deliberate.
W.: (Here he made a comment about "licking" a woman.) Would you

make love with me if I asked you?

_.: No. No way. You're married. Don't you love your wife?

W.: Love has nothing to do with lust.

_.: Oh . . . Mr. Walcott, I really should be getting to dinner.

W.: I'll walk you back.

_.: You don't have to. I'll go by myself.

W.: You have to show me where the Faculty Club is. I'll walk you back.

(By Memorial Church)

_.: Do you ever go to church?

W.: No, I don't go to church, but it doesn't mean that I'm not a believer (pause). You know what I'm thinking about?

_.: No, I don't.

W.: Yes, you know.

_.: Oh . . .

W.: Are you sure you won't change your mind?

_.: I'm sure.

W.: If you ever change your mind, tell me.

_.: I know I'll never change my mind.

While passing Lamont, he told me he would continue to ask me, and devised a "secret code" where I could answer him in class. He would ask me "Oui?" and I would answer him with a "Oui," or a "Peut-être." I refused to play any part in this game. He then left for the Faculty Club and I went into the Freshmen Union for dinner.

Upset and angered by Mr. Walcott's behavior, I told my proctor, Jennifer Hillman, about it later that same night, and she had me speak to Missy Holland, my Senior Advisor, a few days later. Missy told me that I had grounds for a formal complaint of sexual harassment. I replied that if I could be sure Mr. Walcott would no longer harass me, I would like to continue in the course, possibly filing a complaint when I finished. Missy advised me to write him a note. If this didn't work, I planned to drop the course and file a complaint. I gave him my note after class on November 16, the day before I was to have a personal conference to discuss my poetry. In conference he was cold and distant. He singled out one poem that he liked and described the others as formless, rhythmless, and incomplete. After assigning me to write a sonnet he told me he was finished, and I left. The conference had lasted ten minutes.

Knowing that he would no longer harass me, I remained in the course. He showed no concern for my education, and did not fully evaluate my work as he did with other students of the class. My emotional discomfort was so great I missed three classes in a row because of anxiety. At the end of the course I handed in all the required work, a ballad and a sonnet, and the poems I was writing on my own. I received a course grade of "C."

My emotional discomfort did not end with the course. A month ago, in a conversation with a male friend in the course, I discovered that another woman had been harassed. I don't know how many women were harassed by him at Harvard last semester, and what they did about it. All I know is that *no woman student should have to put up with a teacher's sexually harassing behavior.* I have therefore decided to file this complaint.

I ask that Harvard College redress my situation and I recommend the following actions to be taken:

1) that Mr. Walcott be no longer appointed to a teaching position at Harvard College.

2) that I be given the opportunity to have my work re-evaluated if I choose to.

3) that Mr. Walcott write me a letter of apology.

4) that Boston University's English Department be officially notified by Harvard College of my complaint and Harvard's actions toward Mr. Walcott.

Thank you,

As in the Kilson case three years earlier, Harvard Dean Henry Rosovsky investigated the complaint, reprimanded the professor, and required him to write an apology to the student. Rosovsky also notified Walcott's permanent employer of the incident. The student complainant released to the *Crimson* a letter from Harvard Assistant Dean Marlyn Lewis that illustrated the complexities of student, faculty, and administrative viewpoints surrounding sexual harassment on the campus.

Dear____,

I am writing to let you know that Dean Rosovsky has reviewed your complaint and has found it to have merit. Dean Rosovsky has therefore taken formal action against Professor Walcott.

As you know from our May 10 conversation in my office, Professor Walcott preferred that I not go to see him personally to explain your complaint, but wished that I read him your statement over the telephone. I did so, and he acknowledged that you had described his conduct accurately.

When you and I talked on May 10, I passed along to you a couple of Professor Walcott's reactions that I think it worth repeating here. Both help to explain, although not to excuse his unprofessional behavior toward you.

Professor Walcott's first response was that his teaching style is deliberately personal and intense. He believes that his success as a teacher is due largely to his ability to develop close personal relationships with his students, and to "drive" them to include "everything in their lives" in their poetry. From talking with you about Professor Walcott's course, I understood that this intensity was part of the course's appeal. I do want to underscore here the difficulty faced even by the most well-meaning instructors in striking an effective balance between personal interest and professional distance from students.

Professor Walcott's other reaction is related to the first. He reported to me that you had confided in him much personal information about your background and feelings. Indeed in the conversation you described in detail in your statement, Professor Walcott said that he sensed no reluctance in you to pursue the topic of sexual relationships. He told me that your note was the first clear indication he had that you did not welcome such conversations.

I think this last point is worth some careful reflection. Even in a teacher-student relationship, in which the burden of professional restraint must be with the teacher, the behavior of the student is likely to have some effect upon that of the teacher. Had you informed Professor Walcott at his first display of interest that you were unwilling, for example, to share with him the details of your personal life, you might have avoided the discomfort you suffered during the Science Center conversation and subsequently. Although hindsight cannot alter what has occurred, it should be possible to learn some useful lessons from this painful experience.

In talking with you about your complaint, I have explained the importance of keeping a separation in your mind between the complaint itself, in which you asserted that you were made to feel uncomfortable by Professor Walcott's excessive personal interest in you, and your disappointment with the grade of C you received for the course. I have, however, outlined for you the general procedure for having grades reviewed, and I know Missy Holland [the student's Senior Advisor] has discussed with you that process as well. I should mention here, however, that Professor Walcott told me on the telephone that your grade reflected only his evaluation of your work, and nothing more.

I expect you are relieved that the complaint process is at an end. If you have any questions, or if there are any aspects of the situation that you would find it useful to discuss, I hope you will let me know. I

should like to be of help in any way I can.
With best wishes.

Sincerely yours,
Marlyn McGrath Lewis
Assistant Dean of Harvard College

When asked, Dean Lewis maintained to the *Harvard Crimson* that sanctions against faculty should be kept secret because punishment is "a family matter [between the professor and the Dean]. We try to give instructors the privacy to recover." On October 19, 1982, after a review of the student's work in Walcott's class, Harvard's Administrative Board changed the student's grade from a "C" to a "pass." This was reportedly the first time the college took such an action because of a professor's possible bias in grading.[25]

In October 1982 the Florida Ethics Commission found Hillsborough Community College President Ambrose Garner guilty of sexual harassment after four women employees and one student accused him in separate charges of making sexual advances at Hillsborough and in his previous job at Miami-Dade Community College. In a five-day public hearing, reported in detail by the press, more than a dozen women told the commission that Garner had made sexual advances or suggestive remarks to them, but only five testimonies were considered because the other alleged incidents occurred before 1974, when the commission was created. Charges ranged from fondling and French-kissing women to suggestions that one should check into a hotel room and have "some fun" with the accused.

Garner had been granted a leave of absence from his duties in April 1982, when charges against him first became public. Garner maintained that he was "affectionate" and frequently kissed people, but he denied making passes at students and employees. His attorneys described two of the complainants who filed complaints after they were discharged from their jobs as "desperate people striking out for what they perceived to be their survival."

An assistant attorney general accused Garner of conflicting testimony on several occasions. One example she cited was Garner's contention that a back injury would have prevented him picking up a student who charged that he had told her he was going to carry her to a bedroom and "make love" to her. After Garner testified he hurt his back in 1976, the attorney showed him a form he had filled out at Hillsborough in 1980. In answer to the question, "Have you ever or do you have back trouble or complaints?" Garner had responded, "No."

On the recommendation of the Ethics Commission, the Hillsborough Community College trustees publicly censured Garner and suspended him for ninety days without pay. The penalty was, in reality, much more severe The head of the college's trustees remarked after the commission hearings, "We'll seek advice from our attorney as to what we can do legally . . . There's nothing to preclude us from beginning a presidential search."

It was not, however, only the titillating allegations and counter-charges that made the Garner case so interesting. Attracting equal attention was the male-female conflict that developed on the Ethics Commission, composed of four men and one woman. In the 4-1 vote that found Garner's action "corrupt," William O'Neil III was the dissenting vote. O'Neil suggested that the woman who had complained about being touched and French-kissed by the accused may have "unconsciously invited whatever conduct there was." O'Neil contended that Garner's behavior might at times have been "grossly improper" but added, " I don't think it rises to the level of corrupt use." Bernadine Spanjers, the only woman on the commission, was the dissenter in a 4-1 vote to suspend Garner because she wanted to recommend dismissal. "He didn't act like a college president should," she said.[26]

The few sexual harassment cases that have been publicly reported demonstrate the ambiguity and confusion that pervade the issue. No case to date has achieved the notoriety surrounding that of Sidney Peck, Associate Professor of Sociology and department head at Clark University. This case of alleged sexual harassment began in 1980, when Ximena Bunster, visiting Associate Professor of Anthropology, charged Peck, her department head, with unwanted sexual advances and propositions, promising her academic support in exchange for sex and retaliating when she rebuffed his advances.

Peck was well known on the campus for his radical politics; he was active in the antiwar movement and in negotiating increases in faculty pay and benefits. The campus erupted in controversy when supporters of Peck claimed that Clark was using the sexual harassment complaint to punish him for his political activities. During a formal inquiry before a faculty committee on personnel, four additional faculty, student, and staff women testified that they also had been harassed by Peck. The hearing resulted in the committee's recommending to Clark's president that a statement of charges be issued against Peck. This was done in December.

A month earlier, Bunster and Betsy Stanko also filed discrimination complaints against Clark with the EEOC. In January 1981 the University moved to have these dismissed. In the same month, Peck filed a complaint with the National Labor Relations Board. Because Clark is a private college with collective bargaining, the NLRB has jurisdiction over labor disputes. Peck claimed that he was being investigated because of his politics and his role in negotiating faculty pay raises.

In March lawyers representing Bunster and Stanko declined to participate further in Peck's campus trial. They objected to Clark's handling of the case and its treatment of the complainants. They charged that the women were not permitted to call witnesses on their own behalf, to receive a copy of the decision or to comment on the composition of the hearing board. They objected to the school's alleged refusal to address the problem of sexual harassment and its failure to hold hearings adequate to resolve the women's complaints.

The next day, the university signed a settlement with Peck. He agreed not to serve as a department chairman of any department at Clark and to take a leave of absence beginning in March 1981 and a half-year sabbatical at full pay beginning in September. A day later, Peck filed a defamation of character suit against Bunster and Stanko for $23.7 million. They countersued for $1.3 million each for alleged sexual harassment.

In July 1982 Clark University announced that Stanko, Bunster, and Peck had "agreed to an end to all legal proceedings related to previous complaints filed with the Federal Equal Opportunity Commission under Title VII . . . In addition, all parties . . . agreed not to file new charges or claims against each other with respect to the matters previously in dispute, and Clark . . . agreed to pay for a portion of the legal fees incurred by Bunster and Stanko. No money damages [were] paid by Clark University, and all claims against the University [were] withdrawn."[27] In the fall of 1983, Stanko began a sabbatical in Great Britain; Bunster, having completed her duties as a visiting professor at Clark, began teaching at the University of

Maryland. Sidney Peck, after completing his leave, returned to the campus, where former Boston University sociologist Ruth Harriet Jacobs replaced him as chair of the Department of Sociology.

The women involved in the incident were adamant about its personal and professional costs. At one point, Betsy Stanko expressed concern that she might not be granted tenure at Clark and she worried about the effect that Peck's suit might have on other victims of sexual harassment: "Any woman who knows the pressure we've been under would be crazy to come forward." The graduate student who testified against Peck had a similar response: "I was just trying to get an education and because of this case my life has been turned upside-down."

The purpose of reviewing the details of these well-publicized cases is not to revive their notoriety or to establish guilt or innocence. It is to point out the recurrent themes of sexual harassment. In all but one of the cases, complaints came from multiple sources, sometimes as many as a dozen or more; complainants described incidents that occurred over extended periods of time — frequently years. The charges were serious; educators were accused of propositioning, kissing, and fondling. In every case, peers hearing complete testimonies from accused and complainants found evidence sufficient to support charges of sexual harassment. Though some admitted to the behaviors of which they were accused and others denied them, all minimized or dismissed accusations. Jacklin claimed his behavior was a response to students' sexual advances. Hermassi, Garner, and Peck asserted that they were persecuted for their political views and activities. Garner and Kilson maintained that their affectionate natures were misconstrued. Walcott's defense was that a student misunderstood his teaching style. Institutional handling of the cases varied, and sanctions differed greatly.

Whether or not they are publicized, the student and faculty casualties of sexual harassment are mounting. Whatever the outcome in any of these cases, the academic community as well as individuals suffer. The questions facing higher education seem increasingly complex. How can higher education maintain its credibility and status in society if it admits to the presence of harassers? How can it pretend ignorance of the problem when so many know it exists? How can it devise fair sanctions when the precedents are so few and so varied? How can it assess the ultimate academic and psychological damage to victims, and how can it hope to compensate them for their distress?

As the questions multiply and threats of litigation and government intervention increase, higher education must reexamine its own organizational structure, traditions, loyalties, and morality. The struggle to solve the problem of sexual harassment is one it cannot afford to lose.

2 : *Inside the Ivy Walls*

A SEPARATE REALITY

No, he inwardly shouted to himself: Keogh, keep out of this, or they will get you. *The chapel clock struck one. Within twenty hours he perceived, they had succeeded in leading him up the garden path into one of their academic mazes, where a man could wander for eternity, meeting himself in mirrors.* No, he repeated. *Possibly they were all very nice, high-minded, scrupulous people with only an occupational tendency toward backbiting and a nervous habit of self-correction, always emending, penciling, erasing; but he did not care to catch the bug which seemed to be endemic in these ivied haunts.*

Mary McCarthy,
The Groves of Academe

Sexual harassment of women students can be understood only by examining the organization and traditions of the college campus. Higher education is a peculiar institution. At the same time traditional and avant garde, moralistic and libertarian, rigid and flexible, it is neither as highly organized nor as clear in its priorities as the public and the campus assume. Sexual harassment is affected by an environmental context that parents and students, as well as faculty and administrators, need to understand.

The organizational character of the campus has been analyzed by several social scientists. In *Leadership and Ambiguity*, Michael Cohen and James March characterized academic organizations as "organized anarchy."[1] J. Victor Baldridge, a sociologist, described them as "fluid, changing, and confused . . . [with] lines of authority [that] are often blurred . . . [A]cademic organizations are splintered and fragmented around an ambiguous, changing and contested set of objectives."[2] These descriptions help to explain why sexual harassment flourishes in an environment where many people least expect it.

The character and structure of the campus help determine the nature of sexual harassment of women students. The purposes of higher education are assumed to be as distinct and enduring as the Latin motto chiseled on the cornerstone of the college library. While this might once have been true, today higher education suffers from the attempt to be all things to all people. Scholar Jacques Barzun observed:

> All [universities] tend to suffer from similar and unexampled difficulties. They spend huge sums and are desperately poor; their students attack them; their neighbors hate them; the faculties are restless; and the public, critical of their rising fees and restricted enrollments, keeps making more and more preemptory demands upon them. The universities are expected, among other things, to turn out scientists and engineers, foster international understanding, provide a home for the arts, satisfy divergent tastes in architecture and sexual morals, cure cancer, recast the penal code, and train equally for the professions and for a life of cultured contentment in the Coming Era of Leisure.[3]

AMBIGUITY OF MISSION AND METHOD

The original purpose of academia was to educate and to pursue knowledge, but in the last half of the twentieth century the mission has become much less clear. The complexity of the faculty role is compounded by the notion that faculty must nurture as well as educate students. Professors' tasks are ambitious, indefinite, and paradoxical. Faculty are challenged not simply to teach traditional disciplines but also to clarify "values," to develop "character," to impart "wisdom," to nurture "good citizenship," to foster "creativity," to encourage "growth." It is no matter that few agree about the meaning of these terms — faculty are expected to inculcate them in their students.

When a professor assumes or is told that he should foster the moral, social, and spiritual as well as intellectual development of students, he can lose sight of the proper limits of his interest and authority. The distinctions between his professional jurisdiction and the student's private life become blurred, and a faculty member can readily convince himself that he is acting appropriately when he may in fact be violating the parameters of proper relations with students.

David G., a professor of engineering who advises several college organizations, is very popular with students. His comments emphasize the faculty dilemma.

> I think I ought to spend time with students. Most of us seem so aloof and remote to them. So when they invite me to an organizational function, like a skating party or a potluck, I'll go. And I think it's good for them to feel free to talk about their problems — their coursework is pretty demanding and the job market is very competitive. But it gets a little crazy sometimes, and I find myself being asked to advise them about their girlfriends or views about religion. I barely know what to do with my own daughters, let alone their problems. But I at least think I should listen.

Not only are many faculty members ambiguous about *what* they are supposed to be doing, they are equally uncertain about *how* to do it. Assuming that the professor does have the right to involve himself in a student's life, and that is an enormous assumption, there are no standard procedures for accomplishing that end. College professors are trained in specific academic disciplines but rarely receive any instructions about teaching or counseling. The advising of students requires skills in counseling and psychology which faculty never study, so many of them improvise as they go along. Often the results are disastrous.

An associate professor at the University of Massachusetts commented:

> We're continually being told by administrators that we'll be evaluated on the basis of how well we "relate" to our students. We're supposed to be "accessible," and during the late sixties and early seventies, education became a highly personalized profession. There's no question that we see young women at their most inexperienced and susceptible, as well as most attractive, and it's extremely tempting to overlook the innate disadvantage of their position. If you're a really good teacher, you're going to touch them deeply. You're *supposed* to; that's your job.

Many faculty members, male *and* female, sincerely believe, perhaps correctly, the best learning environment is one which is emotionally, even sexually, charged . . . but it's also true that some professors take their D. H. Lawrence lectures out of the classroom and into the nearest motel.[4]

Especially since the 1960s, when higher education was criticized for its impersonality and irrelevance, professors have been told to "relate" to students and to involve themselves with development of the "total" student. They have little direction about what they are supposed to do and how to do it. Inevitably, some can become confused about the genuine reasons for their behaviors. The professor whose intentions are less than honorable can take advantage of the situation. Using the rubric that he is an adviser and caretaker as well as a teacher, a lecherous professor can justify to himself and others all sorts of contacts with a student. He can involve her in discussions about family background, personal problems, romantic relationships, and sexual experiences. He can touch her, invent reasons for seeing her outside the classroom, and suggest private unconventional meeting places. There is always the coffee lounge or the corner bar to serve as a blurred boundary between campus and off-campus.

Women may not realize until too late that interest in them goes beyond the purely academic. Students are hard-pressed to know how far professors can be permitted to intrude into their lives. They are conditioned for twelve or more years to believe that teachers are nurturing and benevolent, so it is easy to regard an intimate conversation, a physical gesture, or an invitation to a private meeting as an extension of that caring. And, of course, there are many faculty who *do* nurture through a pat on the hand, who *do* become valuable guidance counselors, who *do* sacrifice private time for students.

Even when it becomes obvious that a faculty member's interest in a student extends beyond legitimate professional concern, she may still be confused. The college professor is, after all, something of a paragon in society; refusing his advances is different from rejecting a pass from a classmate. A student may worry about how a rejection will affect her grades or status in the college. She may fear that refusing a professor's advances is a denial of her own growth, a rejection of the intellectual maturity that the instructor represents. To be propositioned by a college professor can be a heady experience; to muster an appropriate response is a formidable task.

PROFESSIONAL AUTONOMY

The role of the teacher demands that he be set apart or, in a sense, "above" the student. In colleges and universities, however, the power of the professor is even greater. Unlike high school teachers, whose activities in school are carefully monitored by administrators, college professors have a long tradition of autonomy and self-regulation in their classrooms. The tradition is generally sound, but in cases of sexual harassment it can lead to problems.

College faculty seldom admit one basic truth about their work: few professions guarantee so much potential for exerting control over so many other human beings. There are not many professionals who have such individual power and simultaneous freedom from constraint. Politicians, whatever their transgressions, are ultimately answerable to the ballot box. Even physicians are more accountable than professors. If an illness persists or treatment fails, a patient may seek a second opinion. But how many students question the quality of instruction they are receiving?

As long as faculty do not abuse their professional autonomy, as long as they use it legitimately in the classroom and laboratory as teachers and scholars, it is laudable, defendable, and essential to the academic endeavor. But this autonomy demanded by faculty is illusive. The most subtle of its effects is the distorted self-image it can create for some. A professor can develop an exaggerated sense of self-importance; he may feel like a deity in his profession. The classroom, laboratory, and office are sanctuaries. He resists, except under the most controlled circumstances, any invasion of the privacy of his classroom. To students he dictates attendance, study, and grading policies; he has absolute control over content, interpretation, and methodology in his course. Students are completely at the mercy of his judgment or whim. And both he and they know it.

Autonomy offers sanctuary for him and hazard for them. In the course of a college education a student may encounter an average of twenty to fifty professors. No two will be alike. Each has a unique set of goals and a highly personal philosophy of education. Professors differ on even the most petty rules and procedures. In a four-year degree program, an undergraduate will have from 35 to 60 separate courses, depending on her major and whether the college has a semester or quarter system.

When sexual harassment occurs in this extraordinary setting, the result can be devastating. "I didn't even know what he wanted on tests. How was I supposed to understand what he meant when he got me to come to his office?" one student at a Big Ten university asked. The inherent inequality of the student-teacher relationship often leads the student to assume that college professors are different from males her own age. She is shocked when forced to recognize that their intentions are actually quite similar. One sophomore commented, "I couldn't believe it! He [an English professor] grabbed for me just like guys do when they're sixteen. You'd think someone his age would at least have a little class about it."

Because faculty enjoy so much freedom, they are quick to defend the concept of autonomy for the entire profession.The American Association of University Professors (AAUP), the national association guarding academic freedom and tenure, has fought to secure faculty freedom. The 1940 AAUP statement on Academic Freedom and Tenure was tested through almost bloody battles before it became a tradition of academic life. Professors know how hard tenure and the right to self-regulation were to secure, and they are not about to risk them for quick resolutions to sexual harassment or any other problem that threatens those privileges.

Yet this autonomy tempts arrogance. It is easy — and convenient — to confuse the principle of academic freedom with license to behave and speak irresponsibly. There is little that is "off-limits" in the classroom, and a clever instructor can justify even the most offensive behavior. Leslie K., a student from a rural area studying at a Midwestern college, relates how she was humiliated in class:

My Survey of English Lit professor was talking about the development of the romance in Medieval Literature when we were analyzing *Gawain and the Green Knight*. There were about fifty people in the class, and I didn't know any of them. He looked at me and said, "You know, the funniest things people do are either in bed or when they're trying to get there. Don't you think so?" I was really embarrassed because all these people I didn't even know were looking at me and laughing. He just kept staring at me, so I said something like "I don't know." Then he said, "Don't know because you haven't done the reading or because you've never been in bed with anyone?" That just made everyone laugh harder.

A college graduate told the National Advisory Council about a physics professor's offensive behavior in class:

> One physics professor gave his students a lecture on the effects of outer space on humans. His example consisted of crude drawings of a shapely woman supine in a vessel; the effects of vacuum were demonstrated by changes in the size of her "boobs." This man — a "mature" adult — told the story with all of the sniggering, head-hanging, and red-facedness I might have expected from an adolescent.[5]

The graduate school seminar setting can allow a professor the opportunity for extended intimate conversations the student can't avoid. Another respondent to the National Advisory Council discussed this problem:

> This semester one of my graduate course professors . . . started the first class session asking the women in the class if they liked recreational sex. The second session went the same way. The third session, after he found out which women were married, he asked me why I wasn't married. During the fourth session, he asked me what I thought love was. I told him love to me was when a child has a fluffy rabbit that the little boy or girl loves dearly and takes care of. I was trying not to apply the term to myself in a sexual manner, even though I felt that is what he wanted me to say. Then he said, "Well, what would you do if I said that I loved you?" I said that I would say no, but because it was my choice to remain independent, and not because I dislike him as a person. He then said, "Well, what would you say if I said that I wanted to make love to you?" Again, I said no. Then, after he made reference to how a large man could just overpower a smaller woman, he gave an example of how he could just go ahead and rape me. When I asked him what he would do when he was brought in to be tried, he said that he would just lie. When he adjourned the class that night he told everybody that they could all go except [me]. I did stay after and asked him what he wanted. He just started complimenting me on what a fine lawyer he thought I would be. As we left the classroom, he started toward his office while trying to continue his conversation with me. I then turned the other direction and said goodbye.[6]

The more sophisticated student senses that the professor's autonomy in the classroom extends potentially to the campus grievance process. She suspects that complaints about sexual harassment will be reduced to a conflict between her word and that of an older, educated, established, and prestigious figure.

Elaine C., a graduate student at a Midwestern university, described the autonomy of the professor as "prick power."

> I met Dr. ___ accidentally at a social function we'd both been invited to. I had a dress that was cut in a low V-neck. I guess he would say I bought it to entice men. I thought I bought it because it looked good on me. Anyway, he kept following me around all night even though his wife was there and asking me if I was wearing a bra. I don't know what it was supposed to prove if I wasn't, but I just kept changing the subject. He kept getting more and more personal until finally I asked my fiancé to take me home. When I saw him two days later at a meeting of my [doctoral] committee, he was horrible to me. He challenged everything I said and acted as if he was getting some sort of thrill out of putting me down. I'd never seen him behave like that before, and it took over two days for me to figure out that he really did want to put me down — literally. He couldn't screw me physically, so he made up his mind he was going to do it academically.

DIFFUSED INSTITUTIONAL AUTHORITY

In the fragmented organizational structure of the typical campus, "screwing" students professionally and psychologically is really quite simple. Rather than having one dominant professional group, like physicians in hospitals, the modern university is populated with academic departments that are highly independent and resistant to centralization. They are housed within equally independent colleges. Even in a small liberal arts college, there are dozens of departments and programs, with separate administrative structures. In a comprehensive university, there can be 15 to 20 colleges, each with a dean, and 10 to 20 departments in each college. One result of this diffused structure is that governance is extremely difficult. Hazard Adams, English professor and former administrator, observed that a basic principle of higher education is "that *no one has the complete power to do any given thing* . . ."[7]

Baldridge made the same observation: "The academic kingdom is torn apart in many ways, and there are few kings in the system who can enforce cooperation and unity. There is little peace in academia; warfare is common and no less deadly because it is polite. *The critical point is this: because the social structure of the universe is loose, ambiguous, shifting, and poorly defined, the power structure of the university is also loose, ambiguous, shifting, and poorly defined.*[8]

Role Conflict

One consequence of this poorly defined power structure is role conflict. Faculty are caught among the diverse expectations of students, peers, department heads, deans, provosts, and presidents. A department head has responsibilities to the administration, the department, and students. A dean confronts different expectations from the same groups. The president and trustees must juggle constituencies that include parents, alumni, community, and politicians. Despite the difference in size, the smallest liberal arts college and the largest multiversity share the same complexity of roles. The consequence of this role conflict is not only confusion, but in the case of sexual harassment, institutional paralysis.

The father of a student who had been propositioned by her history instructor inquired incredulously of a dean, "But you're the dean! Why can't you just fire him?" The father does not — cannot — understand that the dean is a man whose authority is interpreted differently within every level of the bureaucracy. He must protect the student, but he must also consider the welfare and rights of the individual faculty member. The central administration and the trustees — if need arises — will judge his ability to balance all factors. Usually, the dean does not even dare consider what might happen should alumni and the public become alerted to a sexual harassment problem, and the threat of court action seems remote and theoretical until it happens.

Lack of Accountability

Although this diffuse power structure is partially responsible for higher education's poor record in coping with sexual harassment, it remains to be seen whether most campuses are *unable* or simply *unwilling* to deal with the problem. To the discredit of higher education, the latter is probably more accurate. Because accountability is so indirect and grievance procedures so time-consuming and cumbersome, true resolution in academe is rare. Sexual harassment problems are more easily resolved through attrition. The process of formal complaint wears the victim down, the issues become confused, and time erodes anger. The student transfers or graduates, and the lecherous professor feels safe and even sanctioned. His publications list follows him wherever he goes; his reputation for sexual harassment does not.

Asked their responses to specific charges against colleagues, faculties' and administrators' responses are predictable. An associate professor of English complained:

> Come on! What am I supposed to do about ____? Everyone knows what he's doing. They've known it for years. I'm not the head of the god-damned department. Let *him* do something about it.

A dean resisted assuming an informal role:

> I'm not sure it's an administrator's function to approach faculty with what are just rumors. Then if a grievance does ensue, my impartiality appears diminished.

A mathematics professor reflected his concern for protecting his relationship with a colleague:

> I have to work with _____ . We're in the same department. We serve on a committee together. He's been here a year longer than I. I'm supposed to take rumors from 19-year-old girls more seriously than my working relationship with him? Even if he does say a few off-color things now and then, I doubt that he realizes that he's offending anyone. He's a good person and a dedicated teacher. He wouldn't hurt anyone on purpose.

Higher education is not truly impotent in the face of sexual harassment. The power to effect remedies exists, but it is easier to deny authority and responsibility. If a faculty member engages in questionable behavior with a student, colleagues assume it is *his* business. She is *his* charge — as if a student is intellectual chattel — and any intrusion into that relationship violates a colleague's professional authority. Department heads, deans, and provosts hesitate to intrude on a faculty member's domain; questioning of one professor's behavior is often viewed by his colleagues as a violation of group autonomy.

THE MYTH OF COLLEGIALITY

Higher education has long affirmed its commitment to the concept of collegiality. Educators see themselves as a community of scholars bound together by common interests and goals. At times, however, this image of internal community or professional bonding contributes to the problem of sexual harassment. The "we-they" mentality of higher education, the tendency to regard the campus as separate from the "outside" world, causes college professors to diminish or deny complaints about members of their profession. The irony is that except in cases of "invasion" from without, there are few professions that are less cohesive. Individual rivalries are common and bitter; specialists within departments struggle for dominance; departments compete for power; colleges within universities vie for preeminence within the institution.

But let a single 110-pound nineteen-year-old muster the courage to complain about being fondled or threatened by a Shakespeare professor, and Latin professors, geographers, physicists, architects, engineers, and lawyers are likely to rediscover the bonds that unite them. They will as a chorus mouth platitudes about loyalty to the institution, academic freedom, and due process. They will suddenly remember the lyrics to the alma mater.

"There's one of me, and all of them. You're crazy if you think I'm going to go to the ombudsman and put myself on the line. They'll hang together, and then they'll hang me," a graduate student protested when encouraged to file a complaint. She was twice cornered in a laboratory by a biology professor. A women faculty member, seeking advice and help from her department head, was rebuffed when she complained about a male colleague's bragging about his sexual conquests with undergraduates. The department head told her, "I don't want to hear anything about him because I won't believe it. I've known him since he was a graduate student, and he's our colleague."

Whether colleagues tend to support one another out of self-preservation, personal insecurity, or professional or institutional loyalty is not the issue. Evidence from across the country and on the grapevines of individual campuses indicates that faculty response is predictably supportive of colleagues and unsympathetic to women complainants and their advocates.

TOLERANCE OF ECCENTRICITY

The concept of collegiality is closely bound to another characteristic of the academic environment. Higher education is more willing than most institutions to tolerate eccentric behavior from its members. At first glance this live-and-let-live attitude seems open-minded, even commendable.

Colleges and universities are dedicated to the communication of ideas, the pursuit of truth, and the expansion of the frontiers of knowledge. Since no one can predict who will be successful in the pursuit or who will push the frontiers furthest, the institution must rely, insofar as feasible, upon universal intellectual investment in its faculty. No one can successfully predict which scientist will discover DNA, who will write a definitive literary biography, or who will devise a new method for teaching learning-disabled children. Protecting individuals from internal or external limitations on scholarship and research entails a high degree of tolerance, even respect, for eccentricity. Innovation and creativity are the positive values of the community.

The danger is that the concept becomes too loose and too many behaviors fall under this protective mantle. Every campus has its proverbial lost-in-thought, absent-minded professor. Unfortunately, many also have an equally well-known "lecher." The first may be the one to redefine our understanding of space; the second will be too busy stalking co-eds to concentrate on the sky. A student's complaint about papers returned late by the former should be considered far differently from a student's charging the latter with fondling her.

Tolerance of eccentricity should extend to intellectual and personal freedom only to the point that they do not adversely affect others. The autonomy of the biologist to pursue new methodology at odd hours does not include the right to bargain with women students for sexual attention. The difference seems obvious, but few institutions have statements that draw the line. On the contrary, academic freedom and individual autonomy are so sacred to the educational community that there is no such thing as summary dismissal for faculty who abuse the concept of autonomy. The professor accused of abusing students has only to cry "academic freedom," and the system tends to rally to his side.

Professors are likely to be more concerned about due process for the accused than they are about the sexual harassment or the victim. One dean, who is also a lawyer, described what he termed faculty "paranoia" about fair play: "College professors are always eager to go further than the law requires. They demand due process for colleagues beyond all legal necessity because they're so concerned about anyone's getting a bum rap." Perhaps this assessment is too optimistic. If professors' concerns for fair play and due process were so great, they might extend it to students as well as to their colleagues and thus curtail abuses such as sexual harassment.

PERCEPTIONS OF STUDENTS

Higher education's attitude toward students has a serious impact on the ways in which it deals — and, more often, does *not* deal — with sexual harassment. Traditionally, students are viewed as learners and subordinates, clay to be molded by the genius of the academician-potter. As a group, students are terribly heterogeneous; despite the media portrait of student power, most students are only marginally interested in the operation of their institutions. Their voices within the system are far more subdued and diffused than the public realizes. A common assumption is that noise from a few students represents or will result in advantages for the majority; the reality is that on most campuses, student opinions are heard only sporadically and often inaccurately.

The only organized, officially sanctioned, and visible student voices on most campuses are student governments and the student newspaper. But these are ephemeral and seldom speak for the student body as a whole. Even on a small campus, the high-profile student leaders are a special group within the student body. Student government leaders often function without any seriously interested constituency. The typical student on a large campus probably does not even know the names of student government officers. On a small campus, they may know the names but think their representatives inaccessible.

Exam schedules, tuition increases, and homecoming festivities are within the accepted jurisdiction of student governments. Behaviors of professors and their relationships with individual students are not. Unlike faculty, students are processed and turned out by the institution. Their movements within the system are rapid and unpredictable. Once they have graduated, they move on to new environments and new endeavors where they forget and are forgotten. In many ways, students are individually and collectively invisible.

Most are sophisticated in their recognition of the gap between them and the institutional hierarchy. This realization underlies the comment of a student whose mother insisted she see the dean of her college about a series of sexual incidents with an instructor. She observed, "I wouldn't even know the dean if I fell over him, and she wants me to go tell him Mr. ____ keeps calling me up."

The predominant attitude of many students and faculty is that because students reside within the system temporarily and lack a clear or unified voice, they can be taken less seriously than those for whom the campus is a permanent home. This view is at the heart of one of the most commonly heard faculty responses to news of a harassment grievance: "So ____ gave her a little trouble. Nobody's perfect. But his whole career is at stake. He's 52 years old, and she's 20. In a year she will have forgotten all about it."

Faculty are uncomfortable and even hostile when students protesting sexual harassment step beyond their prescribed roles and demand to be treated as citizens and consumers with moral and legal rights. Higher education's long-standing resistance to the notion of the student-as-consumer betrays much about its inability and unwillingness to take students and their complaints seriously.

THE PASTORAL SELF-IMAGE

The dilemma for educators is that the sexual harassment issue threatens one of the campus' most cherished self-images. American colleges and universities inherited from the cloisters of Europe the concept of themselves as removed from the world. They tend to see themselves as Edens and this pastoral myth is so widespread that, until recently, few questioned such romantic conceptions of the college experience. This is the reason the campus protests of the late 1960s were so shattering to the public. They belied all of society's stereotypes of professors, students, and collegiate institutions. In popular mythology, the campus is a cloistered, protected environment dedicated to the nurturance of the young. Inside the ivy walls people are supposedly open, natural, and good; catalogs and recruiting films exploit the stereotype as much as possible.

Jocelyn College, scene of battle and intrigue in Mary McCarthy's *The Groves of Academe*, was portrayed in typical fashion as "a picturesque campus — a group of long, thick-walled, mansarded, white-shuttered stone dwellings arranged around a cupolaed chapel with a planting of hemlocks, the remains of a small, old German Reformed denominational college that had imparted to the secluded ridge a Calvinistic sweetness of worship and election."[9]

Describing Yale as "built to withstand attack . . . by mobs of storming townspeople," John Knowles in his novel *The Paragon* developed the familiar campus-garden image.

> There were symmetrical inner courtyards and blooming shrubbery and tended trees and clipped lawns, stained-glass windows and minstrel galleries and Gothic towers, little and big bells in little and big belfries, fieldstone sunken patios, pillared loggias, winding staircases, sealed rooms for music and for squash, ornamental gateways and echoing tunnels, built-in town houses, stranded gazebos, organs surrounded by immense hanging banks of pipes, sculptural figures, mostly clothed and mostly seated, Victorian porte cochères, a defenseless and historic eighteenth-century dormitory completely surrounded by a fortified perimeter, subterranean passageways, white marble Greek temples, numerous bizarre windowless redoubts, greenswards and croquet lawns.[10]

Higher education takes great care to maintain its image as a verdant island removed from the corruptions of the outside world. The college catalogs of the most urban campuses focus on the greenery, not the concrete. Some academics regard preservation of that myth as essential to survival in an age of declining enrollments, financial crisis, and pessimism about the value of a college degree. The predicament facing educators is that when a snake enters the garden, all the trees and ivy in the world — real or imagined — cannot hide its presence forever. Sexual harassment exists, and no public relations campaign is skillful enough to disguise it once it is revealed.

The campus is no longer a walled garden, and now that attention is focused on sexual harassment and women are more vocal in their resistance to it, the subject will not be permitted to sink back into obscurity. Business, industry, the federal government, and the public have economic, as well as psychological, fingers in the academic pie. So long as sexual harassment remains a highly visible issue, colleges and universities must deal with it or risk loss of financial aid and public support — impossible sacrifices at a time of diminished resources and declining enrollments.

ACADEMIC CONSERVATISM

Rapid response to a problem, even a highly serious one, is not easy for most college professors. Both their educations and professional practice instill respect for painstaking analysis and deliberation. College professors are people who work in an environment where ideas are tested, critiqued, and retested by others before they are accepted or put into action. They are not hostile to change as much as they are cautious, convinced that the best changes are the most deliberate. Higher education is, after all, the institution that expresses society's respect for its roots. Its perspective is not the present but rather the entire history of ideas. Because the scope of its vision is universal, it perceives an issue in terms of what has endured over time and what a current decision will entail for the future.

This perspective sounds impressive but is little consolation to the parent who sends a daughter off to college where she is propositioned by her calculus professor while assorted faculty and deans debate the ramifications of developing special institutional policies to deal with harassment. Concern for context and traditions causes the campus to move cautiously, but the student's distress is immediate and undebatable. The problem is exacerbated by the use of committees to analyze issues such as sexual harassment. Individuals who suffer through participation in these august bodies usually attest to the fact that nothing moves more slowly than an academic committee.

As if slow deliberations on policy are not sufficient to discourage efficient response to sexual harassment, there is the additional impact of the campus calendar. The education establishment moves at a much slower pace than that of the rest of the world. Academic life moves in cycles where much is predictable and even more is repetitious. The autumn is needed for organization of committees; meetings depend on diverse schedules and other priorities; recommendations for policy are reviewed again and again. There is no sense of urgency. There is always, for the campus, another homecoming, another Christmas break, another spring vacation, another graduation. Students' faces change, but their habits and abilities are relatively stable. When changes do occur, they are so gradual that the professor rarely notices.

The professor himself lives in a world where much is circumscribed, where the parameters of time are narrow and knowable from the start. He begins by being appointed to multiple-year terms. After seven years, his colleagues determine his lifelong value to the institution. If the decision is positive and he is granted tenure, he knows that he can expect two more promotions and that his remuneration at the height of his career will give him little more buying power than he had as an assistant professor. Some, in pessimistic moments, compare the process to a line in Beckett's *Waiting for Godot*: "Nothing happens, nobody comes, nobody goes, it's awful."[11]

Others take an opposite view. One student affairs official contends that rather than being narrow and dull, the academic lifestyle appears safe to those who choose it and that this influences their reactions to high visibility issues like harassment. She theorizes, "Maybe the pool is so still that even a little ripple can be disturbing. Maybe sex harassment is such a big deal to them because it threatens their calm."

INEQUALITY AND TENSION BETWEEN THE SEXES

A final characteristic of higher education that influences its response to sexual harassment, perhaps more than any other, is the paucity of women faculty. The National Center for Education Statistics reported that during the 1980-1981 school year, 23.8 percent of higher education faculty were women. Women were 9.2 percent of all full professors, 19.7 percent of associate professors, 34.2 percent of assistant professors, and 53.3 percent of instructors.[12]

These percentages do not apply equally to all academic disciplines; there are many areas in which there are almost no women. On individual campuses, women faculty exist as isolated individuals in all but a few areas such as nursing, education, literature, and English.

Not only do they constitute a minority, they clearly have less status than men within the profession. Women are clustered in the lower, untenured academic ranks, where their ability to influence policy and behavior is limited. As a group, they are less-rewarded financially. Annual studies by the National Center for Education Statistics and the AAUP demonstrate that women faculty's salaries are consistently lower than those of men.

Women are no more prevalent or valued in administrative posts on campuses. In a Center for Education Statistics listing of over 50 campus administrative jobs in 1981-1982, women were paid from 50 percent to 5 percent less than men in all but four positions.[13] The women in administration were also concentrated in the traditionally nurturing roles in student services, such as counseling and advising.

Having few women in high places has enormous implications for sexual harassment. Higher education is a man's world, and males traditionally feel less concern about harassment because it usually happens to women rather than men. When a campus does acknowledge sexual harassment, it is typically discounted as a women's issue, not an institutional concern.

Older women faculty, especially those who entered the environment before the onset of the women's movement, learned to survive by directing attention away from their sex. By degendering themselves, they were more likely to be accepted in the predominantly male environment. They learned that presenting themselves as sexless could mean the difference between success and failure, tenure and nonreappointment.

These women, and some of their younger colleagues, may not be eager to involve themselves in the controversial, gender-related problem of sexual harassment. In fact, they may be even more inclined than their male colleagues to avoid the issue. Women have been realistic, not cowardly, in this assessment. In the risks of challenging a male environment about male sexual harassment, women recognize the odds and know who would be the likely losers.

Younger women faculty may be more aggressive and likely to speak out on issues like sexual harassment and to advocate for general equity and policy. But they are still subject to one of the most basic facts of academic life — to be successful, one must be a colleague first and a woman second. Women who do not subscribe to this rule frequently alienate the male power structure and perhaps diminish their effectiveness in helping combat harassment. Assessing the situation as "almost impossible," an administrator in her late thirties commented:

> The problem is the men in a college almost never meet *real* women at work. They define their women colleagues as androgynous. Men faculty think of their women colleagues in ways that make them most comfortable — one of the guys. That's why they can't work with their female colleagues to find a solution to this thing.

The campus is not an environment in which the sexes relate very easily to one another. The tension is made more acute because it is rarely acknowledged by men, who think of themselves as nonsexist. Women professionals, despite the realities of differential treatment, keep hoping they are and thus avoid direct confrontation.

The first colleges were exclusive male clubs where life had a cloistered quality. When women finally scaled the ivy walls, they were not greeted with enthusiasm — as students or colleagues. To many academicians, women represented at best an unwelcome intrusion and at worst a serious threat to men committed to the life of the mind. Where reason and intellect reign supreme, passion and emotion are suspect. And who but women — young or old, bright or dull, beautiful or ugly — pose a greater threat to the equilibrium of men?

The first women hired into all-male departments were recruited grudgingly, regarded with suspicion, treated like intruders, and reviewed cynically. "I was an 'affirmative action' hire," said a woman political scientist. "That meant they felt I got the job because I was a woman, not because I was competent. Despite my publications list, I've never been accepted."

In the sexually uptight environment of academe, men and women may know their Freud or even Hite, but that understanding has not relieved the tensions in their workplace. There is seldom healthy sexual give-and-take among professionals on campus. Perhaps this is so because of some puritan desire to preserve the innocence of the young, perhaps because of some grand commitment to the image of the scholar as dignified ascetic. It may be that some people who are attracted to the profession have never been comfortable with members of the opposite sex. It may be that they really do believe the life of the intellect can be carried out without reference to gender differences in colleagues. Whatever the reasons, the result is clear.

Where there are already internal frustrations and tensions over sex-related issues, the ambiguities surrounding sexual harassment cannot easily be resolved.

Even if these tensions did not exist and male and female educators were unified in their attitudes about sexism in the institution, their power to influence the harassment issue would still be limited. Effective action in the fragmented political structure of the campus requires the ability to forge coalitions that can accomplish change. Women academicians, the most likely to have interest in confronting sexual harassment, seldom possess that urge toward unity or the institutional security to be successful.

Despite higher education's grandiose claims about its concern for students, life on campus is not always as college recruiters portray it. The institution, by its own biases and organizational structure and cultures, contributes to sexual harassment. Students appear to recognize the indecisiveness and weakness of their institutions and are likely to endure the indignities of harassment rather than risk seeking remedy. By their silence, they assert not only their own feelings of powerlessness, but also their convictions that campuses themselves cannot cope. One student summarized this viewpoint best when she told a discussion group, "They can't even figure out how to find places for all of us to park, so what can they do about the things these jerks say to us in class?"

The odds on educators' "figuring out" how to resolve parking, scheduling, or academic problems are not good. They are even worse when one considers sexual harassment. The ambiguities surrounding this issue make it one of the most difficult problems facing college campuses.

3 : Contemporary College Women

MYTHS AND REALITIES

"Listen, Nick; let me tell you what I said when she was born . . . I woke up out of the ether with an utterly abandoned feeling, and asked the nurse right away if it was a boy or a girl. She told me it was a girl, and so I turned my head away and wept. 'All right,' I said, 'I'm glad it's a girl. And I hope she'll be a fool — that's the best thing a girl can be in this world, a beautiful little fool.'"

F. Scott Fitzgerald,
The Great Gatsby

The college campus is believed to be an ivory tower, a haven in the midst of a grubby world. But once one looks beneath appearances and glimpses some of its darker realities, perceptions of the campus are forever altered. Replying anonymously to a question about sexual harassment, a sophomore provided an example of the darker side of academic life:

Well, my freshman year I took a class. I didn't understand all of the readings, and by the time the final came around I found myself with an F. So I asked him if I could talk to him about grades in his office. So I went to his office and he gave me a choice — either be with him or take the F. I was attracted to him a little, but there was no way I could take the F. So I met him at his house, and I spent three hours with him in his bed. I had to close my eyes and pretend that I was with my boyfriend. I

59

felt dirty, but I didn't get the F. He gave me a D. Was it worth it? Yes and no. I felt it was something I had to do to save myself.

There are those for whom this college sophomore exemplifies the "loose" morality that they fear is driving society and helpless scholars toward ruin. They see her as someone willing to sell herself for a grade or a recommendation, just as prostitutes sell their bodies for money. For others, who know her and thousands like her, she is the victim of a world so confusingly competitive that it dictates bad choices to resolve seemingly worse dilemmas. In the midst of her terror over grades, three hours of unwanted sex somehow seemed less punitive, less humiliating than the omnipotent F she dreaded. Going to bed with a stranger was "something [she had] to do to save [herself]."

The student's description is simple but deserves close scrutiny. She resigns herself to the only alternative given her and takes responsibility for the choice. She does not question its fairness and does not think of seeking help from the institution. She does not condemn the professor. His demands are, to her, perfectly predictable, logical, and acceptable. He is a man. He is a teacher. She is a student with an F. If she goes to bed with him, she can pass the course. It is a matter-of-fact, possibly even familiar scenario to her. *She* feels dirty; the adjective applies more logically to him, but that does not occur to her.

Nor does it occur to her male classmates. A seldom-mentioned consequence of sexual harassment is its harmful effect on male students. Some are sophisticated enough to see the embarrassment and panic felt by women students targeted by instructors. Some feel frustrated as men because their status as students prevents them from intervening on behalf of women. Others are less sensitive. They conclude that women possess unfair advantages. Subordinated to the sexual power of the female and the academic power of the professor, men students feel bewildered and angry. Frequently, their social conditioning and self-interest lead them to turn their hostility toward the victims rather than the offenders. Marc B., a student in broadcasting, voiced the ambivalence:

Every now and then I would see this one girl from one of my classes with a professor standing with him (very close) and then kissing him goodbye. For me this was something I had never seen before and I was surprised at my own reaction, although I felt no need to attempt to change it. I have read articles on this subject but the articles I read only dealt with the professor approaching the student, instead of the situation I was seeing which was the opposite. In the former situation I always felt kind of sorry for the girl. But now I resent certain girls for flaunting their sex. I also found myself to be very angry with this professor for "using" his position as an authority figure.

It is easy for male students to become embittered about the advantage women students appear to have. An interior design major reflected:

> In one of my studio classes the male teacher had a habit of taking out the girls from the class. I never actually saw him take out a student but I have heard about him from seniors, juniors, pre-juniors, and sophomores. They have all said that his classes were mostly girls and I found this true. In my class there were thirty students and six of us were guys. From what I was told all of his classes were about the same as mine as far as the ratio of male and female. He took out the female students and from what I have heard these were the students who received the A's. If you were a male in his class and getting A's on the projects you would receive a B for a final grade. If you were female and doing B work, you would more than likely receive an A.

A freshman at a small liberal arts college encountered a similar situation:

> A teacher last quarter was having a fling with one of his students. I saw them together all of the time and this really bothered me. The girl never showed in class and yet I heard she did well.

A senior in a business administration program experienced similar exasperation:

> My English prof really likes the women. You don't have to be a genius to figure that out because he makes it obvious in class. To tell you the truth, what really pisses me off isn't him getting off on the ladies. We all do that. What I don't like is they know it and use it to get the grades. How am I going to compete with that?

How indeed! When professors themselves assume that women use their sexuality to further their college careers, it is little wonder that their male students become confused about the motivations of women. In a *Psychology Today* article, "Seduction in Academe," a poet-in-residence at a university complained, "The girls come into my office flashing their thighs, wriggling about in the chair, talking about poetry. Perhaps they're doing what nature tells them to do. Perhaps they don't know what they're doing. But I know — and I notice it."[1] In this case, the professor reads the women's body language, and he assumes that his interpretations of their motivations are the only valid ones.

The attitudes expressed toward sexual harassment are greatly affected by individuals' views and assumptions about contemporary college women. While peers, parents, and professors have direct acquaintance with some college women, their perceptions derive from a mixture of limited personal experience and the influence of cultural myths.

A basic source of the imagery of college women is the media and literature. For the past several decades, the movie portrait of campus coeds has been consistent. In films like *Carnal Knowledge* and *Tall Story* to *Animal House* and *Change of Seasons*, the college woman overwhelms men with her irresistible loveliness and cheerleader voluptuousness. She may be cast as wholesome or erotic, but she always seethes with sexuality. In the pages of Philip Roth, John Barth, and Bernard Malamud, the coed devours birth control pills like candy and, given the opportunity, would spend lunch hours fornicating beneath the football stadium. In popular film and fiction images, the college woman uses the classroom or lab to meet men and appears to be on campus primarily to have a good time and to improve the scenery. Film and television images also foster the fantasy of coeds as wriggling seductresses. The voluptuous coed image is promoted by advertising which portrays college women as ultimate consumers of beer, liquor, and the leering men who surround them. The portrait on the nightly news is equally one-dimensional. Whether at an NCAA basketball game, a nuclear disarmament rally, or an ERA march, the news camera focuses on college women as pretty faces in the crowd or bouncy well-proportioned bodies.

Because of these complex and even contrasting perceptions, it is easy to understand why there is so much confusion about students' roles in sexual harassment. Are they seductive, or is that the fantasy of wishful thinkers? Do they regard their college professors as sexually, psychologically, and socially compatible? Must they use their clothing and sexuality to survive academically, or are they intellectually fit for higher education?

The popular images are so pervasive that they confuse both the public and the campus about women students' roles in sexual harassment. The mythology that is created about college women can help to "explain away" sexual harassment or to diminish its damage to victims. Thus the myths must be tested against reality and, where necessary, debunked.

THE BEAUTY MYTH

The beauty myth has much to do with cameras, models, movie stars, and novelists and little to do with colleges and universities, where gorgeous women are as rare as elsewhere. The myth is that college women are so sexually compelling and youthfully beautiful that men cannot resist them. This image is nurtured in the pages of books like Bernard Malamud's *Dubin's Lives*. Fanny, a college dropout, is described by Dubin, her aging mentor:

> [Dubin] was surprised at the time he had given [Fanny]; and it annoyed him a bit that he had felt her sexuality so keenly. It rose from her bare feet. She thus projects herself — the feminine body — beautifully formed hefty hips, full bosom, nipples visible — can one see less with two eyes? . . . She was gifted in femininity, Dubin decided . . . When she bent it was a gracious act. A beautifully formed female figure suggested ideal form — her ass a bouquet of flowers . . . Afterward he reflected that this intense unexpected response to her occurred at the thought she would soon be gone . . . A momentary source of innocent pleasure lost — the beauty of a vital young woman.[2]

A common explanation for sexual harassment on campus is that faculty are daily bombarded with the temptation of young women who are so physically desirable that they cannot be ignored. The reality is that the proportion of women "gifted in femininity" is no greater on the campus than anywhere else and that youth does not automatically guarantee sexual appeal. Yet people typically respond to a report of sexual harassment by asking if the victim is pretty. After hearing a coed's complaint, deans and department heads frequently express shock at a faculty member's behavior by commenting, "She isn't even that attractive." The attempt to establish the woman's beauty as a cause of sexual harassment diverts attention from the real power issue. It is a standard way of discounting the professor's responsibility and shifting blame to the victim.

The irony is that college officials most experienced in dealing with the problem report that complainants are seldom exceptionally good looking. Mary Dean S., ombudsman at a southern college, commented, "We very seldom get the campus-queen type in our office. My guess is that they are less likely to be harassed than those who are average in appearance. I think professors avoid them for the same reason a lot of college men hesitate about asking them out. They don't know how to act with them, and they're afraid of being rejected."

Linda W., a professor who advises a campus social sorority, expressed a similar opinion: "The young women in Tri-Delt are unusually attractive and tend to have been that way in high school too. The result is that they become sophisticated about men earlier than most women, and they are not easily intimidated by male faculty. I think professors sense this and tend to seek 'safer ground' when they decide to harass."

THE CLOTHING MYTH

The beauty myth has a corollary that is used to explain away the sexual harasser's responsibility. The clothing myth is the belief that college women dress in ways that invite and provoke sexual advances. Certainly it is impossible to discuss American women, young or old, without mentioning the role of dress in their lives. The cultural, sociological, and psychological implications of women's dress are complex. From infancy, clothing is an expression of sexual identity. Mothers dress little girls as if they were dolls; in childhood, little girls dress their own dolls; and in adolescence, girls relinquish the dolls and dress themselves. For teenagers, wearing the "right" clothing is almost an obsession, and it becomes seemingly impossible for a woman to separate who she is from what she wears. In an article titled "Dressing Up," Shane Adler remarks, "Traditionally, males found satisfaction through achievement, whereas females could only find theirs by wearing the most fashionable gown."[3]

Females learn that clothing communicates and that attractive dress increases self-esteem. They can never ignore these lessons.

Jessie Bernard captures this point in *The Culture of the Female World*:

> Beauty matters . . . [B]eautiful clothes remain an important value in
> female culture. Success in the areas of sensing fashion trends, finding
> good clothes, wearing the right thing is the kind of success women can
> appreciate in one another; it is in this sense that it is sometimes argued
> that women dress for one another, not men. It is a form of competition
> and, as do other forms, it offers its own kind of exhilaration. Early in life
> the pink world starts to process the little girl to value it. She learns early
> the punishment meted out to the unattractive child. And also the fact
> that there are few areas of life in which injustice is more blatant and
> failure more painful than in the area of physical beauty. There are few
> agonies more excruciating than the wallflower's. Or the fading
> beauty's.[4]

An attractive appearance is a positive expression of a woman's
self-confidence and competence. The problem for women is that
some people have trouble distinguishing seductive attire from that
which simply emphasizes beauty and self-esteem. Susan Jacoby
wrote in an article on professional women's wardrobes:

> In most of the "how to dress" books, there is a basic confusion between
> overt sex appeal — the special way a woman might dress when her lover
> is coming over for dinner — and the normal, everyday sexual attrac-
> tiveness and attraction that are intrinsic to the image of any woman who
> takes pride in both her mind and her body. This sort of sex appeal is
> just as much a characteristic of proud and competent men as it is of
> proud and competent women.
>
> Setting up a dichotomy between sexual attractiveness and profes-
> sional competence places women in a no-win position. A woman can
> try to look as neuter and neutral as possible, but a body-concealing suit
> and an attaché case will not conceal the fact that she *is* a woman.[5]

The sexual message of clothing is in the eye of the beholder, and
women have suffered great misunderstanding from the opposite
sex. A 1980 study at the University of California at Los Angeles found
that of 432 blacks, whites, and Hispanics between the ages of 14 and
18, none viewed a male's open shirt, tight pants, tight swim trunks,
or jewelry as indications that he was seeking sex. But males generally
assumed that low-cut tops, shorts, tight jeans, or bralessness meant
that a female was encouraging a sexual reaction. Females, however,

contended that such dress simply indicated they were trying to be in style.[6]

The bra symbolizes women's predicament best. Women have not always worn bras, but when some discarded them during the late 1960s, the world reacted with shock. Many older people and males read into the symbol of the "braless woman" the opposite of what she intended. To them, it was a come-on, an erotic message, a solicitation. To the millions of young women who followed the style and began going braless, those interpretations did not apply. Bras came off on campuses across the nation because the women there knew what was "in" and discovered that without them they were more comfortable. In retrospect, it was "no big deal," as one student expressed it:

> I don't wear a bra a lot of the time because it's comfortable. Why shouldn't you be allowed to be comfortable? Guys run around everywhere in gym shorts without jock straps, and no one says that's seductive. A guy never wears baggy jeans, and you can always see the outlines of his penis because his jeans are so much tighter than ours, and no one says that's seductive.

The young women who decided to go braless understood one of the most important lessons of being female: clothing language, like beauty, is in the eye of the beholder. Dress *does* give information about the wearer — whether she feels attractive, fashionable, sexy, athletic, young, even physically well. But a statement is not an invitation, and those who contend that it is delude themselves. A fitted sweater clearly asserts, "I am a woman. This is how my body is made." Nowhere in that message is the statement, "Therefore, men have a right to my body." A student's clothes may affirm her sexuality and her comfort and display her youth and attractiveness, but that visual communication does not give men permission to touch or grab.

Just as clothing does not give permission for others to act, it does not signal what the student wearer wants or will do. Attitudes toward exposed skin have changed radically since the Victorian era, but some still assume that a woman's morality can be measured by the amount of skin she chooses to reveal. While few in higher education would actually defend the notion that certain kinds of clothing excuse unwanted touching, there are those who hold that women's clothing can be a cause of sexual harassment. Their argument is simple: "When a woman wears tight jeans (or tight sweaters or short shorts or . . .) she's asking for it," said a Spanish professor who was attempting to defend a colleague accused of propositioning a student. This thinking is convoluted. A student's clothing choice is cultural communication, not a manifesto on her morality.

Obviously, clothing may be used to attract sexual attention. This is one of the first steps in the elaborate process of establishing male-female relationships. But the assumption that a student's clothes are an invitation to teachers rather than male peers is wishful and muddled thinking by college professors. Perhaps men tend to overstress sexual motivations in humans. A 1982 article in the *Journal of Personality and Social Psychology* that reported experiments with male and female college students revealed that males tended to see the behaviors of both genders as more sexually motivated than did females. After observing female and male factors in heterosexual interchanges, male observers rated both sexes as more flirtatious, seductive, and promiscuous than did females. There is little reason to believe that older men conditioned in the same social patterns as young men, would respond any differently.[7]

Sexual harassment is neither caused by what students wear nor is it excused by adult professionals' misreading the messages of attire — especially if they choose to act on their interpretations. "Provocative dress" has nothing to do with sexual harassment. Whether women wear high collars, dresses that flatten their breasts, skirts that hide their ankles, or veils that cover their faces, they are forced to endure sexual harassment. It did not begin with tube tops and short shorts, and it will not cease as long as society insists on believing that men cannot restrain their sexual impulses and that women, by their dress, invite sexual advances.

THE PROMISCUITY MYTH

The myth that college women's "provocative" dress invites sexual harassment is the most polite tip of the iceberg. Underlying it is the third myth, the view that college women are sexually promiscuous, unfettered voluptuaries with hedonistic philosophies. Malamud's Fanny, a college dropout, is a classic example. Her attitude toward life and sex is simple:

I think we're entitled to have sexual pleasure any way we want.... To me life is what you do. I want it to enjoy, and not make any kind of moral lesson or fairy tale out of it . . . I just wanted to say that the real truth about my own sexual experience, at least as I am now, is that I have become a better person because of it . . . I don't do everything for a purpose. I do some things for fun.[8]

Fanny is quick to point out that sex is "the most satisfying pleasure of life."[9] Her lover Dubin is so awed by her sexual experience that he imagines her "lying nude on her double bed [while] a line of men coiled around it, a long line of types and ages extending into the hall and down a flight of stairs."[10]

Fanny, however, is not an accurate portrait of the contemporary college woman. Ten years ago, in the largest national survey of sexual behavior since Kinsey, Morton Hunt and Research Guild, Inc., reported evidence that debunks the promiscuity myth. They were commissioned to assess changes in the sexual behaviors of American men and women eighteen years of age and older. Their results established that females 18 to 24 were more sexually active and experimental than those in Kinsey's report; nevertheless, such behavior was regarded as acceptable only within very definite boundaries. Hunt concluded:

But if young women are much more likely than their mothers were to feel they have a right to a complete sexual life before marriage, they do not exercise that right in a lighthearted and purely physical way . . . The new norm [is], in sociologist Reiss's words, "permissiveness with affection." In Kinsey's study, 46 percent of all married women who had had premarital intercourse had had it only with their fiancés; in our sample, while twice as many had had premarital intercourse, an even larger proportion — slightly over half — had limited it to their fiancés, and among the youngest women in our sample the figure was still higher. It is very likely that in absolute terms there are more single young women today than formerly who are willing to have intercourse without any emotional ties, but in relative terms it remains true that most sexually liberated single girls feel liberated only within the context of affectionate or loving relationships.

To the majority of Americans, sexual liberation thus means the right to enjoy all the parts of the body, the right to employ caresses previously forbidden by civil or religious edict and social tradition and the right to be sensuous and exuberant rather than perfunctory and solemn — but all within the framework of meaningful relationships. Sex, for the great majority of Americans — including the liberated — continues to express loving feelings, or to engender them, or both. It has not been successfully disjoined from love and remade into a simple appetite, except by a tiny minority of swingers."[11]

Hunt's report that Americans continue to discriminate in their choice of sexual partners and to attach great emotional significance to their sexual acts is corroborated by findings of the Astin survey, a joint project of the American Council on Education and the University of California at Los Angeles. The largest ongoing empirical study of American college students, the Astin survey annually accumulates demographic and attitudinal data on freshmen entering representative institutions of higher education. In the data collected in 1982,[12] answers of men and women students to questions concerning sexual relationships included:

	Agree Strongly or Somewhat
People should not obey laws that violate their personal values.	30.0%
Abortion should be legalized.	55.9%
The activities of married women are best confined to the home and family.	17.6%
A couple should live together for some time before deciding to get married.	35.5%
Divorce laws should be liberalized.	42.5%
If two people really like each other, it's all right for them to have sex even if they've known each other for only a very short time.	32.8%

The portrait of the college woman that emerges from the Astin study further dispels the myth of the promiscuous student. The survey for 1982 indicates that 67.2 percent of freshman women do not agree that having sex is all right if people simply like each other; 64.5 percent of them are not enthusiastic about cohabitation prior to marriage. These attitudes are moderate and conventional and held by the majority. It seems unlikely that a significant number of these women would consider seducing their professors when 70 percent of them do not think people should disobey laws which violate their personal values.

The reality reported in these research studies contradicts the myth of the promiscuous college woman. Yet even if the myth were true, sexual harassment could not be explained away. The myth of student promiscuity is an attempt to defend the characters of harassers by impugning the reputations of women students. History and common sense should prevail. Sexual harassment on campus occurred long before anyone conceived of the pill, long before women were allowed to have sex drives. College women's attitudes toward sex may have undergone transformations, but that does not mean their sexual liberalism extends to relationships with professors.

THE UNFIT-FOR-COLLEGE MYTH

College women also suffer from myths about their motivations and competence to pursue higher education. The most long-standing of these is that women go to college "to find a man" and to get a "Mrs." degree. Despite overwhelming evidence to the contrary, women are still suspected to be intellectually and psychologically unfit to withstand the rigors of academic life.

The Astin freshman studies address this myth and undo it. According to the thousands of college-bound women surveyed every fall, their reasons for deciding to go to college are the same as men's: "to get better jobs, to learn about more things, to gain general educations, and to make more money."[13]

Both men's and women's choices of colleges are influenced most by the school's academic reputations (53.5 percent) and the availability of programs that meet their special educational needs (25.5 percent).[14] Women's average grades and academic ranks in high school are superior to those of males. Freshman women are as, if not better, prepared than men to succeed academically. Comparison of college freshmen grades and class rank in high school shows a significant difference between men and women.

Average Grade in High School	Male	Female
A or A+	7.5%	10.8%
A−	9.4%	13.3%
B+	16.6%	21.8%
B	25.4%	27.9%
B−	16.6%	11.9%
C+	14.8%	9.1%
C	9.2%	5.1%
D	0.5%	0.2%

Academic Rank in High School		Male	Female
top	20%	34.5%	43.8%
second	20%	24.7%	22.5%
middle	20%	32.5%	28.4%
fourth	20%	7.2%	4.7%
lowest	20%	1.1%	0.6%[15]

The figures speak for themselves. The assumption that women are unfit for college is pure myth. Students with the qualifications reported by the Astin study do not need to use seduction as a survival strategy in college.

THE GALATEA/PYGMALION MYTH

Another myth some use to explain away sexual harassment is that women students turn to male faculty as necessary and desirable guides to maturity. The myth portrays college women as formed but lifeless creatures, wanting and needing the professor's touch to give them intellectual and sexual vitality. This view allows the sexual harasser to see himself as a modern-day Pygmalion, which can be very flattering to his ego but dangerous to the student he chooses to see as Galatea. The Pygmalion role allows the professor to assume even greater power in his relationship with the student and encourages him to discount as naive any view that doesn't match his own.

The myth ignores basic truths about youth and student culture. Youth has distinct preferences in music, language, and style. Young people tend to prefer their peers. Women students are not likely to be universally attracted to male faculty. The barriers that separate the coed from her professor are simply too enormous. Often she views him from a chronological distance, but the social, intellectual, and cultural gap can be even more significant. Few nineteen-year-olds eagerly abandon the tastes and interests to which they have been committed since puberty in order to pursue men with whom they have so little in common.

Whether or not students are physically attracted to faculty is an obvious but seldom-asked question. At a large Midwestern university, 189 college women wrote anonymous responses to the following instructions: "Please discuss briefly the reasons that you do *or* do not find yourself sexually attracted to college professors. Have you ever considered or engaged in seduction of an instructor? If so, explain your motivations." Only four expressed attraction to their professors; even in these cases, their feelings could hardly be classified as passionate:

> On occasion I find myself sexually attracted to one of my professors. I am attracted by maturity, charisma, a sense of humor, etc. On one occasion I have engaged in the seduction of an instructor. My motives were simply my attraction to his personality and my desire to be with him and spend more time with him. On this occasion I was 18 and right out of high school and eager to "grow up." He was attracted to me and was very gentle and made me feel safe. Maybe I did carry the "teacher" concept too far.

• •

> I have never been physically attracted to any of my professors. I really don't know if there is any reason why. I have, however, found myself liking certain ones over others simply because of their personalities. I can't remember any terribly attractive professor that I have had.

• •

> I have never really thought about seducing a male professor. When I stare at a professor for hours a day, I begin to ask myself what he would be like as a companion. However, if the man is not handsome or good-looking on the outside, the thoughts never cross my mind. Underneath though, I guess I wouldn't mind finding out. The attraction would begin because of his control of the class and his easygoing style. I never have had an experience of the sort though.

• •

> Most of the college professors that I have come in contact with are elderly, and for mostly that reason I have not been sexually attracted to them. But I can see how a young attractive professor could turn your head because he has established himself, and this sometimes would look good to some girls.

All of the students who reported any sort of interest in men faculty indicated an awareness of the role differences between themselves and faculty. Describing the professor as "established," "mature," in "control," and possessing knowledge was a way of acknowledging his power. A student's interest in a professor might evolve from curiosity, from hero worship, or from the desire to be noticed or cared for. It does not automatically result from an interest in bartering for academic success.

In this particular survey, no one expressed a proclivity for older men. On the contrary, most were repelled by professors' ages and physical appearances. The following comments by five different women demonstrate their lack of sexual response to faculty:

> No, I never have [been attracted to college professors]. None of my profs were nice looking. Most were rather rude and some very obnoxious. I don't hang around school and have never had any desire to see more of a prof than in class and some not even then. Besides all of this, most male profs at _____ are either old or ugly.

> • •

> I have never had any interest in college professors. I cannot find any attractive qualities in them. Usually, they are older men, weird, and unattractive. I could never feel close to them for we have nothing in common.

> • •

> I do not try to attract professors. To me, all of the professors are too old, ugly. Older men at least in the late thirties on are old enough to be my father. College professors are all ugly. I would never seduce any professor.

> • •

> I am not attracted to male college professors for the simple reason that they don't do anything for me. I respect male professors as I would any professor, but that's about as far as it goes. Besides, most male college professors are weirdos!

> • •

> I do not find them attractive because I am 20, and they are too old for me. Anyway, my father would shoot me if I had anything to do with an older man!

"Old, weird, and ugly" — this was the portrait of the professor that emerged from this particular group of students. Obviously, no generalization or even hypothesis can be derived from these responses. The male faculty at this particular university might be homelier than most, or its undergraduates' standards more rigorous than most, but neither is very likely. What is likely is that most college women, like college men, do not experience extraordinary physical attraction to members of the opposite sex who are not peers. Herbert Livesey wrote in *The Professors*:

> The incidence of sexual liaison between college faculty and students is difficult to assess. Given its status of taboo layered over taboo, professors are reluctant to estimate frequency, and some insist professorial-undergraduate fornication to be the rarest of aberrations . . . Conversely, to accept the picture suggested by some professors, one must visualize a pen of rutting chimpanzees maddened by Spanish fly . . . Lacking valid evidence, it can be fairly speculated that students of the present rarely require the extracurricular erotic tutelage of their professors; they have each other.[16]

THE CONSENTING ADULT MYTH

Occasionally there are women students who are attracted to faculty. There are husbands and wives who were once teacher and student. These relatively few examples are cited again and again as proof that relationships between professors and students are private matters and that the concept of sexual harassment should give wide berth to such liaisons. The faculty role may be attractive to some, because it combines intellectual attainment and power, but being attracted to an individual's role and consenting to a relationship are vastly different.

If a professor becomes involved with a student, his standard defense is that she is a consenting adult. Few students are ever, in the strictest sense, consenting adults. A student can never be a genuine equal of a professor insofar as his professional position gives him power over her. Access to a student occurs not because she allows it but because the professor ignores professional ethics and chooses to extend the student-faculty relationship. Whether the student consents to the involvement or whether the professor ever intends to use his power against her is not the point. The issue is that the power and the role disparity always exist, making it virtually impossible for the student to act as freely as she would with a male peer.

In a normal romantic situation, both the man and woman make efforts to assess each other's reasons for pursuing the relationship, to understand their true feelings and desires, and to predict their own and the other's future behaviors and attitudes. In a faculty-student relationship, the enormous role (and frequently age) disparity inhibits the woman so that she herself may have trouble understanding and predicting her feelings.

Penny F., a woman in her mid-thirties, a suburban housewife and teacher's aide in her young son's grammar school, recollected her "consenting" role in an encounter with a professor.

> I was so young then, just a sophomore, and so mousy. I had dishwater hair, a flat chest, and legs so skinny I was embarrassed to wear short skirts. Everyone at _____ was so into the Peace movement, and I was so out of it. My mother freaked when my best friend and I were found smoking a Camel in high school. Then I got to college and found people smoked stuff I'd never even heard of. I guess I had enough of my mother in me that that didn't bother me.
>
> What did upset me was all the people on my floor who seemed so sophisticated about sex when I'd had three dates in my entire life. I felt like such a little mouse. Everyone seemed to be sleeping with everyone else, and I went around in this permanent wallflower daze. I don't know whether that's what made me get involved with Dr. _____ or not. Maybe I'm just trying to excuse myself, maybe I just wanted to rebel. Who knows?
>
> Sometimes I don't remember what happened between the times he was so gentle and nice in class and that afternoon. I guess I was too out of it. Anyway, he seemed to care about me and take so much interest in me, and pretty soon I was making up all sorts of stories in my head about how I'd take him back home and prove to everyone I wasn't dull, mousy little Penny after all. I guess I missed something in between that should have been there.
>
> The only thing I remember now is finding myself in his apartment and seeing dirty dishes on the table. I thought, "So this is it," and I'm sure that everything that happened I wanted to happen. Only it wasn't the way I thought it would be at all. He didn't talk much. I guess I wanted him to say he loved me or something. Remember I was pretty young. All I remember is that it hurt and there was blood and I was embarrassed because I didn't know what to do about the sheet.
>
> I called my parents that night and told them I wanted to transfer. I took the bus home that weekend and never saw him again. I finished my degree at _____. And you know, even after all this time, I don't remember anything that hurt worse — not even having my kids.

People who promote the consenting adult myth seldom mention that true consent demands full equality and full disclosure. Students lack not only power and equality; they are also frequent victims of professors' distortions of truth. A student may understand and agree to limits in her relationship with a professor, but faculty Casanovas usually forget to inform the woman that she is only one in a long procession of "consenters."

A male student affairs dean at a branch campus of an Ohio public university had observed the romantic career of a middle-aged professor for years. The professor's pattern was first to invite a student out for coffee, then to begin meeting her for tennis, and eventually to establish a sexual relationship with her. The dean commented:

> Women are sincerely attracted to him, fall in love with him. If I were to try to speak to them and say, "You're just part of a pattern I've watched for ten years," they'd tell me it's none of my business, and they'd be right. When the affair breaks up, maybe they just feel the normal heartbreak over the end of a love affair, but I get so angry seeing the same pattern over and over again. Maybe they don't see the overall pattern. Maybe it's not as harmful as I think it is.

It is impossible to assess the effects of these relationships because so few women involved are willing to discuss them. Donna C., a graduate of one of the seven sister colleges, described her student experience with women students who had affairs with faculty. She found them devastating to the self-esteem of the women:

> Perhaps this is shocking, but an accepted norm in our institution was faculty-student affairs. Ours was a small campus in a somewhat isolated town, and very bright young female students were forced to spend considerable time with the extremely intelligent, predominantly male faculty. When affairs inevitably resulted, there often appeared to be an element of glamour in them for some of the women. Frequently, these were their first sexual experiences. I suspect that their previous encounters with men their own age had been problematic, and the faculty reinforced their sense of alienation from their peers. The women were told that they were too bright, that they would be too threatening to men their own age. In some ways, that was true, so they often responded to sexual attention from younger male faculty by supposing that intellectual equality implied the male could be trusted to guide them into other areas of life.
>
> However intelligent they were, the students were actually at an

emotional disadvantage. In fact, most of the affairs were sad to watch because the women didn't really know what was happening. The relationships were usually fairly visible, since there wasn't any real disapproval. They might last two or three months, and the student would appear to feel totally in control of the situation, almost proud of it. It wasn't unusual to see the faculty member right in the dorm, using the floor john.

Then when the affair broke up, the student would often be a basket case. She would have to watch the next affair, see her ex-lover go on to another student, possibly even in the same dormitory.

In the four years I was there, I remember only one case of "true love," of a faculty-student relationship that lasted with any integrity. It was an older female in her mid-twenties and a new faculty member who was single and just a few years older. All the others were just casual affairs for the men, and the women who became involved with them never realized that until it was too late.

Attraction between professor and student may occur, but it is almost impossible for that attraction to be acted on successfully given the average campus environment and the restrictions on student-teacher roles. If legitimate attractions do occur, the couple's regard for the relationship should lead them to restrain themselves until their roles change. Students do become alumni. If the faculty member and student choose to be involved, they must be prepared to withstand the criticism and professional risk that inevitably accompany faculty-student relationships. Responsible faculty understand the need for caution in acting on their desires and feelings. Sexual harassers just act.

VULNERABILITY

College women may suffer because of misconceptions about their behaviors and characters, but do they also somehow permit themselves to be sexually harassed? An important factor in understanding womens' responses to harassment is the education and socialization of females. For over half a century, studies of female development — from language acquisition to sexual behavior — have emphasized women's docility, passivity, dependency, and avoidance of risk. A twenty-five-year project by Moss and Kagan[17] revealed that passivity patterns in females were remarkably high and that dependent orientations to authority figures continued from adolescence into adulthood. Elizabeth Douvan and Joseph Adelson's *The Adolescent Experience* compared 1,045 boys from ages fourteen to sixteen with 2,005 girls from eleven to eighteen and concluded that dependency is a way of life that increases as females mature.[18]

One of the primary places where females learn to respect authority figures is the school. David Bradford, Alice Sargent, and Melinda Sprague stressed that educational institutions are primary sources of reinforcement for male-female stereotypes:

> A substantial body of research demonstrates that from birth boys and girls are consistently treated differently. The types of games, toys, and books given to boys, as well as the kinds of behavior for which boys are rewarded and punished, teach boys different values, aspirations, and behavioral skills than girls. Boys are supported for being aggressive, assertive, analytical and competitive, while girls are praised for being helpful, passive, deferential and concerned with interpersonal relationships. Teachers as well as parents support these differences. One example is the research by Serbin (1973), who found that elementary school teachers, both male and female, responded more often to questions raised by boys than girls, and gave the boys longer answers that were richer in content. Girls received more perfunctory answers often accompanied by a pat on the head or arm around the shoulder — as if support and not cognitive content were the important response.[19]

Women's vulnerability to harassers becomes clearer in light of this stereotyping process. The education system, from nursery school through college, reinforces women's dependency and reliance on authority. Women are taught submission, not aggression. They learn that being "good" implies not acting but reacting, not trusting oneself but entrusting oneself to the authorities — parents, clergy, teachers — that promise reward. Forced into a choice between a teacher's wishes and their own, some students do what they have learned to do best — defer, submit, agree. In their own peculiar ways, they once again act out the roles of "good little girls," doing what teacher says is best.

Even Fanny, the classic young temptress in *Dubin's Lives*, shows dependence on authority. Early in the novel, she walks into Dubin's study, throws off her clothes, and waits for him to respond. Later she writes to him of confusion and fears typical of the college-age woman:

> I have ideas about what I ought to be doing but am afraid of the next move. I don't want to get into something I can't get out of if I make the wrong choice. Or into something that won't come to much, and will make me feel, again, that I am up Shit Creek in a leaky rowboat. William, please advise me about my life . . . Could you specifically say what I ought to be thinking about in the way of a job or career, or recommend books that might be helpful? Or give me the names of courses I could take when I get back to New York City? I'd like to be better organized and enjoy my life more . . . I'm afraid of my day-to-day life. A day scares me more than a week or a month. But the truth of it is I want to be responsible, to work my life out decently.[20]

In addition to the burdens imposed by sexual stereotyping, many women confront new and greater pressures upon entering college. College is not a particularly quiescent juncture in anyone's life. Alumni view the experience far differently from those who are living it. For most students, it is a time of uncertainty, pressure, and confusion, a time in which joy is counterbalanced by despair and achievement, by defeat. Students must decide successfully about academic programs, careers, and personal independence and relationships. College is a period of constant trial and judgment by oneself and others, in truth a far more harrowing experience than students care to admit. But for some women, it is particularly trying.

One of the most comprehensive analyses of the psychological differences between men and women is Eleanor Maccoby's and Carol Nagy Jacklin's *The Psychology of Sex Differences*,[21] which examines the results of more than 1,400 research studies to probe the myths and facts of gender distinctions. One finding was that women of college age (18 to 22) exhibit less sense of control over their own fates and less confidence in their probable performances on school-related tasks than men of similar age. This was *not* observed in either older or younger women.

It should not surprise anyone that many women feel less self-confidence and control once they reach college. Most academic environments are patterned after male interests and male behaviors. Since the turn of the century, cognitive rationality and the scientific mode of enquiry have dominated higher education. Women, socialized in humanistic and intuitive forms of knowledge, are at a psychological disadvantage in this kind of environment. The institution's emphasis on competition and intellectual aggressiveness runs counter to all that they have been taught.

There may be a link between women's vulnerability to sexual harassment and their diminished confidence and sense of control in academic settings. Because higher education is a male-dominated institution, college women are often treated less seriously. A man who hopes to become a physician is taken at his word. A woman elicits raised eyebrows and questions about her marriage and child-bearing plans. Her intentions meet with skepticism, so she is forced to prove herself and to endure more from faculty.

Nonassertive women are not the only likely victims for sexual harassers. The data are anecdotal, but there are overwhelming similarities in accounts of counselors, ombudsmen, and administrators who deal with the problem daily. Women who are experiencing serious stress are vulnerable, as are women uncertain about academic programs. Women who are loners, without visible friends, seem to be sought out by harassers. One ombudsman commented, "This will sound really crazy, but I think we tend to have more blondes coming to our office. They aren't beautiful or necessarily even pretty and I haven't kept a running count, but I'm almost sure that's the case." Others note that the nontraditional woman student, the individual attending college after some time has elapsed, also seems to be a target for the lecherous professor.

Harassers are influenced by multiple characteristics in women — physical characteristics, economic status, marital status. However, from analysis of stories of sexual harassment collected from college women, two particularly vulnerable groups arise: minority women and females enrolled in traditionally male fields. The reasons they attract harassers are easy to identify.

A racist stereotype of minority women is that they are "easier" and more responsive to sexual advances. For some males, the sexuality of women of a different race reportedly appears mysterious. Either of these conditions could account for what one counselor describes as some harassers' "quick-target" attitude toward minority women. An even more insidious possibility is that the lecherous professor may sense the unease experienced by some minority women entering the academic environment. If the self-esteem of women students in general is on trial during college, then that of minority females is sorely threatened as they seek to establish credibility in institutions that are not only traditionally male but also white-dominated.

Women in nontraditional fields exhibit some of the uncertainty and vulnerability of minority women. Male-dominated disciplines are governed by a fraternity of men with strong credentials who until very recently were unaccustomed to the presence of women in their classrooms. Women entering these fields tend to be high achievers, often academically superior to their male counterparts. Disconcerted by this new situation, some male faculty are openly hostile to such women; others ignore them. At any rate, female students in engineering, architecture, accounting, medicine, law, and a variety of other historically male disciplines report discomfort in their environments.

The sense of being an intruder can have consequences beyond the classroom. Women who feel themselves "outsiders" are especially vulnerable to displays of interest or kindness from instructors. Some faculty prey on the distress of such students for their own ends. One administrator observed, "These women feel like such pariahs that they'll hang onto any shred of human kindness, and a lot of faculty are not beyond taking advantage of that fact."

A story told by a black woman professor of accounting reflects the environmental stress. She recalled her own freshman collegiate days when she was singled out by a faculty member who was very arrogant about his five degrees and his predominantly male profession. She was the only one in class whom he did not address by first name; he preferred calling her, "Miss _____." At the end of the quarter he asked to speak with her after class. She was 17 at the time, and he was a middle-aged married man. She described her shock when he asked her to attend a dance with him: "I just looked him in the face and said, 'You're the wrong age, the wrong color; and if you want to take someone to a dance, it ought to be your wife.'"

ATTEMPTS AT COPING

Whatever her age, appearance, race, or field of study, there is vulnerability in the student's status that makes sexual harassment by teachers a most intimate betrayal of trust. In case after case, students report their initial reactions as disbelief and doubt about the most blatant acts.

College is a time when students question their sexual identities and relationships and evaluate their values and self-images. Most see faculty on the other side of the threshold called maturity, part of the adult world, more parents than peers. Sexual harassment by faculty, even in its most impersonal, generalized forms, injects a note of unexpected, incestuous sexuality that shocks the average woman student.

After shock comes the feeling of powerlessness. College professors are older, more adept verbally, more sophisticated socially, and certainly more knowledgeable about the workings of the college or university. A student at a Midwestern university asked, "Who was going to believe me? I was an undergraduate student and he was a famous professor. It was an unreal situation." A graduate student complained to her college counselor:

> What was it that I did that led him to believe I was interested in him in anything but a professional sense? I am quite outgoing and talkative; could that be interpreted wrongly? I realized how utterly vulnerable I was in a situation like this . . . Everything that happened would be interpreted in his favor, if it ever became public. It would be said that I got my signals wrong, that he was just truly interested in helping me in my career.[22]

Closely related to women's feelings of powerlessness are those of guilt. Student victims report feeling responsible, feeling at fault somehow. Some have an almost childlike fear of having broken some rule they did not know. They wonder what they should have known or done to prevent the harassment. "I keep asking myself what I did to get him started. There were twenty-two other girls in the class. Why did he pick on me?" Michelle Y., a student at a Southern university, asked.

Women recognize early that power and sexuality are equated by society. Some students are unsophisticated and fearful about the possibilities suggested by their sexuality; they may develop conflict about it and, correspondingly, guilt about their intentions and behaviors. They know that in cases of sexual harassment and rape someone always asks, "Did she encourage it?" and "Did she enjoy it?" The questions linger in the minds of even the most innocent and make them impotent to confront the harassment. Too many members of both sexes assume that women say "no" when they really mean "yes," that they secretly savor squeezing, patting, and pinching.

Men are not misunderstood or vulnerable to the same degree. An average woman of fifty would never be expected to whet the sexual appetite of a twenty-year-old male, and he would not be accused of seducing her. But people believe a twenty-year-old female can easily be transported to rapture by the attentions of a fifty-year-old male. After a while, the culturally induced confusion makes some women actually begin to doubt their own motivations. They then discover that their abusers prey on their uncertainties.

Paramount in the minds of many student victims is fear of what will happen if they resist or report the professor's behaviors. Victims often believe that the authority of the professor equals power over their futures — in a sense, their lives. Ambivalent about her academic capabilities, the typical student may be devastated when a professor, the symbol of intellect, treats her as if she has only a body and no mind. Even the best students worry about reprisals by the harasser and his associates. They fear that grades, jobs, careers, and sometimes even their physical safety will be threatened. Kelly H., a pre-med student, observed:

> It's easy for someone else to say I should do something about Dr. ____, but how can I? He was the first person at ____ to take my work seriously. At least I think it's my work that made him notice me. He's the one who's pushing for me to get into med school. If I refuse him, then I ruin my whole life.

Another repeated reaction of women victims is their ambivalence about and sometimes sympathy for the harasser. Women students, especially if they are considering making a formal complaint, worry about the professor's career, marriage, and future. Over and over, they comment, "I don't want anything bad to happen to him." A major source of this guilt is the harasser himself; when confronted by a student, harassers often distract them with discussions of personal and professional costs professors pay. Students may also feel guilty because they are flattered by the professor's interest in them. They may find him physically and socially unattractive, but being the object of attention from an older man can be a heady experience. A student may worry that she is stepping out of her proper place by affecting a faculty life, or she may have a certain amount of gratitude for the interest he has in her. This, as much as compassion, may lead to students' frequent pleas that deans or counselors "make sure he doesn't get in a lot of trouble."

Given this complex set of reactions, victims of harassment respond to their experiences in different ways. The important point to remember about their coping strategies is that because they feel frightened, guilty, complicit, powerless, and alone, most victims usually attempt to deal with harassment, however serious, on their own. The significance is that for every reported incident, there are innumerable others, some even more serious, about which no one ever knows.

A frequent coping tactic is refusal to acknowledge that harassment exists. Some students are either too naive or too self-deluded to admit that sexual exploitation can occur in their relationships with teachers. The students explain their intimate relationships with faculty in idealistic terms. They use hyperbole to describe the professor — he has "given life meaning," he has taught them "what it is to be an adult." They may know the definition of harassment, but what happens to them is "different" or "special."

A woman engaging in this kind of denial would be wounded if anyone suggested that a forty-year-old professor who works in a highly cerebral environment must have interest in something other than the stimulation of her mind. Confronted with her hero's record of previous lechery charges, she would refuse to accept the accusations. This naiveté makes her especially vulnerable to manipulation.

Another coping strategy is to deny the seriousness of the problem. Many students attempt to ignore incidents in the hope that they will not recur. Their optimism usually proves false, since most harassers are encouraged by a student's failure to resist. One professor, enraged that students were disturbed by his sexist remarks in class, contended, "No one has ever complained to me! Obviously, they like what I do and enjoy my humor, or someone would have said something by now. I'm certainly not going to change my whole teaching style on the basis of a few rumors." Ignoring harassment usually produces similar results. The offending individual interprets silence as assent or even encouragement to continue his behavior.

Often women who do acknowledge the seriousness of harassment try to cope through avoidance. They invent appointments, enlist the presence of friends, cut class, or even hide to prevent encounters. Another tactic is "dressing down," trying to appear asexual and unattractive to avoid notice. Each of these maneuvers is a passive-aggressive strategy; the student attempts to control external factors in the environment because she realizes she cannot control the professor.

Avoidance strategies indicate that students are sensitive to the power imbalance. They take friends to meetings with harassers because another person can provide reinforcement. They avoid meetings with harassers by claiming obligations equally important to those imposed by faculty. In both cases, students are trying to convince themselves and to communicate to their professors that powers can be offset.

Dressing down is a form of avoidance that demonstrates women's use of clothing to symbolize self-perceptions. A woman may make herself unattractive to escape the attention of an undesirable male, but dressing down may also be a way of declaring feelings of inferiority and victimization. It can express self-doubt as well as desire to deal with a threatening situation. Making oneself unattractive can be a way of declaring, "I don't feel good about myself. I feel inadequate and incompetent to cope with this problem."

Even when students do try to resist more directly, their intentions are frequently misread or intentionally misunderstood. Women tend to reject romantic overtures from their professors by talking about their boyfriends, expressing reluctance to become involved with faculty, contending that their families or friends would disapprove, or explaining that they lack time for social activities. Barbara H., a senior in an agricultural program, described her experience:

> I kept making up all kinds of excuses to keep from going out with ____.
> I told him that my mother was sick and I had to work on weekends. The times he called me at home I said I had to study for big tests. I guess he didn't believe me or didn't care because he just kept on calling me and staring at me and talking to me in class. Finally the only thing I could do was drop the course because I knew he was never going to let me alone as long as I was in his class.

Seldom are students willing to resist emphatically. But an adult who is confused enough to make advances toward a student is likely to misinterpret subtle as well as overt expressions of rejections. This was the case with a student who responded to the National Advisory Council:

> I had a class with ____ when I started my doctoral program. He left notes on my papers asking me to come in and see him. I was really impressed — he seemed to take such genuine interest in my program. I asked him to be my chairman. He changed. He began to touch me, my arms and legs, giving me neck rubs, kissing me. I would try and pull away, he'd pull closer. He kept asking to come to my house. He came and brought wine. He began touching me again only going farther. I told him I didn't think a sexual relationship for us was a good idea because he was my chairperson, married, etc. He assured me it was a good idea. I got him to leave without having sex but his pursuits became heavier. He frequently said he wanted to be sure I knew that I didn't have to make love to him to get through the program. (Ha!) Finally when I couldn't take it any longer I tried to politely but firmly tell him no. Once again I was chastized for my "coldness." About three weeks later, out of the blue, he threatened to give me an incomplete in a class. He began to be bitter and sarcastic with me. I confronted him with what I thought was unfair behavior. He told me he was angry because I hadn't been "straight" with him — he said he knew now I didn't want him so why hadn't I told him. It was obvious the man was out of touch. I tried to placate him but keep distance. I have not finished my program so I still have to deal with him. I have married . . . which I have really played up to keep him at a distance. He remains periodically unfair to me, was a complete jerk during my comprehensives, and generally makes life difficult. I stay away from him as much as possible.[23]

"Staying away" is not as simple as it sounds. Staying away means that women are forced to drop courses, to alter schedules, sometimes to change majors or colleges because they feel they have no other recourse. Frequently they transfer to other institutions without admitting their reasons. Worst of all, there are students so unable to withstand harassment and so estranged from the institution that the only solution they discover is leaving school. There is no way to determine the number who eventually adopt this drastic measure. Few colleges have adequate exit interviews of graduates, dropouts, or transfers, so information about sexual harassment is not likely to be collected and assessed by proper authorities. Nevertheless, counselors in a variety of schools state emphatically that the number of women who leave college because of harassment is substantial.

Herein lies the tragedy of sexual harassment on the campus. It is not a minor inconvenience soon to be forgotten by the women compelled to deal with it. Sexual harassment has the power to change lives, and what few inside higher education face is that the costs it exacts from victims are too enormous to estimate. Karen F., a senior, found the price high:

> Prof. M. was my adviser and taught several of the required courses in my language major, so I didn't have any choice about taking his courses. He used a lot of obscenities in class — taught us how to say "fuck" five different ways, for instance. And he used to embarrass women in class — I think he liked that. Finally he started flirting with me in class. He'd make comments about my hair or my hands, saying he wanted to touch them. The real trouble came on the trip that summer. There were 20 of us and he was the program coordinator. We got academic credit and a chance to speak the language for real. I borrowed money from my folks to go. Within the first week, he started coming on to me, saying he wanted to make love to me, inviting me to go away with him for a weekend, telling me I was prudish, saying his wife was frigid. I'd try to be nice but I told him I didn't want to do that, that I was engaged. He'd get really emotional and upset and cry and I'd tell him we could be friends. But then it would start all over again. He'd talk to the other students about me. I guess at first I was sorry for him and I didn't want to make trouble. But he kept at me and wouldn't leave me alone. One night he got really drunk and came into my room. My roommates were asleep. He made this big scene, grabbing me all over. I wasn't really frightened, just really embarrassed. After that, I stayed away from him the rest of the trip. I had classes from him the next term, but I thought he'd leave me alone, especially because I got married. But fall quarter he started again, telling me now that I was married I could have an affair. I cut class to avoid him, but I still feel nervous and can't sleep. I want to go to graduate school here — I've been accepted — but I'd have courses from him and I just can't take any more.

Much is heard from educators concerned about the reputations and livelihoods of those accused of harassment, but there is little discussion of the long-term effects it has on the women abused. Sexual harassment obviously has the power to damage careers; women leave colleges every day because they cannot deal with it. It alters their attitudes toward institutions and may have longlasting effects on their perceptions of men and sex. Perhaps most insidious are its influences upon the self-images of those forced to endure it. Higher education has been able to ignore consequences of sexual harassment because the victims' damage and pain are often felt years later, long after women have left the institutional environment and forfeited their claims to its protection.

4 : *Voices of Women*

DISSONANT CHORUS

"Do you believe any of this? It is not the stuff of fiction. It has no shape, it hasn't the balances so important in art. You know, if one line goes this way, another must go that way. All these lines are the same. These lives are like threads that get woven into a carpet and when it's done the weaver is surprised that the colors all blend: shades of blood, shades of tears, smell of sweat. Even the lives that don't fit, fit.

We half believed there was something terribly wrong with us. We crept into our holes and learned to survive."

Marilyn French,
The Women's Room

To understand sexual harassment, one must listen to the accounts of its victims. Eventually there may be surveys that quantify the problem, but nothing can capture its meaning and truth better than the voices of women who have endured it. The voices are sometimes halting, sometimes angry, sometimes reproachful, sometimes self-deprecating. They come from across the country, from all kinds of women, on campuses large and small, private and public.

A professional writer, recalling her college days, depicted sexual harassment as a basic reality of collegiate life:

Any woman who goes in for higher education, unless she goes to Bob Jones University, is bound to tangle sexually with a professor.

Life in the groin of academe is never simple. Instead of making the pitch like an ordinary man, the professor must try to seduce a girl by giving her a special assignment. This is his way of getting her into his office.

Thanks to his habit, I had to plough through Henry George's treatise on the single tax. When I entered the professor's office, he emerged from behind a huge pile of papers and books on his desk and gave me a glittering smile. As his pipe punctuated his sentences with puck-puck he mumbled the professorial version of the sweet nothing.

"Special assignment for you . . . couldn't give it to any of the other students . . . not your caliber . . . puck-puck . . . it's an oral report . . . just your cup of tea . . . puck-puck . . . requires a little supplementary reading . . ."

I had thought that the War of Jenkins' Ear was crazy-making, but it couldn't compare to the single tax. It was the most ghastly subject I ever tackled. I don't know how I managed to make my oral report, and I don't remember what I said, but somehow I got through it. When I went to the professor's office to return the book, he gave me another glittering smile.

"Excellent report . . . solid grasp of the material . . . most unusual . . . nobody understands Henry George as a rule . . . puck-puck . . . *Progress and Poverty* is one of the few really great books . . . puck-puck . . . I like his theory of cartels . . . puck-puck . . . you ever had a dick in your mouth?"[1]

The details of sexual harassment situations are sordid, like the melodrama of a bad soap opera. But for an inexperienced nineteen-year-old undergraduate working part-time as a secretary to a professor, the drama was real, and the professor's office became an insidious trap:

When I first started working for him, I thought it was nice that he was always so friendly and interested in me. He would always stop at my desk on his way into the office and say good morning or compliment me on my clothes or something like that. I liked the way he would make a point of talking to me — sometimes about his kids, sometimes his wife, sometimes just about his work. If I didn't have a lot of typing to do, he'd ask me if I wanted to take a break and come sit in his office, and he was real easy to talk to.

When he started making sexy comments I didn't like it, but he didn't seem to mean anything by it. He'd say things like my breasts looked really inviting in a certain sweater or that I had the kind of mouth men really like — stuff like that. I'd notice him staring at my breasts, but there didn't seem to be any point in saying anything. I started to feel really funny when he'd come in in the morning and say he was really tired because he'd had a really wild night. He'd sort of wink at me like I was supposed to know what that meant. That happened a couple of times, and I just pretended that I didn't know what he meant.

One day he asked me to come in his office because he really needed to talk to somebody. Instead of sitting behind his desk, he sat in the chair at the side of the desk so we were facing each other maybe six feet apart. He seemed really upset and nervous and told me this long story about how he got married real young, and it hadn't worked out, and they got divorced, and he thought he'd never ever really get married again until a few years ago when he met his new wife and fell in love and his whole life seemed like a new start. They got married and adopted two kids. He said they had this perfect relationship. They were true soul mates, and she was the most wonderful woman he could imagine except — and he got real upset — they didn't have sex. He said that wasn't really important to him except he was a real man, and he had natural desires that he had to satisfy. He said it didn't have anything to do with his marriage and that he really loved his wife, but that real men need certain things.

He talked about fantasies he had and how when he looked at some women he thought about making love to them in his office, or he thought about sucking on their nipples and stuff like that. He said one of the things he'd always wanted and never had was to be with two women naked and have them sit on his face. I was really embarrassed because I'm not used to people talking like that, and I didn't know what I was supposed to say.

I didn't like being there, and I was trying to figure out a way to leave when all of a sudden he said, "Now that I've told you my fantasies, you tell me about your fantasies about men." I said I didn't have any, and left his office. I felt mad and sort of messy. I promised myself that I'd never get caught in that kind of situation again. I tried to be friendly but cool. I didn't want him to fire me or anything because student jobs are hard to find. I asked my boyfriend to pick me up when I was through working, but I was still nervous around him. He still acted the same — like we had some kind of secret.

When I got engaged a few months after that weird talk, he congratulated me, and I thought everything would be okay. But one day he stopped by my desk and started talking about how he hoped we'd really be happy and everything. Then he said, "But, honey, you're the kind of woman that will never be satisfied with just one man." I was so mad I wanted to spit at him or something, but I just walked away because I didn't want him to see me crying. When my boyfriend came to pick me up that afternoon, he sort of pulled Jim aside and shook his hand and said he was really lucky to have a woman like me and he hoped Jim knew how to be a man to me.

The next day I went to the department head and said I really needed to keep my job for the rest of the semester, but I couldn't handle that stuff anymore, and I wanted to get a transfer. I asked if he was going to do anything about [the faculty member]. I told him I thought he did stuff like that with a lot of other students. The department head told me that if I wanted to sign a written complaint, then he could do something but that if I did that, it might be really hard to find another job. I guess he meant people would think I'm a troublemaker.

Most harassers are less elaborate in their sexual approaches. The behaviors students report are crude, predictable, and mundane. Julie W., a history major, felt herself a captive in a required course:

I think he put me in the front row because he wanted to get his body near to me. I know that sounds conceited, but I guess I think it's true. He always came and stood right in front of me when he was lecturing, and sometimes he would move his foot so it was touching mine. He used to be standing right over me so I could hear his breathing, and it was so awful, like some big jungle animal that was waiting to attack me.

Again and again, student accounts of sexual harassment describe the classroom as having become an unavoidable problem. Laura S., a math student, tried to cope by changing the way she dressed.

Dr. P. gave me the creeps. Whenever we took a test, I'd look up from my paper, and there he would be staring at my top or my legs. I quit wearing skirts to that class because I was so uncomfortable around him. I felt like I was some kind of freak in a zoo.

Even outside the classroom, faculty have a certain access to students. A community college student, Karen S., resented her professor's street-corner behavior:

One day I was walking across campus with a T-shirt that had "California" on the front. I met one of my professors, and he just stared at me for a minute before saying, "My, I've been to California but I don't remember it being so mountainous." I felt the teacher was being very silly. In the first place, my breasts aren't that big. If he gets off on that more power to him, but not on me. I felt like saying, "Doesn't your wife please you?" I was angry because I wasn't coming on to him. I felt sure of myself and very secure.

Some, like Susan N., an art history student at a liberal arts college, understand their professors' intentions but feel more disillusionment than anger and choose to ignore rather than confront them:

> I've had several experiences with profs staring at me, bumping into me, making suggestive remarks. They're silly and boring, but they also repulse me. When I talk to my friends, they're not surprised; they just say that it happens all the time. For the type of harassment that I've experienced, the only thing you can do is ignore it and make professors understand that it isn't a turn on and that you're not a sex object. Mostly it makes me feel disappointed in a professor.

But students' natural trust of teachers can make them oblivious to even the crudest forms of sexual harassment. Claudia G., a university administrator in her late twenties, works with women's programs and counsels harassment victims. With some amusement and amazement, she recalled an experience she had as a student in the early '70s:

> Looking back, it seems almost funny that I was so naive. I was taking a logic course and really didn't understand the material. My boyfriend and I would spend a lot of time with the graduate student who was the teaching assistant in charge of our discussion section. I thought he was just being extra helpful to me; he'd see me any time, even when there weren't special study groups. One day he said, "Come to my house and I'll make sure you get an A." I remember thinking, "I wonder why he has a blackboard in his house." It never occurred to me at the time that he meant anything. It was years later before I realized that it was a proposition. I guess it was a good thing I just ignored it and thought it was a joke. I would have been really upset to think that he was saying anything sexual.

When students decide to ignore blatant propositions, they often find themselves doubly harassed — first by the professor and then by their own sense of helplessness. Mary Ann Y., a criminal justice student, couldn't find resolution in silence:

One of my professors had singled me out in the classroom and would detain me after the class — always to talk. I was brief but polite. But one day he saw me on campus and stopped me. He made some very suggestive comments, off-color remarks. Then he proceeded to tell me how he would like to come in my room with me at the dorm. At first I ignored the comment, but he repeated it. I shook my head no and tried to laugh it off. After that I tried to ignore him and make my intentions as a student obvious. I was very angry and disgusted and shocked. I also felt very helpless and trapped. I talked about it with people —women police, etc. — but it didn't really seem to resolve the situation. As far as grades go, I made sure that I got good grades in class so he couldn't possibly flunk me.

One of the women who answered the National Advisory Council's call for information was the victim of a professor's very overt bartering for sex:

Mr. _____ and I walked out of the classroom, then he asked me if I had any suggestions to help my grade (a D where a C had been earned). I told him I didn't know what my options were. He said he didn't give any suggestions only took them. I asked him if I could write a report for extra credit. He answered with, "I can't give that option to you unless I give it to everyone." I didn't have any other suggestions so I excused myself saying I had to go to class. He stopped me and said, "Some people have suggested they take incompletes and take my class in the fall." I asked him if I could do that and Mr. _____ again stated, "I can't give that option to you unless I give it to everyone." I was confused, wondering why he even mentioned it and said goodbye again. He interrupted me again and said, "I've given you three options and you've discounted two of them." At this time, myself really confused and trying to think of what option he had given me, he asked me to step into the classroom. When we went into the classroom he walked to the door and looked down the halls. By this time I was becoming nervous. He then walked up to me and said, "There's one option I can give to you that I can't give to the males in the class. Sex?" I was shocked and said, "I can't answer that." He asked, "What do you mean you can't answer that, yes or no"? . . .

I was glad I did not have any other finals to take as I probably would not have done well on them . . . This incident has unfortunately left me feeling disillusioned and wary of male professors. I know it isn't right to generalize like that, but I can't help the uneasy feeling.[2]

Social occasions offer opportunities for graduate students to establish professional connections. A Ph.D. student reported to the National Advisory Council the sexual harassment that occurred at a party she attended:

> I see male colleagues and professors chumming it up and hear all the talk about making the old boy network operate for women, so I thought nothing of accepting an invitation from a professor to attend a gathering at his house. Other graduate students were present. Should I have stayed home? Was I asking for whatever I got? I say no. Anyway, the professor made a fool out of himself pursuing me (it took me a while to catch on) and then blurted, "You know I want to sleep with you. You know I can do a lot for you; I have a great deal of influence. Now, of course I don't want to force you into anything, but I'm sure you're going to be sensible about this." I fled.[5]

Although many accounts of sexual harassment are repetitive, some professors devise kinky methods of inflicting themselves on students, and their victims' stories read like scenes from a John Irving novel. The bizarre qualities of these accounts make them no less serious or repulsive. If anything, they are more insidious because faculty abberations are added to the insult of harassment. A history major, Nancy S., had this experience at a Big Ten University:

> My professor asked me to collect the exam papers and bring them to his office because he had to leave early to run an errand. I didn't think anything about it because he had asked me to do stuff like that before. When I took the papers to his office, he was looking out the window and maybe he might have been a little nervous, but I'm not really sure. Anyway, he asked me to sit down, and I wasn't in a hurry, so I did. He just started talking about little things, but I didn't think anything about that either. Finally, he asked me if I knew he could read palms. I said no. He asked if I wanted him to read mine, and I said okay. No one would ever believe this, but when I put my hand out to him he grabbed it and put my finger in his mouth and started sucking. I didn't know what to do. I think I yanked my hand back pretty quick, but it seemed like a century before I did while he just sat there staring at me and sucking my finger. I ran out of the office. It was so weird and awful that I still don't believe it. I told my roommate and we sort of laughed about it, but I don't know if I can ever go back to that class again.

Many academic disciplines require students to work with faculty outside the classroom in labs, clinical settings, studios, or on field trips. Sexual harassers often capitalize on their access to students in these situations and even tailor their approaches to these opportunities. Sarah V., a professor of psychology, recalled an experience of ten years ago:

> When I was doing the research for my dissertation, my adviser, Dr. G., was continually harassing me, both sexually and otherwise. My worst memory is of the day he asked me to do hospital rounds with him. We went into a room where the patient, an indigent black man, was comotose. Dr. G. had made several advances toward me, but I had always managed to slip out of them. This time, he pulled back the sheet — the man was totally naked — and instructed the orderly to bring him equipment to catheterize the patient. The patient was dying, and there was no way this was relevant to his condition. He went ahead with the procedure describing it in great detail, while I was forced to watch. To this day I have always believed that the incident was a means of both shocking and chastising me for not responding to him.

In these nontraditional settings, faculty can isolate students and remind them of their dependence on the professor. Linda F., a 40-year-old university administrator, recalled her inability to confront her professor-adviser:

> In the mid-1960s I was a graduate research assistant to an internationally famous professor at a Big Ten University. My job was to proofread the galley proofs of his research before they were sent to the publishers. There were several times when he called me late on Friday afternoons and asked if I would be available to proof Saturday morning. I was just married and we were both graduate students and assumed that you worked when the professor wanted you to. So I would meet the professor in the empty building in his office, always with the door open. While I worked, he would read aloud pornographic passages from novels and stories that he had gotten from Grove Press. He would start off by saying, "Isn't this amazing?" and then would go on reading. Nothing else ever happened, he never made any off-color remarks to me — only that reading of those strange passages that I had to sit and listen to because there was nothing else I could do and nowhere I could go.

Chris G., a fine arts undergraduate, was comfortable with the liberal environment in her art classes. But when her professor introduced a private agenda into the environment, Chris found herself on guard and nervous:

> Professor S. always liked to make little sexual innuendoes in class or to individual students. Most of it was just funny, perfectly harmless. The rest could be easily ignored. Once, however, we were doing some life drawing in my basic drawing class. The model was clothed, and we were outside enjoying the fresh spring air. Professor S. had mentioned that we would be drawing a nude female figure later in the quarter. I expressed my wish to draw a nude male figure as well.
>
> After class, I stayed outside to finish my drawing. About fifteen minutes later, the professor came back outside, sat down with me, and offered to pose nude for me in my own home. In return, I was to cook him dinner.
>
> As usual, I pretended I never heard the offer. "Normal" teacher-student relations continued but I always feared that he would try to put me in an ultimatum/threat situation.

Kinky sexual advances are rarely reported to anyone. They are unusual, seem unbelievable, and often require years to be fully deciphered by women. Also rarely reported are the unexpected assaults by some faculty members. A community college student recounted to the National Advisory Council an episode that continued to plague her. The head of the department in which she was majoring pressured her to continue discussions and to work during coffee and lunch appointments:

> On the first such occasion, I rejected his attempt to kiss me, but relations remained pleasant. On subsequent occasions, during which he helped me with the research for a paper, he behaved with propriety. Finally, after repeated requests, I agreed to meet with him for a drink at a nearby restaurant. At the last moment, he phoned to say his car had broken down; could I stop by and pick him up. When I turned up he invited me in to hear a tape on the subject we had been discussing. After 45 minutes and a drink, I went to the door to leave. He grabbed me and we wrestled for quite a time until I submitted to intercourse with him. I received an "A" from him every quarter for the remainder of the year, even though I virtually stopped attending his class. A few months after I left the institution, I received a call from a girl I scarcely knew. She said that she had seen me with this instructor, and noticed his attentiveness

and my later absence from the class. She went on to say that he had attacked her and that she feared she was pregnant. She wanted to know if I had had similar problems with him, and asked for advice. She was nineteen. We discussed the matter but decided not to report him if she wasn't pregnant. Fortunately she was not pregnant and we dropped the matter . . . I am now sorry that I did not have the courage and sense of self I needed when [this incident] occurred.[4]

When a faculty member masks his sexual intentions with academic or personal attention to a student, the consequences are complex. Not only does the student have to deal with an unexpected and unwanted sexual encounter, she also feels betrayed by someone she trusted, and, perhaps most distressing of all, she feels complicit in her own abuse. Lured by a professor's offer of personal concern, a student may be unable to interpret cues until time has given perspective to the incident. Recounting her experiences, Janet S., a student in a highly competitive engineering college, struggled to understand what had happened to her:

Fall quarter I had some very serious personal problems which severely affected my studies. One of my professors seemed very concerned. I decided I would have to drop his class. He talked me into keeping his class because he said he'd let me take a make-up exam. Then he started pressing me about my personal problems, so I finally gave him a basic rundown on my situation. Before I left, he invited me to come back to his office to chat any time.

When I turned in the make-up exam he said to stop by and he'd tell me how I did. I stopped by about 5 or 5:30 that afternoon. He didn't have the exams graded yet but said to come by Saturday. We talked for a while and I told him I had a date that night. He said he would've asked me to have dinner with him otherwise.

Saturday I stopped by. He graded my paper while I was sitting there and I thought he was too lenient. In lecture he said a couple of times he wouldn't give partial credit, but he gave me partial credit. He invited me to study at a table in his office while he worked and I said okay. Then he asked if I'd have dinner with him and I said yes, thinking we would go out. But he meant at his apartment. At that point I felt uncomfortable but told myself that he was too old to play games with me and that he was really concerned about me and wanted to be friends. So I didn't say anything and we went to his place. We were alone most of the evening. Nothing physical happened, but looking back I can see where he hinted. I didn't catch it then, because I believed he was nice and thought that I must be reading something into his words. He asked a few times if I still thought of him as a professor because, according to him, the quarter was over. I asked him to walk me home about midnight and he did. I don't know... I don't know what to make of it. I feel embarrassed and a bit hurt.

Even when a professor's intentions are obvious, a student can find herself helplessly entrapped by course requirements or her desire to complete a particular academic program. Kathy W., working to earn an associate degree, also found herself struggling with harassment. Her determination to cope finally turned to anger when she realized the professor had repeatedly abused students:

The course, required in my major, allowed the instructor to be physically close to students. Each student sat at a desk with a particular machine. One day my instructor leaned over and put his hand on my inner thigh while he was explaining the machine to me. Then he put his hand around my upper arm so that his fingers were on the inside of my arm, with the tops of his fingers touching my breast. As each class came, and I had a question, he would continue to pull up a chair next to me and put his hands on my legs, upper arms, and sides. I can remember when I wore bib overalls to class one day and he put his hands down the back of my bib overalls and pulled them up.

I tried to think of ways to lessen the opportunity for him to touch me. I began going up to his desk if I had a question. He still managed. I began to realize that he was going to touch me if he damn well pleased. A pat on the ass on the way out of class, a smirky smile and a glare at my breasts — he made me sick! I would come to class late in hopes that he had found someone else that interested him, and sometimes he would. I skipped the maximum amount of classes that I could without being dropped from the class.

After talking with a few good friends, and seeing that their reactions were the same as mine, I decided that I was going to report it. After a few conversations with the head of the department, I could see the attitude that he had developed: "Oh, this is one of these supersensitive females who always thinks males are out to get her." I became aggravated and guilty that I had said anything at all about it.

Now that it is in the past and I have heard that there have been other girls with similar experiences with the instructor, I realize that what that S.O.B. did was wrong, unjust, and perverted. If I only would have been strong enough with my own thoughts and impressions at the time I would have tried my damndest to nail his ass.

Linda S., aware that women are just emerging as students in industrial design, felt captive to her professor:

> Although there are more and more women in my field every year, we still feel unusual, out of place. The teacher in charge of one of the major studio classes made me feel very uncomfortable. Every time I walked into the classroom, he greeted me with some embarrassing remark, like "Hi, sexy," or "Welcome, sensual being." It was deliberately loud enough for all the other students to hear. I didn't say anything or look at him. It made me really uncomfortable, but I didn't know what to do. I've got this studio for the entire year and he'll be critiquing my work for the next three years. I'm afraid to speak to him about it because I can't afford to make him angry.

In rare cases, the pain of sexual harassment can have positive results. A social worker in her mid-thirties, Nancy B., turned a sexual harassment experience with an English professor into a professional insight:

> I had just enrolled at the University. One professor was exceptionally warm and friendly. He frequently asked me to stay after class and would walk me to my next class. After a couple of weeks he asked me very personal questions about men. I told him I was engaged to be married at the end of the quarter, feeling this would discourage any possible overture.
>
> One day this professor requested that I come to his office and discuss a paper. When I arrived, he escorted me to a chair and closed the office door. He walked over to me, put his hands around my face and told me I was a very beautiful woman, then kissed my forehead. We never discussed any of my academic work. After that, I avoided being alone with him. I disregarded his constant requests to visit his office, and I hurriedly left his classes.
>
> The first quarter I received an A. After the exam, he stopped me and said, "Well, you will be a married woman the next time I see you," and put his arm around me and kissed my cheek. Since I was getting married, I felt this would end his obsession with me. His attention continued. I avoided him completely except in the classroom, and I never went to his office again. The second quarter I received a B. The third quarter I received a C, the lowest grade I ever received in that program.
>
> I was so upset. I guess I'm still angry about it. The funny thing is I met him on campus the next year, and he didn't even remember my name!

Some "beautiful woman" I was to him!

Now that I'm older I realize that sexual harassment is a kind of rape. This experience gave me the incentive to become involved with problems of rape and domestic violence. I began to realize that if you keep women afraid, they're more likely to be victims.

Few harassment experiences have educational effects, however. Usually, sexual harassment forces a student to forfeit work, research, educational comfort, or even career. Professors withhold legitimate opportunities from those who resist, or students withdraw rather than pay certain prices. An assistant dean in a liberal arts college described how a student gave up a rare opportunity rather than withstand possible harassment:

> A senior in psychology, interested in graduate work, applied for a part-time research job with a professor in her department. Her hope was that she would be able to show her abilities in the field, increase her chances for graduate school admission, and earn some money all at the same time. The professor held interviews for the job in his office. The student said the professor stared at her legs throughout the entire interview. He didn't really ask any questions about her experience or training. The student found herself giving a monologue, getting non-committal nods and grunts in response. She said that she became increasingly uncomfortable and awkward. After fifteen minutes, she left, deciding she didn't really want the job after all.

Ann S., a graduate student in biology working on a research team funded by a professor's grant, found her life changed as a result of an encounter with a teacher:

> In the lab he would stare at me, rub up against me, make crude remarks. He repeatedly asked me out and would make public comments on how well I looked in a certain blouse, dress, and so forth. He implied that I could get a higher grade if I dated him. I refused to go out with him and I got a lower grade than I deserved. The harassment was so intense that I withdrew from school for one quarter to assess the situation and get counseling. When I returned, I quickly finished the research project and refused to deal with anyone from that laboratory, thereby forfeiting any possibility of publishing my work.

The isolation of sexual harassment victims is sometimes shattered when students accidentally compare notes or when they seek support from classmates. Students are shocked to discover that they are not alone or unique, and they are frequently relieved. Fear, embarrassment, and guilt reinforce silence until some inadvertent comment or isolated grievance action reveals a pattern. One woman told the National Advisory Council:

> When it finally came into the open I was amazed . . . The room was full of women who had been victimized, and almost none of us had ever told anyone but a few close friends.[5]

Sometimes it takes such accidental comparison to shed light on a pattern of seemingly innocent activities. A group of university women who were joking about "all-time great lechers" discussed a residence hall counselor who was also a history instructor. Donna C. remembered the experience of a friend who had worked with him as a student resident adviser:

> It was a kind of friendly counselor job. He was in charge of about ten of us and lived in an apartment in the dorm. He was in his late twenties then, pretty good looking, and we used to sort of compete for his attention. It got really complicated for some of the advisers because they would really get psychologically involved with him and wanted to be special to him. When he would pay extra attention to one of us, others would feel really rejected, almost like they were girlfriends. But they'd complain about surface stuff, like he was treating them unprofessionally or something. One time he showed up in the adviser's dorm room at 2 A.M. It really was upsetting to her because there wasn't any problem or crisis, no real reason for him to be there. He said he just wanted to talk, and he didn't say anything off-color or suggestive. But she said she felt uncomfortable the whole time. She kept wondering what the students would think about his being there or if anyone had seen him in the halls because his wife, who is also a friend of mine, must have been right upstairs in their apartment. Anyway her relationship with him deteriorated after that. After she left, she found out he had given her a bad recommendation because she was "uncooperative."

Another woman, Elaine M., described how the same man had arrived unexpectedly one evening at the apartment of a friend of hers who had been registered in one of his classes: "He just came in and sat down and said he wanted to get to know her better. He didn't do anything else, just sat there for a while, and finally got up and left."

A third woman, who was his professional colleague, explained still another encounter: "We were in my office discussing some student affairs problem. All of a sudden, he said, 'Can I give you a hug?' I sort of looked at him and said, 'Sure, why not?' So he did, and then he left and that was that."

In addition to the problems colleges face with student victims, they have known the fury of faculty wives whose husbands direct attention to women students. A professor known as a harasser by students over the years became involved in what appeared to be a serious relationship with a student. One colleague commented, "It's really humiliating to have to pass them plopped all over the floor of the hall outside other people's classes. I don't know how to respond. I know his behavior is unacceptable, and I get so damned mad at myself for not having the courage to tell him he's a disgrace to the whole profession."

The situation became more complicated when the professor's wife assumed that he was having an affair with the department secretary. The secretary reported she became the target of a series of unusual incidents:

One day I was home sick, and the phone rang. Someone asked, "Who is this?" I gave her my name, and the person hung up. A little later the phone rang again, and the same voice identified herself as Mrs. X. She said that Mr. X was evaluating another professor and had given her his schedule, but she had lost it. It was something ridiculous like that. I was kind of annoyed and said, "I'm sick today, and I really don't think I can help you." She said, "Oh, I'm sorry." Then I felt kind of bad and told her to call the department head and get it from him. The next day when I went back to work, I couldn't believe it. Mr. X came up to me and said he thought his wife thought we were having an affair. I couldn't believe anyone would think I could seriously be attracted to someone like him. I almost laughed. I don't know whether he used me to hide the thing with the student or not. I think he must have brought me up to Mrs. X or mentioned me in some way; but with him you never can guess what he might do to set her off because his reasoning is so bizarre. Anyway, I told the department head about it, which was a good thing because one day soon after that she came flying into the office. She was headed for me, but the department head got her into his office and took care of it somehow. I did ask her on the way out if she found Mr. X and she acted sort of flighty and said it had been taken care of or something screwy like that.

The preceding anecdotes and the patterns they reveal help to convey the nature of sexual harassment on campus. Yet the brevity of these comments can give the impression that such incidents are isolated. Nothing is further from the truth. Most faculty who are identifiable as sexual harassers have repeated patterns of easily recognizable, predictable, and persistent behaviors.

In bringing a formal complaint at a multicampus university, fourteen women — graduate and undergraduate students, clerical staff, and faculty — submitted written statements about a faculty member who taught and supervised staff and students in a clinical setting. Their documents revealed a coherent pattern of unprofessional language, behavior, and attitude.

One fellow faculty member summed up the professor's inappropriate behavior:

> The working environment within the department has deteriorated to the extent of nearly total dysfunction directly as the result of Dr. ____'s behavior. These are some of his behaviors:
>
> Dr. ____ has repeatedly cleaned his glasses with a pair of men's jockey shorts while I have been sitting in his office.
>
> He volunteered to guess the bra size of each member of the Department.
>
> He "complained" that a certain trainee's blouses were too small for her; she was always popping buttons.
>
> Discussing how he and his wife have an understanding that he may "date" when he is away at conventions.
>
> Nearly constant sexual references in conversations with students and staff such as: (a) comparison of hair pattern on his chest and his son's and (b) description of the body of his daughter as he observed her and her mother dressing in a motel room.
>
> Continually tells dirty jokes, especially in the presence of younger female employees/students.
>
> One day he noticed that my badge was clipped on "wrong" and that my blouse was actually a man's shirt and, therefore, buttoned "backwards." He asked if I was having a sexual identity crisis.
>
> Persistently touched me on hand, arm, shoulder when he talked with me — much more frequently than might occur casually.
>
> Repeatedly urged an older female trainee to become involved with his son because he needed experience with an older woman.
>
> Advised me that once he and another man rented a "secret" apartment to entertain women.

He has described the "bedroom" games that he plays with his wife such as chasing her around naked.

Has remarked on the improvement in his sexual relationship with his wife since she lost weight — especially makes these remarks to people who are heavy.

Repeatedly has discussed his vasectomy, remarking that the scar is very small.

The statements by women students, faculty, and staff led to a campus grievance hearing and a cursory disciplinary action by the administration. A year later, a complaint was made that the same professor was asking students out for dates and making overt sexual remarks to them. Several of the complainants left the department because of the hostility directed toward them. The legal and medical bills they had incurred during the grievance process were an additional hardship.

The costs of sexual harassment to victims are financial, psychological, and professional. Anecdotes are limited in their ability to convey the frustration of weeks, months, and sometimes years spent dealing with sexual harassment. An account by a psychology graduate student in a nationally renowned program revealed the tension and discouragement of complainants. With two years in the program, the woman was completing her master's degree when her ordeal began. She was working under a research contract to Dr. X when she had her first problematic encounter with his colleague, Dr. Y.:

May, Dr. Y asked me if I wished to share a motel room with him at meetings to be held in the spring. Following our return from these meetings (at which I did not share a motel room with him), he began criticizing my work, suggesting that there was something wrong with my master's thesis data, suggesting that my experimental groups would not replicate, etc.

June, I had set up a schedule for completing my master's thesis when Dr. Y. asked me whether I had completed the analyses. I indicated that I had done so. He indicated that he did not think that I had completed the work. I said that I was aware of the fact that he held that opinion. I was very sensitive to the fact that someone had gone through my desk earlier in the week. That person left the statistics papers in considerable disarray. Dr. X, who was present for the above exchange, found it very funny. Dr. Y and I went to a room across the hall to work on the study, for which frozen brain tissue is used. He asked me how many brains I had. I said that I had just one. His eyes rolled back in his head and he said that he would like to take it out and freeze it.

June, I approached Dr. Y several times and attempted to discuss his hostility toward me. He said that he didn't know what I was talking about. He began commenting about the fact that I did not seem to be having any problems with graduate school, and he said that it was too bad that no one had given me any trouble.

July, Dr. Y approached me with a suggestion about the one night per week that his wife is out of town. He was interrupted . . . Dr. Y's criticisms of my work continued. When pushed he admitted that the criticisms were unfounded, and he began to make references to how difficult it is to fire people. He told me repeatedly that when he was a graduate student, he did whatever his adviser wanted in order to get his Ph.D.

August, Dr. Y suggested I come to his home and help him with some work. I spoke with some of the other women in the lab about the incidents. One woman said she had been approached some months earlier, and with some physical force, by Dr. Y. A second woman said she had encountered some physical harassment from Dr. X . . .

(The student's September and October accounts described Drs. X's and Y's refusals to support her attempts to collect data for her thesis.)

November, Dr. Y approached me and began telling me that in his opinion I did not seem to be doing anything. He said that I was becoming quite marginal as a graduate student. I mentioned to him that I had had to repeat the statistical tests. He said that he would not want anyone to treat him the way that he had treated me but that he and Dr. X were very traditional and would do the same thing to their first-year graduate student when she started working on her master's thesis . . .

February, I received a letter from the graduate director saying that my committee was becoming concerned because I had not completed my thesis.

February, I asked Dr. Y if he thought that we could be civil to each other until June. He declared that there would be no more hostilities. I asked him why they had started. He said that there had been a conflict between his personal feeling and his feelings about me as a graduate student.

February, Dr. X phoned my home and asked me to talk with him, which I did that afternoon. He asked me about the problems with Dr. Y. I told him of some of the incidents and that I had attempted to talk with Dr. Y.

Eventually I had concluded that his actions were deliberately destructive. Dr. X suggested that I not be so upset about it. I told him that had I not been so involved in the lab I would not be so upset. He officially declared I would not work with Dr. Y. I talked with Dr. X later that afternoon after he had talked with Dr. Y. He said rather vehemently that no one was trying to break my self-confidence.

I began working on my thesis in the library. Before I left the lab, the first-year graduate student told me she had been invited to attend meetings and that Dr. X had told her that she could choose with which of three professors she wished to share a motel room. She also told me of an incident of physical harassment from Dr. X.

(The student's March, April, and May accounts relate her meeting with the director of graduate students to protest her treatment.)

May, I met the department head, I gave him a written account of most of my experiences at the lab. He suggested that Dr. X and Dr. Y were simply teasing. He suggested that I was upset because I was going through a divorce and that I was misperceiving the incidents. He then suggested that my behavior was controlled and that it was obvious that I hated someone. He pointed out to me the serious nature of my charges against Dr. X, and he expressed concern for Dr. Y's reputation.

(During June, the student was given a new thesis committee which did not include Drs. X and Y.)

June, I told the new committee head that I wanted some commitment that the department would address the problems that I had encountered. I told him that without such a commitment I could only assume that all women students in the department were treated as I had been treated. I told him that until some action was taken I would not be able to finish the thesis, and I said that if the department would not act, I would. He told me that if I took any action it was very possible that I would not receive my master's degree, as no one in the department would be able to work with me.

July, I talked with [another professor]. He said that if I tried to do anything about the problems I would get hurt. I became very angry when he said this, and he told me that I had better leave.

August, I spoke with several members of the committee about the problems that I had encountered, and about getting the department to address the problems. One committee member sympathized with the fact that I was being "treated like dirt." Another suggested that I repress the entire thing.

September, I was informed that Dr. X wanted my master's thesis data. A woman graduate student had worked with Dr. X in 1974-1975, and she had encountered problems at the placement. Chief among these was a dispute over the analysis of her master's thesis data. After she had completed the thesis, Drs. X and Y took the data. They discarded some, reanalyzed the rest, and produced a significant study presented at a meeting in 1977 and published in 1978. I told Dr. A that I would give Dr. X access to the data after the study had been accepted for publication.

October, I asked whether any action had been taken to address the problems that I had encountered at the placement. I received a negative response.

October, I informed the committee in writing that I intended to (1) terminate my teaching assistantship and (2) terminate my training in their program upon completion of the master's degree. [One professor] threatened to terminate me prior to the master's degree. [Another] also suggested that the committee might again terminate me prior to the degree, in order to mar my academic record and to make it more difficult for me to complete the degree.

October, I was informed that my resignation had been accepted.

Over the summer the first-year graduate student had prepared a proposal of her master's thesis. She brought this proposal to the department, and she encountered problems. She left the lab at the end of the summer. In September she left the psychology department on a leave of absence.

There is now another woman graduate student there. She works only with Dr. E. Drs. X and Y are now working with undergraduate students.

The statement, "I was informed that my resignation had been accepted," summarizes clearly the predicament of victims of sexual harassment. They resign themselves to the situation. In this case, the student's life and future are radically altered; but the individuals accused of harassing her and others remain in academe, where their careers are presumably undamaged.

For those familiar with sexual harassment on campus, there is a dismaying predictability in student responses. When asked to simulate the reactions of harassment victims, students who have not been sexually harassed replicate the real victims' feelings. In an undergraduate psychology class studying the phenomenon of sexual harassment, Dr. Dee Graham, Associate Professor at the University of Cincinnati, prepared a guided fantasy based on a true experience told to her by a student. The class, composed of different majors, ages, and sexes, was asked to assume the identity of the student. There was a pause after each episode in the story, and students were directed to reflect on their probable feelings. At the end of the reading, they reported their reactions. (Unless indicated, the responses were from women).

Q : Imagine yourself as an undergraduate student taking an afternoon class in the English Department. Dr. Mann is your professor. You are sitting at your desk, and Dr. Mann is handing back the exam papers which he has graded. As he hands you your paper, he smiles and says, "On both of the exams we've had this quarter, you've scored the highest that any of my students have ever scored. You're very expressive." You take the paper and say, "Thank you, Dr. Mann." What are you feeling? What are you thinking?

A : I wouldn't think anything at all.

A : I'd be pleased with the grade.

A : I'd be embarrassed at being singled out.

A : Surprised.

A : Flattered, I guess.

A : Good grades are a neat deal.

Q : During the next class meeting, he calls on you. You answer his question. He says, "Yes, that's an important point." As you volunteer your own perspective regarding the novel being discussed, he tells the class that you have good ideas and that he hopes others will give as much thought as you do to the material being read. As the class ends, you gather up your books and prepare to leave. Dr. Mann approaches you, puts his finger on your books, and says, "I would like for us to get together and discuss your ideas some more. Would you like to join me for a drink this afternoon?" What are you thinking and feeling? What do you say to him?

A : Would I go? To talk, yes.

A : I wouldn't go. I'd be intimidated by the fact that he was a professor. I wouldn't believe I was that smart. I'd anticipate that he had other intentions.

A : The part about "getting a drink" would put me off. That seems suspicious. Coffee or a Coke would seem okay.

A : It's a clear invitation to go out. A prof has to be a little deceptive, use his position. He can't just make moves on students. He has to be subtle. (Male Student)

A : I'd be flattered he was interested in my ideas.

A : I'd hesitate about whether something funny was going on but I'd tell myself I was being silly and dismiss it as my own paranoia.

A : I'd be worried, not sure how to say no, how to get out of the situation. I'd make up excuses, but I'd worry about grades, making him angry.

A : If I was attracted to him, I'd accept. It'd be neat, but scary. There'd be the excitement of checking out what might happen. There is with anyone new. But I'd figure I could handle whatever happened. I'd make the decision.

Most students struggled with the decision to accept the social invitation. The professor was injecting ambiguity into their relationship. Nevertheless, the students assumed that they were responsible for resolving the conflicts they felt.

Q : During your next class, Dr. Mann calls on you to present your views about the new novel being discussed. You do so, and he responds, "That's an excellent analysis. Thank you." As the class ends, you prepare to leave. Dr. Mann once more approaches you and says, "Perhaps this afternoon you will join me for a drink." What are you feeling? What do you say to him?

A : Don't know how sure I'd feel about myself. I'd try to figure out where he's coming from, try to get a total perspective on it.

A : I'd still be figuring out what to do, how to get out of this situation. I might go just to avoid a hassle.

A : If I went the first time, I guess I'd go again. I mean, how could I say no?

A : I'd be confused, worried about grades.

A : If I went, I guess I'd be complicit in whatever happened.

A : I wondered when she'd catch on. Didn't seem to catch on so quick. It's obvious the guy's just baiting the hook, making his moves. It's typical stuff. (Male Student)

A : If she accepted, she'd be giving him signals, misleading him, accepting dates and stuff. (Male Student)

A : She should be flattered. Just laugh it off. I don't know why this is such a big deal. (Male Student)

A : I guess it'd matter if he were older. If he were a father figure, it would remind me of incest or something and I'd be scared. If he were younger, I'd think he's more attractive and I wouldn't be scared.

A : I don't think I'd feel so vulnerable. But she should be pleased. It's not some dreadful thing. (Male Student)

The repeated invitation increased confusion and concern, but the students continued to feel responsible for the relationship.

Q : At the end of your next class period with Dr. Mann, once again he asks
you to join him for a drink. He then says, "I'm noticing that the quality
of your work is sliding. Is there something you would like to talk about?
You appear depressed about something." You tell him you have no
more problems than usual. He answers, "It's important that you keep
your grades up if you want to go to graduate school. Look, you're a
special student to me. If there's something wrong, I want you to tell me
about it. You can talk about anything with me . . . Tomorrow I'll take
you to lunch. We can eat off-campus so that you can talk freely."

The next day you and Dr. Mann go out to lunch. As your food is
being prepared, he asks you questions about your background, and especially about your past relations with men. You are flattered that he's
interested — you want him to like you. He asks you, "What were your
relations with these men like sexually?" You answer, "I'd really rather
not talk about that." He says, "Are you uptight about sex?" You
answer, "I don't think so, but I consider my sexual life to be private."
You ask him about his life. He responds by asking you another
question about the problems you are having with an important man in
your life. He seems so interested in you and so understanding. You
think to yourself, "My friends and family aren't even this understanding." So you begin to talk with him about your problems. How
much do you self-disclose to him? What are you feeling?

A : Because of the class, I wouldn't have thought anything until the
questions about boyfriends and sex. Then I'd be scared, try to figure
out how to get out of here, what do I do now?

A : I'd feel naive, think how did I get into this.

A : I'd feel stupid, like I didn't know the ropes.

A : I'd tell him those things are none of his business. I came to talk about
work.

The injection of intimate topics by the professor triggered self-
deprecating reactions from some students who felt foolish for
believing the interest had been "sincere." In the fantasy situation,
students tended to resist the offer of an "understanding" conversation about their sexual relationships. In real life, many students
reported that they engaged in such conversations and were flattered
and pleased when a professor was interested in details about their
lives. In the classroom situation, students knew to be on guard. In
real life, their defenses are down; they are much more vulnerable.

Q : As you and Dr. Mann wait for the waiter to bring the check, he tells you, "You are very bright. I think you have *real* potential. I can help you realize your potential to its fullest." He continues, "In the future, we're going to be working together closely. Perhaps we should get to know one another well. Really well." And he suggests the two of you go to a nearby hotel. What are you thinking? What do you say to him?

A : The hotel stuff would make me rethink everything, I'd go back over everything and be suspicious of his intentions.

A : I'd question myself. I did respond in a friendly manner and he took it sexually. It's socially acceptable to interpret it that way. I'd feel guilty because I'd been friendly and I'd think about what I'd done.

A : I'd feel naive. That I should have known all along. I'd be mad at myself for accepting a social engagement.

A : I'd tell him where to get off, like I would any guy that made a wrong move.

A : I'd be angry that I'd accepted the first drink.

A : That's really crude. (Male Student)

A : It's hard for guys. They don't know the limits. Maybe he was just trying to understand things.

A : Maybe he just misinterpreted me.

The actual proposition, put as bluntly in the real episode as in the fantasy, set off multiple reactions from individuals. Initially, most reported a single response; but in group discussion, respondents stated that they had a number of reactions at the same time. Those who were angry or confrontive said they also wondered if they had misled the professor or misunderstood his statements all along. The students whose first responses were self-blame and complicity also admitted feelings of anger and betrayal that they feared were illegitimate or inexpressible.

Q : Several days later, you begin to feel angry about Dr. Mann propositioning you. You go to his office and confront him. He tells you, "You led me on, and now that I'm responding as any normal man would, you're outraged. You were just pretending to be interested in me. I had to sit and listen to all your problems. You told me all about your sex life. And now you're trying to get me fired . . . You've been using your body, not your mind, to make a grade in my class . . . You're just like the female character in the novel we're reading. You're manipulative! You're hysterical. You're evil! You use men without caring about them. Now you're making up these lies to ruin my career . . . I think you're sick and you need therapy. I feel sorry for you." What are you feeling?

What are you thinking? What do you do?

A : I'd feel guilty, take the blame for it.

A : Why would she go back to the office? Why would she want to see him again? (Male Student)

A : I'd be disgusted that men can do that.

A : I'd be angry. I know when I'm flirting and when I'm not.

A : I'd make him defend what he said. My body had nothing to do with it.

A : I'd want to clarify the situation, check out my confusion.

A : I'd have grades to worry about.

A : I'd be angry at the betrayal.

A : I'd figure things had gone too far, that I had let them. I wouldn't fight.

A : I'd call him every name in the book. Say he led me astray, blame him for all this.

A : I'd probably find a way to make it my fault. My self-esteem is kind of low.

The confrontation scene in which the professor unleashed a barrage of defenses and counterattacks engendered many angry reactions in the classroom, but few students thought they would express that anger to the professor. Most students took the professor's attack as an indicator that there was nothing more to be done; they were intimidated and reported concerns about grades, their own self-esteem, and the general power of the professor to control even a confrontation scene. Almost all the students in the class, both men and women, talked about the risks to the professor — career, personal reputation, family — as more important than their own well-being and self-esteem.

The women in the guided fantasy exercise had the same diversity of reactions and responses as real-life victims. A few in the class showed their anger and were willing to confront the situation directly. Most, however, had to struggle with their inferior roles as students; they worried about grades, offending an authority figure, and misinterpreting the professor's intention. The student role more than anything else was responsible for their confusion and inability to confront an undesirable situation. As with real victims of sexual harassment, the fantasy victims persistently reviewed their own behaviors and assumed they had responsibility for their own abuse. Perhaps the most shocking aspect of the classroom exercise was how easily women accepted the role of victim and their power-lessness to change or remedy it. In fantasy and in fact, the undertone of resignation is the clearest sign of higher education's indifference to sexual harassment.

5 : *The Lecherous Professor*

A PORTRAIT OF THE ARTIST

"When I use a word," Humpty Dumpty said, in a rather scornful tone, "it means just what I choose it to mean — neither more nor less." "The question is," said Alice, "whether you can make words mean so many different things." "The question is," said Humpty Dumpty, "which is to be the master — that's all."

Lewis Carroll,
Alice In Wonderland

In a recent *Cosmopolitan* article on sexual harassment, Adrian L., a student at a large Midwestern state university described Tom, one of her professors:

> [He's] like a rabid wolf hovering at the edge of a sheep pack — the incoming class of freshmen.
>
> When he's selected a girl who's unusually attractive, intelligent, and naive, he moves right in. Believe me, he's *predatory* — I've seen him in action. First, he'll "rap and relate" with the freshman over drinks at the college bar. In a couple of weeks, he has her dizzy with the "existential nihilism of Sartre" or "archetypal patterns of Jung." All this may sound exciting, but the results are tragicomic. Two years ago, he "shared" a girl with a friend of his, another faculty member. The three of them made it while watching a particularly beautiful sunrise — very aesthetic, you know. His current ploy is backgammon. You see him shaking those dice at a table in the rathskeller with this hazy-eyed kid. Several

dormitory assistants have seen him leaving her room at six in the morning, and the campus security guard once caught him with a student in the stacks of the library. You can guess what he found.

Is Tom exploiting his pupils? You bet he is. Does he know what he's doing? Of course. Is the administration aware of what he's up to? Sure they are, but these days, to get fired for what they used to call "moral turpitude," you'd have to rape an entire cheerleading squad at half time. Tom's like a pothead turned loose in a Twinkies factory.[1]

Although there is limited evidence of the number of harassers who may be "loose" on the nation's campuses, one point is clear. They are tolerated because society doubts that men are capable of sexual restraint. Sexual harassers are often defended with the shrugged observation, "After all, they're only human." A middle-aged professor, notorious for pursuing sexual relations with female students, offered a variation on this view: "If you put me at a table with food [with coeds], I eat."

The appeal to "human nature" is a reminder that even in an era of ostensible sexual liberalism and freedom, both men and women suffer and stereotypes die hard. Even in the 1980s, society has not freed itself of the Victorian notion that men are creatures barely capable of controlling their bestial appetites and aggressions. All the contemporary rhetoric about liberating the sexes from stereotypes has done little to change the popular view of the male as a kind of eternal tumescence, forever searching and forever unsatisfied.

Such an attitude demeans the notion of "human." To be human does not mean that a man is at the mercy of his genitalia. Whatever it is that constitutes "humanness" is located in the mind and heart, not the libido. "Human" implies reason, compassion, control — all the qualities that distinguish college professors from their cats and dogs. Without these, they are "only animal," a defense few find appealing. Sexual harassment unquestionably harms females, but men are equally debased when it is allowed to flourish. On the college campus, a very small number of men damage the reputations of colleagues who perform difficult tasks for relatively low wages without "succumbing" to the "irresistible" temptations of women students.

The professor-as-lecher is so much a part of the folklore of higher education that it appears consistently in popular writing. One of the most telling examples is Anna Sequoia's *The Official J.A.P. Handbook*.

The work is intended as a parody of the Jewish American Princess stereotype, but in order to accomplish the parody, the author relies on the universally familiar stereotype of the lecherous professor. According to Sequoia, Marsha Lynn, the typical J.A.P., "looks for love in all the wrong places." One of the most predictable is college:

Marsha Lynn and the Professor. Marsha Lynn often meets her professor during the first term of her freshman year. Usually, Professor Maisel is teaching an art-survey course or a freshman English course. He may be a painter or a poet: probably the first real painter or poet Marsha Lynn's met. Professor Maisel, of course, won't put the touch on Marsha Lynn that term: he'll wait until she has her (well-deserved) A, but they'll become friends. Perhaps they'll have long, passionate conversations about Faulkner. Perhaps Professor Maisel will introduce Marsha Lynn to *Roethke: Collected Poems*, or *The Selected Poems of Margaret Atwood.* Maybe when Adrienne Rich or David Ignatow come to read on campus, Professor Maisel will invite Marsha Lynn to the party afterward and get her as drunk on the proximity to Real Poets as on the cheap white wine. Little by little, Marsha Lynn will become incorporated into Professor Maisel's world, visiting him in the afternoons in his office, perhaps stopping by on occasion — usually with two or three other bright students — for a dinner of homemade pasta and intelligent conversation.

And coming from what Marsha Lynn will perceive as her intellectually limited suburb, in (temporary) rebellion against her parents' milieu of conspicuous (even if tasteful) consumption, hungry for the stimulation and surface glamour of the Literary Life, Marsha Lynn will fall into Professor Maisel's carefully laid trap. Poor Marsha Lynn really has no adequate defense. Professor Maisel is an old hand at seducing students and makes a regular, if moderately discreet, practice of it.

JAP parents have few resources against the Predatory Professor. If they withdraw Marsha Lynn from that college, she may refuse to leave and move in with her Older Man. If Daddy goes to talk to the professor, he'll embarrass himself and have no effect. Usually, the dean or chairman of the department or even the president of the college will do nothing: they know that every campus has its share of Professor Maisels, and they choose to do nothing about it. Usually, the only resource is to have a powerful friend on the college's board of trustees: sometimes that works.

But generally it's just a question of time. Sooner or later, Marsha Lynn will realize that Professor Maisel drinks too much, or sleeps with other students, or is just too old for her (even though he may be in his late thirties or early or middle forties), or too condescending.[2]

Popular fiction also perpetuates the lecherous stereotypes. Jacob Horner, John Barth's protagonist in *The End of the Road*, described his opening day of classes:

> Indeed! One hundred spelling words dictated rapidly enough to keep their heads down, and I, perched high on my desk, could diagnose to my heart's content every bump of femininity in the room (praised be American grade schools, where little girls learn to sit up front!). Then, perhaps, having ogled my fill, I could get on with the business of the course. For as a man must grow used to the furniture before he can settle down to read in his room, this plenitude of girlish appurtenances had first to be assimilated before anyone could concentrate attention on the sober prescriptions of English grammar.
>
> Four times I repeated the ritual pronouncements — at eight and nine in the morning and at two and three in the afternoon. Between the two sessions I lounged in my office with a magnificent erection, wallowing in my position, and watched with proprietary eye the parade of young things passing my door. I had nothing at all to do but spin indolent daydreams of absolute authority — Neurotic, Caligular authority of the sort that summons up officefuls of undergraduate girls, hot and submissive — leering professorial dreams![3]

Horner's adventures may sell books, but they miss the point about everyday life in higher education. The truth is that most faculty probably lack the time and energy required for "leering professorial dreams." Literary characters can afford the luxury of "magnificent erection(s)," whereas real-life college professors spend their working hours juggling time between classes, meetings, research, writing, and professional conferences. Those who fit the Jacob Horner stereotype are the exception, not the rule, but lecherous professors repeat their offenses on multiple victims and do so much damage that they claim more attention than professors who simply do their jobs.

A crucial concern for both students and academicians is learning to recognize the characteristics that differentiate the lecherous professor from his colleagues. There are no infallible predictors for recognizing sexual harassment. The most pernicious behavior can occur exclusive of "giveaways," or isolated actions can be misinterpreted as sinister when they are simply examples of clumsy professional or social style. However, a tentative list of warning signs might include the following:

- *Staring, leering, ogling* These behaviors may be surreptitious or very obvious. In any case, college faculty should possess knowledge of social decorum, and must avoid such activities.

- *Frequently commenting on personal appearance of the student* In the academic setting, most professors refrain from discussing the apparel and physical traits of their students.

- *Touching out of context* Every physical gesture should be appropriate to the occasion, setting, and need and character of the individual student. Professional educators may legitimately be expected to possess the ability to make such determinations.

- *Excessive flattery and praise of the student* This behavior, exhibited with others present, is especially seductive to students with low self-esteem *or* high aspirations. By convincing a student that she is intellectually and/ or physically exceptional, the lecherous professor gains psychological access to her.

- *Deliberately avoiding or seeking encounters with the student in front of colleagues* Depending on the type of harasser, he may either attempt to hide from or to perform for colleagues in interactions with the student. The key is that in either case his behavior with the student changes when he is being observed.

- *Injecting a "male versus female" tone into discussions with students or colleagues* A frequent behavior of verbal harassers, this conduct signals a generally disparaging attitude toward women. Its initial effect is to make them feel outsiders in the academic environment, but it may also be an indicator of other potential forms of abuse.

- *Persistently emphasizing sexuality in all contexts* Pervasive, inordinate emphasis on sex can occur in class or outside. For the lecherous professor, sexuality becomes, in effect, the prism through which all topics are focused. Students, male and female, can usually detect this behavior readily, and such professors often acquire a reputation for "being fixated on sex" in papers, tests, and discussions.

Such behaviors can serve as signals to the student. Another key to understanding the lecherous professor is assessing the setting or context in which he works. There are both public and private harassers, and they act in very different fashions. The public harasser engages in observable, flagrant posturing toward women. He is the most likely to intimidate or seek control through sexist remarks and advances that may be offensive but are essentially free from sanctions. Students sometimes refer to him as "hands," "touchy-feely," or "mouth." Colleagues describe him as "patronizing," "always performing," "convinced of his own cuteness." He frequently costumes himself by extreme dressing up or down and seldom employs standard academic vocabulary — except to punctuate a witticism. He is articulate, glib, sarcastic and/or funny. His general image is that of a casual "good guy" or an imposing man of the world.

The public harasser appears always available, always approachable. He spends enormous amounts of time with students — in his office, in the halls during breaks, in the student union or at a nearby bar when the day or week ends. His informality is a welcome contrast to the authoritarian style of most of his colleagues. The more perceptive of them detect but hesitate to question his intentions. This was the position of a male philosophy professor:

> I'm really not particularly comfortable with _____'s style. Perhaps because it's so different from mine and so unlike what we were taught to emulate in graduate school. I do feel a sense of unease when I see him several times a week huddled with a group of young women over coffee in the Union. I have other colleagues who are just as concerned about students and spend equal amounts of time with them, but they don't seem to need to flaunt those relationships before others.

The high profile of the public harasser is his defense. It deters observers or victims from protesting when he touches too often or cracks one joke too many. Even male students hesitate to criticize public harassers. A sophomore at a college in Michigan explained:

> Sure, I was afraid to say anything to anyone about Mr. ____ . They all laughed every time he made some stupid remark. You would have thought he was a burlesque comedian or something. What I really couldn't get, what really floored me was why the girls laughed at him too. He was supposed to be teaching psychology, and there he was making these gross remarks that should have embarrassed them half to death (they sure as hell embarrassed me) and they just kept on laughing all year.

When an individual's remarks to and about women or his physical contact with them appears open, he can easily contend, "I have nothing to hide. There's nothing malevolent in my intentions. Everything I say or do is right out there for everyone to see." The difficulty is that an institution's ability to restrain a public harasser depends upon the level of awareness of those within the environment. Some "see" malevolent intentions and others do not, but the harasser's reputation as communicative, friendly, and open provides a sure defense. Thus he is free to perform and be observed but not challenged or chastized for his behavior.

The style and intent of the private harasser are directly opposite. He may be the more genuinely "lecherous" of the two, for he uses his authority to gain private access to the student. Unlike his counterpart, he deliberately avoids notoriety. He not only seeks but depends upon privacy because he requires a domain in which there are no witnesses to his behavior. He is the harasser of greatest interest to the public and the media, the one who demands sexual favors of students, the one most readily cast in the image of despoiler of innocence and molester of youth.

His personal and professional styles lend credence to the epithets. The private harasser often adheres to academic stereotypes. He usually dresses conservatively. His language and demeanor are generally formal, perhaps even intimidating, to the student. Because he appears so circumspect, he is the last to be suspected by colleagues. The Levi-clad professor who sits casually before the class seems more culpable than the imposing man with the resonant voice who stands behind the lectern.

The lectern symbolizes the private harasser's teaching style. Characteristically removed and aloof, he lectures while the class listens. Just as the public harasser uses his openness to move the student to compliance, the private offender employs authority to lure her into acquiescence. The ability to control the setting gives him special access to the women under his power. He can seduce them into his private domain with a simple oral or written directive. "Please see me" or "I would like a conference with you" are familiar demands.

But, few are prepared for the deception that occurs when the professor closes the office door and sheds the professorial for the male role. Whether he begins with overt sexual advances or the more subtle verbal approach ("My wife doesn't love me anymore," "Young women like you are so lovely"), his sudden role change causes the student surprise and confusion. Her role submissiveness, female self-doubt, and shock combine with the privacy of the interaction to provide a cover for the harasser. When there are no witnesses and the student experiences extreme disorientation, there are seldom sexual harassment grievances.

Another way of understanding sexual harassers is to describe the roles they most commonly assume:

- *The Counselor-Helper* This type of professor uses the guise of nurturer and caretaker to gain access to the student. If she feels lonely and anonymous on campus, she may be flattered or consoled by his interest. He invites her confidence and uses information about her private life to discover her vulnerabilities, commitments, and attitudes about men and sex. Then he can tailor his "line" to her specific need. One professor, after encouraging a student's anguished account of rejection by a boyfriend, replied earnestly, "I'd never treat you like that." To her, it was a terribly moving assertion. To the witness to the incident, it was far less compelling because she had observed the professor making the statement to at least three other female students from whom he later sought sexual favors.

  The counselor-helper may act as a go-between in male-female relationships of students. This behavior, described by one ombudsman as "pimping," encourages the student to see the professor as a broker or gatekeeper in her relationship with a significant male. The professor's intent can be to derive vicarious sexual pleasure from thus involving himself or to use the male as a foil to increase his own stature in the eyes of the female. One administrator describes this as "seduction with an agent." An accomplished harasser in one university was fond of acting as go-between and then reporting to the female that he had advised her boyfriend, "She's a real woman. Are you prepared to satisfy her?" The motive was to win the seduction when the student became attracted to the professor's image of her as experienced and voluptuous.

- *The Confidante* This individual approaches the student not as a superior who can help her but as an equal and friend. Sharing is an essential element in their interaction. He may invite her confidences, but he also offers his own. In an attempt to impress or win sympathy from the student, he may relate or invent stories about his private and professional life. Placed in this role, the student often feels that he values and trusts her, so she becomes an involuntary confidante. Without genuine mutual agreement, the relationship is moved into an intimate domain from which she may find it difficult to extricate herself.

Another method a harasser may employ is creating indebtedness through gestures of friendship. Offers from a professor to lend the student books, money, notes, a place to study or providing her with free tickets or rides may signal an attempt to make her feel obligated.

- *The Intellectual Seducer* Called "mind fucking" or "intellectual intercourse" by some, this kind of seduction results from the professor's ability to impress students with his skill and knowledge. He may use class content to gain access to personal information about the student. Self-disclosure on the part of the student is often invited in disciplines like psychology, sociology, philosophy, and literature where personal values, beliefs, and experiences are easily related to course content. At one college, students told of being required to write about their sex fantasies. Such information may be used to identify areas of vulnerability and/or accessibility in the student. A psychology professor bragged to a colleague about requiring students to take personality inventories. He told them they demonstrated uses of the test, but his real motivation was to gain personal information about respondents in whom he was interested.

  A professor's avocations may also be engaging or dangerous. A common example is the faculty member who uses his knowledge of books or movies to move the student into discussions of erotic topics. Another is that of the professor who hypnotizes students outside the classroom. While some use hypnosis appropriately, it can be dangerous when done by a sexual harasser. Finally, there is the case of the art professor who employs female students as nude models for private studio work.

- *The Opportunist* This person takes advantage of the physical setting and unusual or occasional circumstances to obscure his inappropriate behavior and to gain intimacy with students. He may rely on equipment or subject matter to gain physical access to the student. A serious problem in clinical, laboratory, counseling, performance, and vocational-technical settings, this behavior is often described by students as stealing "cheap feels." The lecherous professor discovers ways to touch the student by using proximity to equipment as an excuse or by employing parts of her body in class demonstrations. One student complained that her woodwind professor persisted in touching her breasts while telling her he was illustrating the movements of her diaphragm; another that her nursing instructor "felt [her] up" while using her body to demonstrate physical disabilities in patients.

The opportunist may also use field trips, meetings, and conventions as occasions to escape institutional restraints. The problem for the student is that these are often described as scholastic or professional honors and/or necessities, and she feels compelled to attend.

- *The Power Broker* The most familiar type of harasser, the power broker, trades on his ability to control grades, credentials, recommendations, or jobs. The assumption that he works only through crude and raw assertions of power is inaccurate. Direct promises of rewards or threats of punishment can exert enormous influence on students, but they feel equally victimized by promises and threats that are implied rather than stated openly. Because so much may be at stake, the student is unlikely to risk a complaint unless the harasser has been very overt about his intentions.

Regardless of the role he assumes or the type of harassment in which he engages, the lecherous professor always controls the circumstances surrounding the student victim. Sexual harassment is a power issue, and the power of the professoriate is enormous. It is easy for some college professors to deceive themselves about the relationship between their power and students' responses to them. Reviewing a number of studies on sexual harassment, Marilyn B. Brewer commented in "Further Beyond Nine to Five: An Integration and Future Directions":

> In general, the participant in a high power position is likely to perceive an interaction — especially one involving positive expressions — as motivated by interpersonal attraction, and to assume that flattering remarks, compliance, and agreement are sincere and attributable to internal causes. The lower-power participant, on the other hand, is more likely to be aware of the external constraints imposed by the threat of abuse of power and consciously to use flattery and compliance as strategies to win approval and/or to avoid the displeasures of persons in high power positions. The low-power participant is also likely to *assume* that the high-power individual is aware of these external causes to a greater extent than is actually the case.[4]

In *Power and Innocence*, Rollo May commented on the environment of higher education:

> If we take the university as the setting, we need only ask any graduate

student whether his professors have power over him, and he will laugh at our naiveté. Of course professors have power; the perpetual anxiety of some graduate students as to whether they will be passed or not is proof enough. The professor's power is even more effective because it is clothed in scholarly garb. It is the power of prestige, status, and the subtle coercion of others that follow from these. This is not due to the professor's conscious aims; it has more to do with the organization of the university and the teacher's unconscious motivations for being part of it.[5]

Sexual harassers are people who misuse the power of their positions to abuse members of the opposite sex. Higher education tends to discuss their behavior in the abstract — as if it were unrelated to real-life human beings. But sexual harassment cannot be understood or curtailed until professors are subjected to the same scrutiny as students. What motivates a man with so much education and power over others to act abusively toward women?

Obviously, there are no simple cause-effect relationships to explain so complex a behavior. There is an infinite number of variables that may intervene in the experiences of individuals to influence their actions, and there is little reliable, verifiable information on the psychology of sexual harassers or college professors in general. There is also no means to gather from individual faculty the enormous retrospective data necessary to establish an image of a prototypic sexual harasser.

What *can* be examined are some relevant questions about contemporary male professors: What traits are generally associated with male academics? Are there knowable similarities in the developmental cycles of a significant number of men who choose the academic profession? How might one or a combination of these contribute to the aberrant professor's decision to harass women students? Although there is currently little information to aid in analyzing the sexual harasser's motivations, this speculation may be valuable in raising the consciousness of the academic community and encouraging new perspectives on the issue. To anyone attempting to understand the problem of professors who harass women, analyses of the developmental cycles of human beings are particularly interesting. Perhaps most worth consideration at this point are unresolved adolescent crisis, professional crisis, and midlife crisis.

ADOLESCENT CRISIS

The socialization that underlies sexual harassment by men is easy to recognize and understand. It would be heartening and convenient to find that the harassers of academe are freaks and outcasts, true outlaws in society where men value equality, compassion, intimacy, and authenticity in relation to women. But the reality, however painful, is that the code of sexual ethics that harassers follow is simply a crude extension of the norms some consider acceptable for males.

By the time the average male reaches school age, he already believes that "real boys" must be assertive, aggressive, competitive, and physically strong. Peers, parents, and society in general influence boys to behave in traditionally masculine ways. The elementary school setting presents them with a serious dilemma, which Herb Goldberg described in *The Hazards of Being Male*:

> While there is great peer pressure to act like a boy, the teacher's coveted classroom values are traditionally "feminine" ones. The emphasis is on politeness, neatness, docility, and cleanliness, with not much approved room being given for the boy to flex his muscles. Teacher's greatest efforts often go into keeping the boys quiet and in their seats.
>
> A recent study of 12,000 students produced some interesting findings along this line. The researcher correlated masculinity scores of boys on the California Psychological Inventory with their school grades. She found that the higher the boy scored on the masculine scale, the lower his report card average tended to be.
>
> Of the 277 students with a D or F average, 60 percent were boys. Of the two boys with the most distinguished scholastic records, one was noted to be markedly effeminate in speech and gesture while the other "gave the strong impression of being more feminine than effeminate." Both boys had very low scores in physical fitness.[6]

The male experience may become especially traumatic during adolescence, which is the period when the masculine stereotype exerts its greatest influence. Adolescence is the bridge between childhood and adulthood, the period during which biological, sociological, and psychological forces converge to produce self-concept and identity. Psychologists like Robert Havighurst and Erik

Erikson used various terms to describe the tasks essential to healthy transition into adulthood. Whatever the language, almost all developmental theories stress the importance of adolescence as the time during which one crystallizes a sex role, develops satisfying relationships with peers of the same sex, forms adequate heterosexual relationships, and lays the foundation for a career choice. Asserting that an identity crisis occurs in its purest form in adolescence, Erikson maintained that if the crisis was not resolved during this period, the conflicts of adulthood would be greater and more difficult.[7]

Although many have studied adolescence in the abstract, few have examined the real-life arena in which it takes place. The American high school is the most significant setting in which the developmental tasks of adolescence are carried out or left uncompleted. Whether it works through formal or informal mechanisms, the high school experience influences adults. Oddly, or perhaps predictably, college professors who study adolescence often limit their observations to issues such as "socioeconomic influences on achievement" and "intellectual-cognitive development." But high school graduates usually recall that the primary effect of the high school is not educational but social. Long after the last geometry theorem has been forgotten, graduates remember the captain of the football team, the prom queen, and their own positions in the status quo of adolescence.

In *Is There Life After High School?* Ralph Keyes stated colloquially a concept similar to more erudite theories about ego-identity formation during adolescence. Arguing that adult values grow directly out of high school, Keyes contended that the imprinting of adolescent peer acceptance remains with Americans throughout life. In other words, people go through life seeing themselves socially as they did in high school — as "innies" or "outies." High school "innies" and "outies" differ from one another solely on the basis of status or power. Keyes reported surprise at discovering, "Power is central to innie status . . . I always thought status in high school had to do with being well-liked, and liking yourself . . . That isn't what status is all about. What it's about is power."[8] And lack of power can leave indelible marks on the self-images of those unfortunate enough to be among the outies.

What constitutes the power and status for which adolescent American males strive? *The Adolescent Society*, James Coleman's classic 1957-1958 study of this subject, provided impressive empirical data to prove what most Americans already knew. Coleman contended that desire for status was the controlling force in the adolescent society and that for males athletic stardom was the highest symbol of success, the surest guarantee of entry into the leading crowd, and the most reliable means of gaining popularity with females.[9]

The masculine myth rests in large part upon equating athletic achievement and physical prowess with masculinity and success. Early in American history frontiersmen and farm and factory workers defined manliness as having the strength and stamina to endure the rigors of physical labor. As conditions changed during the twentieth century and intellectual achievement became more important, the value system incorporated the new without discarding the old. The playing field became the testing ground for masculinity, and American faith in the importance of physical superiority remained so unwavering that no one raised an eyebrow when Robert F. Kennedy, Attorney General of the United States, declared in the early 1960s, "Except for war, there is nothing in American life — nothing — which trains a boy better for life than football."[10]

Males learn very early what Marc Feigen Fasteau in *The Male Machine* described as:

A skewing of values which tend to make sports a compulsion for many boys, the mandated center of their lives. Some boys can live with this... Boys who can't conform easily to the athletic ideal are made to feel inadequate. They either quit completely, developing a compensatory disdain for sports as a result or they keep trying, setting standards for themselves that have nothing to do with their own talents or desires.[11]

Burt Avedon in *Ah, Men* expressed a similar point:

The pressure on boys is most intense during their teens . . . The demands of rapidly budding masculinity reach their heights for the boy in high school (perhaps earlier now), where the laurels of success adorn the competitive athlete, the masculine ideal. (Schools often seem geared toward elevation of athletic endeavor over all activities including academic achievement.)[12]

James Coleman's findings corroborated this. In his studies, scholastic achievement was ambiguously regarded by adolescents. In some institutions it was respected; in others, it was a source of embarrassment. However, it was never in any of his research settings ranked above athletic ability, the primary determinant of recognition and respect.

The recognition awarded athletes over scholars comes not only from other males. Coleman and his colleagues found that adolescent girls overwhelmingly preferred athletes. Avedon supported this view: "In high school, boys find that only those who fit the ideal male image, principally through sports, are able to achieve another conquest of growing importance for adolescents reaching adulthood: the attraction of beautiful, desirable females."[13]

To the adolescent, physical attractiveness in males means looking "athletic," and Coleman found "good looks" to be another key to status and power within the adolescent society. Very early, but reaching a culmination in adolescence, the body becomes a primary symbol of self. A recent poll of sixty thousand *Psychology Today* readers found that "adults who thought they were unattractive teenagers currently have lower self-esteem than those who felt beautiful, even adults who blossomed in maturity."[14] The relationship between physical appearance and self-image is clear. The male who sees himself as unattractive in adolescence does not often acquire physical self-confidence as an adult and may never forget his failure to achieve the masculine ideal in the difficult world of high school and youth. It is, after all, as Keyes quoted one female, a time when "nothing didn't matter."[15]

Keyes, a self-acknowledged "outie," is firm in his view of the placement of college professors in the adolescent status system:

> Here is how the sides break down: we give the innies all of pro sports and its cheerleaders; we concede them the military, insurance agencies, PE departments, and heavy equipment. Politics and show business are divided zones, but we write everybody's lines because outies control American's means of communication. We write the speeches, publish the books, produce the movies, make the music, do the research, report for the paper and comment on reports . . .
>
> Teaching is a field shared by innies, but we tell them how to do it. Our strategy here is to take over the colleges of education [i.e.-higher education], control research, and write all the books about how to teach

high school. In these books we never take seriously any of the values innies used to keep us down. "Popularity" is a topic we're very condescending about and brush under the heading of "Peer Relations." Sports generally get ridiculed, and activities such as cheerleading and homecoming are reduced to "Student Culture: Ceremony and Ritual."[16]

The future professor might easily be recognized in *Fear of Flying*, when Erica Jong described the "brainy boys" at Columbia:

[They wore] flannel shirts with twenty-five leaky ballpoint pens in their breast pockets, [and had] flesh-colored frames on their thick glasses, blackheads in their ears, pustules on their necks, pleated trousers, greasy hair . . . They commuted by subway from their mothers' [kitchens] in the Bronx to the classrooms of Moses Hadas and Gilbert Highet on Morningside Heights, where they learned enough literature and philosophy to get straight A's, but never seemed to lose their gawkiness, their schoolboy defensiveness, their total lack of appeal.[17]

Jong is not the only one to notice the phenomenon. Students, alumni, staff, and women faculty often recognize it too. They hesitate to say that they, like men, observe and evaluate the appearance of the opposite sex; they are also uncomfortable because the idea of characterizing an entire profession as "plain" seems so outlandish. Yet two women professors and a university secretary were among a number of women who admitted to finding male professors physically unappealing:

I'm embarrassed to say this but I really do find most of my colleagues unattractive physically. When I began teaching eight years ago, I thought my standards were probably adolescent or too demanding; but after all this time, I'm still not impressed. If I had to depend on the university for attractive male companionship, I might never have married.

• •

The assumptions that college professors who are women are sexless is absurd. Of course, I look at men; and what I see here is not what you'd call encouraging. There are more short men, more men with glasses, more men with bad skin, more unkempt men here than in any single place I've ever been. Don't ask me to explain. I just know it's true.

• •

When I first became a secretary at the college, my husband was upset because he knew I would be around men so much of the time. If I ever thought it would cause a strain, I know now how silly I was. There isn't a man here anyone would want to look at once — let alone twice. There are days when I honestly wonder where these people come from. I probably sound like a sex fiend, but you can't help noticing things like that. I've had three secretarial jobs, and I've never worked anywhere else where there were so many sexless men.

A woman dean explained the situation more graphically:

You're asking me what I think of the way these guys look? I *don't*. You work with the same types. You must understand why.

It is difficult to determine how the media developed the image of the sexy college professor with the corduroy jacket and the ever-present pipe. He may be alive and well on the silver screen and in the pages of best sellers, but he is not in abundance at the Faculty Club or meetings of the American Association of University Professors. The typical professor does not resemble Fred MacMurray, Elliott Gould, Donald Sutherland, or any other of the Hollywood types who have portrayed him over the years. If there is a star who most resembles the typical accounting, art history, or seventeenth-century literature professor, it would have to be Woody Allen.

Some college professors have been critical of organized team sports on the campus. This faculty hostility probably results from a conviction that sports receive excessive emphasis and financial support from institutions and seem at odds with academic priorities. But sometimes the fervor appears personal as well as political. Is it possible that student athletes can become surrogates for former classmates who captured attention denied the future college professor? One college coach, countering criticism of the athletic program, inadvertently touched on this possibility. While hardly unbiased, his point of view is a reminder that faculty criticism of athletic programs may be motivated by many factors.

You want to know the truth? I don't think these guys [faculty] are upset about these boys' grades at all. I don't think they know or care what happens to them. I think what bothers them, what really makes them come down on these kids is they're jealous. You take a look at them — most of them almost pass out once a week on the racquetball court. You think they like seeing these younger men in top physical condition when they probably couldn't even make manager for the high school team? I don't think they ever forgot that or forgive it, and all the rest of the talk about standards is just that — talk.

A woman professor also noticed how male members of her department raised dubious objections to the football program:

I have to admit when I sit in faculty meetings and listen to the assault on the football program, I detect a certain adolescent hysteria. It's as if the skeletons have come out of the closet, and some of these men are foolish enough to believe they can clothe them with flesh and make them pay for the defeats of the past. If you listen carefully, the debate hinges as much on the perceived ills of athletic types as it does on the economics of football. If I could be certain their opposition to the football program was really based on academic and economic concerns rather than on some perverse need to resurrect and redo the past, my own position would be easier to decide.

There are women professors who are quick to maintain that adolescent attitudes and behaviors color their colleagues' interactions with them. Sometimes they are frustrated and angry for themselves as well as for their students. Jackie T., an instructor in a community college, exclaimed:

There are days when I just want to scream! If I'm late to a faculty meeting, it's like running the god-damned gauntlet or something. There are maybe a hundred people in the room, but all the men in business and math sit together, and having to squeeze past them is a nightmare. These are forty- and fifty-year-old men and they're saying things like, "Hey, you can sit on my lap" or "We've got room for you here, if you don't mind a tight fit." I feel like I'm a sophomore in high school having to pass the greased-up motorcycle gang that used to stand outside until the last bell rang. I really dislike the way they all chuckle and guffaw after one of these remarks — as if to imply that they have some secret bond. They're no different with the students. They make the same kind of disgusting remarks to them in front of other people; and when they talk about some of the attractive ones, it's even worse. Back to sophomorics. I've seen them stand in a group and do everything but whistle when an attractive student walks by. Two weeks ago I walked into a conversation three of my educated colleagues were having, and it turned out to be a discussion about "what a piece of ass" a

> student in the economics class of one of them was. The thing that makes me most angry is that I was embarrassed, and they could have cared less.

These are subjective impressions, and there should be caution about opinions unsubstantiated by statistics. In this case, however, there is previously unpublished data to support the thesis that, as adolescents, a majority of male academicians did not fit the masculine stereotype. Coleman's 1957-1958 study, which was replicated several times, included approximately 9,000 male and female students. In 1975, Lloyd Temme, who was then with the Bureau of Social Science Research, composed *The History and Methodology of "The Adolescent Society" Follow-up Study*. Temme was able to locate a remarkably high number of the original participants in the Coleman survey — approximately 85 percent. In his own exhaustive study of these adults, Temme gathered considerable data on their vocational experiences. These records enabled him and his associate Jere Cohen to isolate from the original Coleman sample those individuals who became college professors. They found 120 males who were actively working in the profession.

The results of their findings are significant. One of the questions asked of Coleman's male adolescents was, "What do you and the fellows you go around with here at school have most in common? What are the things you do together?" Out of several choices, the most relevant here was "Organized outdoor sports — including football, basketball, tennis, etc." Of those who became college professors, 94.2 percent replied they did not share with friends participation in organized athletics.[18]

Coleman provided five responses to the query, "Suppose you had an extra hour in school and could either take some course of your own choosing, or use it for athletics or some other activity, or use it for study hall. How would you use it?" The choices were (1) course, (2) athletics, (3) club or activity, (4) study hall, to study, (5) study hall, to do something else. Future college professors differed most significantly from their peers on the first two items. Most, 41 percent, preferred to use the extra time for a course; only 17.2 percent of the general population selected this item. While 42.6 percent of the total group indicated they would spend the time in athletic activity, 31.6 percent of the subgroup chose this option.

Another item in the Coleman survey read, "Suppose the circle below represented the activities that go on here at school. How far out from the center of things are you?" The number one was the center, and six the periphery. As adolescents, most academicians viewed themselves on the fringes of the "innie" group: 9.4 percent saw themselves at the center (one), 31.6 percent at point two, 41.0 percent at point three, and the remainder in the outer three categories. Keyes and Temme had interesting observations on adolescents who were just beyond the center of status in high school. Keyes reported:

> Temme says it's important to distinguish between those who were at the bottom of the social ladder and those who stood on the 'second tier," one rung below the top. Those lower in the pecking order get used to being dumped on over time, he speculates, and are less resentful of it. But those on the second tier aren't accustomed to being excluded and resent it bitterly. Adults from the second rung don't lose this resentment after graduation.[19]

Another set of statistics from the sample was college professors' responses to the question, "If you could be remembered here at school for one of three things below, which one would you want it to be? Brilliant student, athletic star, most popular." Their responses were the following: brilliant student — 51 percent, athletic star — 22.3 percent, most popular — 25.0 percent. These are considerably different from the aggregate responses of 3,696 adolescent boys of whom they are a part: brilliant student — 31.3 percent, athletic star — 43.6 percent, and most popular — 25.0 percent.

Although the future college professors very early defined themselves as different from their male peers, their attitudes toward females were quite typical. Asked whether they would prefer dating a cheerleader, the best-looking girl in class, or the best student in class, their interest in intellectual pursuits lessened considerably. By a majority of 54.5 percent, they preferred the best-looking girl; the cheerleader received the next highest vote — 32.7 percent, and only 12.7 percent were enthusiastic about dating the best female student. The aggregate responses were very similar: best-looking girl — 63.1 percent, cheerleader — 26.1 percent, best female student — 10.8 percent.

When they have been fully analyzed, the Coleman-Temme materials provide fascinating insights into the relationships between adolescence and adult choices, behaviors, and opinions. For the purposes of this book, they serve as a reminder that adults — even the aberrant ones — may not be as mysterious as most choose to believe. Some sexually harassing behavior may logically have roots in adolescence if Temme's assertion is valid: "I think the rest of our lives are spent making up for what we did or didn't do in high school."[20]

This is not to suggest that all college professors were adolescent failures or that high school stereotypes are necessarily desirable. On the contrary, achievement of status in the adolescent society can be seriously detrimental to those who cannot adjust to the demands of the adult world. Emotionally healthy adults translate the superficial standards of adolescence into mature values. But there are some people who never recover from its trauma, and some sexual harassers may be among them.

If physical attractiveness and athletic achievement are the access to status with adolescent females, what is the long-term effect upon the individual outside the high school mainstream? Education is one of the few vocations in which adult males are exposed for extended periods to large groups of very young women at the height of physical desirability. For the few who have never resolved the ego problems developed in adolescent society, this may become a serious difficulty. How do a professor's recollections of adolescence influence his behaviors and attitudes toward the women over whom he exercises power? If he has painful memories of adolescent females, what are his behaviors when the tables are turned and scholarship is finally a symbol of prestige and authority? Is it likely that the past will trigger misuse of power in the present?

Unresolved adolescent conflict may contribute to the motivation of the harasser seeking sex from students. For him, as for other promiscuous men, young women can represent a means of remaking the past. To the professor denied status in high school, the prospect of a relationship with an attractive, desirable student may be especially enticing. It offers not only sexual gratification but also an opportunity to prove, if only to himself, that he can "score" as successfully as any musclebound jock.

A 1980 *Glamour* article paraphrased the statement of a psychiatrist who refused to use her name because "so many of [her] patients [were] involved in [student-professor] relationship[s], and not happily."[21] She believed that such relationships "arise because of the professor's need to take advantage of a younger person who looks for his approval and is probably quite vulnerable. Consciously or not, he is bolstering his ego by choosing from a crop of 'subjects' who are readily attracted to him — thanks to the showmanship of teaching — and readily available to him." In the same article, Dr. Maj-Britt Rosenbaum, associate clinical professor of psychiatry at Albert Einstein College of Medicine, stated, "the male-teacher is the dominant man on campus and . . . has the chance to preen and show off because of the nature of his position."[22]

Arrested adolescent development may also influence the verbal or gender harasser. In high school, football heroes dominate the spotlight and the fantasies of females, but the academic harasser learns that when the setting changes his image can be altered. In *Ah, Men* Burt Avedon emphasized the male's concern about image:

> The desire for an image of sexual prowess inheres in almost all males no matter what their income or social position . . . Sexual conquest is an essential part of the masculine persona. Sexual prowess, or at least the image of sexual prowess, is the goal. Sex is part of a game men play, much like the games they played as boys. The aim is to score. Once they won on the field of play; now they score and win in the great pastures of prurience. [23]

Those denied the recognition that comes from victory "on the field of play" may discover later in life that power is an aphrodisiac and that words aimed at the right audience can be as much of an ego trip as scoring a touchdown. Some professors use sarcasm and repartee about gender and sex to demonstrate that despite their bookishness, they are nevertheless virile and exciting. Others employ words as a way of asserting control and putting women in their place.

Sue W., a senior at a college in Texas, saw both motivations in the verbal harassment of a psychology professor who was "fixated on the parts of girls' bodies":

> He was always saying these dumb, off-color things he thought were real cute. I don't know if he thought they were going to make us like him or if he just wanted to watch us squirm. I *do* know I've heard funnier

remarks and seen more grown-up behavior from my fourteen-year-old brother.

A botany major at a large university described the behavior of a verbal harasser even more explicitly:

> I was standing in the hall just outside of the student lounge carrying on a discussion with a senior botany major when Dr. ____ walked past, stood by the window and called out my name. He motioned for me to come over and I did. He had a roll of lifesavers. He took a green lifesaver from the pack, placed it in the palm of my hand and said, "The green ones make you want to screw." He then gave me a red lifesaver and said, "The red ones make you want to fuck." I tried to put both lifesavers back into his hand; however, he was laughing and refused them, so I put them on his briefcase and said, "That's okay, you can have your lifesavers." He acted surprised and somewhat taken aback, but I walked away and continued to talk with my friend.

Verbal harassment can also be related to insecurities about male bonding. The adolescent boy whose interests are intellectual rather than athletic has a more difficult time feeling a part of the peer group. In adulthood, he may assume that the way to gain peer acceptance is to "be cool" with the women. Whistles, insistence on eye contact, nonreciprocal touching, jokes, and off-color remarks are standard tactics that unsophisticated men suppose to be masculine behaviors. A well-known professor at a large Midwestern university was fond of beginning his first class with a sweeping glance at the women and an injunction to them to "cross your legs and close the gates to hell." It was his way of declaring to the male community his place in the order of things, and he was said to take pride in his reputation. A similar motivation inspired the language of a business instructor whose department head described him as having "locker-room humor." The department head claimed that the professor needed to "feel himself one of the boys" and mistakenly assumed that salacious remarks to and about women were a way of "making the grade with the group."

Bonding can assume more ominous tones, however. Sometimes protection of turf and preservation of conventions and the status quo are the primary forces underlying harassment. This is the reason that women who enter nontraditional fields suffer so much verbal abuse. Consciously or subconsciously, instructors may try to punish females for invading their ranks, for entering the locker room uninvited. The perpetrators of such offenses claim a standard defense. A law professor stated matter-of-factly:

> Lawyers must learn the element of give and take. Women are no exception to the rule. If they're not prepared to withstand classroom pressure, they don't belong in the courtroom.

A similar view was expressed by an engineering professor:

> If you're going to enter a man's profession, you had better be prepared to take harassment and learn to defend youself. Engineering has been male territory for years, and our job is to teach these young ladies how to live in it with dignity and calm.

PROFESSIONAL CRISIS

Arrested adolescent development is only one concept that can help explain the behaviors of men who harass. Another is the professional crisis contemporary college professors face. The financial crises facing most campuses in the 1980s mean that college professors, especially those who are younger, confront harsh realities over which they have no control. In the foreseeable future, mobility in most disciplines will be limited, promotion and tenure will be harder to achieve, and salaries will not improve significantly. Since the financial rewards of higher education have never been good, such bleak forecasts only add to the professor's dilemma. Because society sees the academic profession as prestigious, rewarding, and influential, there is widespread confusion about realities of the profession.

College professors pay thousands of dollars for educations that, at best, qualify them economically for inclusion in the middle class. *The Chronicle of Higher Education* reported that in 1982–1983, the average salary for faculty in all types of higher education institutions was $26,063. The survey did not include instructors, who receive the lowest pay. Its breakdown of average pay for the other three ranks demonstrated the limited financial mobility of academics: assistant professors — $20,636; associate professors — $24,876; professors —$32,258.[24]

In a 1980 article in *Academe*, Walter F. Abbot, Associate Professor of Sociology at the University of Kentucky, presented a painstaking analysis of recent trends in academic salaries. His thesis confirmed the gravity of the college professor's professional crisis:

> The working poor comprise those who are employed but receive incomes that provide a marginal level of existence. An academic career has traditionally been considered a middle-class occupation that will provide neither an upper-level nor a poverty-level income . . . [H]owever, if 1970–1977 trends in academic salaries and the poverty level threshold persist, lower-ranking American academicians may expect to enter the ranks of the working poor in the eighties and faculty in the professor rank will receive an income in 2000 that compares about as well with the poverty threshold as assistant professors at the present time.[25]

In popular myth and movies, college professors live in Victorian houses with wood-burning fireplaces, oak staircases, and paneled, book-lined studies. In reality, many drive secondhand cars, consider themselves fortunate to afford tract housing, and wonder how they will accumulate enough money to send their own children to college. A party of professors often means moving the department or college meeting to someone's basement family room to nibble cheddar cheese and drink wine from Styrofoam cups. This scenario is not all that bleak unless one considers the discrepancy between the ideal and actual worlds of academics. College professors are the people who teach others to appreciate expensive and sophisticated equipment, books, art, theater, and music — all that society recognizes as manifestations of "the good life" — and who cannot readily afford them for themselves or their families.

In *The Male Mid-Life Crisis*, Nancy Mayer pointed out that "in America success has always meant making money and translating it into status or fame,"[26] and the relationship between financial success, power, and sexuality is a frequent topic of psychologists and organization specialists. In their article "The Executive Man and Women: The Issue of Sexuality," Bradford, Sargent, and Sprague observed:

> An important aspect of the sense of self-identity for both males and females is their masculinity and femininity . . . How do males assert their sexuality? Teenagers resort to fistfighting . . . playing football, and

competing against one another to see who can consume more beer or have more dates. While this may do for youth, an educated adult must find more discreet and indirect proofs . . . For many men, work serves as the major vehicle defining their identity, including sexual identity . . . Status and pay of the job also bear an element of sexuality . . . [Men] strive to advance, build up their programs, and compete in meetings partially to obtain status and financial records that connote masculine success, but also to affirm their masculinity more directly.[27]

A professor who sees himself in a static or unsuccessful professional and financial position may choose to exert his masculinity in negative ways. Feelings of frustration and defeat can be displaced onto the women students under his control. He can affirm his authority by being openly abusive to them, or he can turn to them for solace and ego-gratification. The dean of students at a very selective liberal arts college considered such displacement significant in some sexual harassment:

I guess you might say that many men consider access to females one of the perks of the profession. If you don't make a lot of money, if you can't go to Europe without scrimping and sacrificing, if publication of your dream book seems less and less a reality and even promotion becomes a vain hope, life looks fairly dim. It's also not hård to see why some of these men turn to students for comfort or excitement or whatever it is their egos need. Sometimes they're abusive to students because that's a way to deal with their own anger and despair. It's not right, but it's one of the realities we have to live with.

MIDLIFE CRISIS

The frustration and confusion inherent in professional crisis are similar to and sometimes synonymous with those of midlife crisis. Not surprisingly, midlife crisis is the most frequently — if not the only — explanation offered for sexually harassing behavior. Peter A., professor at a large Massachusetts university, voiced this common defense:

Another problem, and one not easily dismissed, is the fact that many of us are in our thirties and forties and are watching our youth slip away at the very time we're in extremely close contact with women who are just coming into bloom. Let me tell you, it's not easy to hit the beginning of a midlife crisis when you're surrounded by nubile twenty-year-olds.[28]

If a man is going to follow the traditional pattern for male midlife crisis, academe is the best of all possible worlds in which to be. Mayer described this period in the male's life:

> In response to wrenching change, a man at this stage of life is struggling to revise his own self-image and find dignity in the face of undeniable limitations. More than ever, he needs the confirmation of being seen as a powerful and desirable man — a need that the nubile girl is uniquely suited to satisfy. Our culture's most obvious symbol of hot-blooded sexuality, she can meet the aging male's intensified need for reassurance both in public and in private . . .
>
> Seeking refuge from the harsh assaults of this midlife period and release from heightened anxieties that haunt and perplex them, [some men in middle age] confirm their manhood through the worshipful gaze of a nubile girl — who mirrors back an image of their most potent self. Contrary to popular wisdom, men in their middle years are generally drawn to younger women not because they want to recapture their youth, but because they need to reconfirm their maturity . . .
>
> This, then, is the single most seductive reason for the appeal of the nubile girl: A yielding innocent on whom a man can project whatever fantasy he craves, she makes him feel not merely potent, but also omnipotent. A soothing balm indeed. Where else, after all, can the aging male find a sexual partner who will offer applause and adulation without demanding reciprocal attentions? Who will satisfy his emotional needs without requiring him to cater to hers? Only the young can afford to be so selfless.[29]

The enormous advantage that college professors have over men in similar situations is that for them, the stage is already set. Not only are there more than enough "nubile girls" from whom to choose, but they are women who have already been conditioned to regard the teacher as intellectually omnipotent. As individual desires and needs change over time, a wife who is a peer may become intellectually, professionally, or emotionally menacing; the attraction to a younger woman may lie in her lack of competition or threat. A person with whom the professor has no shared history is cleaner, less complicated. If she is also a student, she exhibits all of the deference that comes with discrepancies in roles, experience, and sophistication. A male confused about responding to an older woman's demands may find those of female students more manageable and less intense.

The middle-aged professor suffering from sexual insecurity may find college women especially appealing sexually. Older women may pose not only intellectual and professional threats but also — and perhaps more important — very real sexual pressure. Their sexual demands are greater, and they increase the anxiety of the male in crisis. One man explained to Mayer:

> One thing that's true, though, I think you can get a younger woman to respond to you very strongly. She's going to be less appraising than an older woman. She's had less experience. There are fewer men in her life to which she can compare you. You can dominate her more, sort of impose your myth on her. And you can feel you're initiating her into all sorts of things and blowing her mind and enslaving her — or whatever the hell it is that you want to do with a woman.[30]

The professor whose sexual insecurity contributes to his harassment of students can easily delude himself. He has heard that women students today are freer and engage in intercourse earlier, so taboos about despoiling or deflowering the innocent can be rationalized. At the same time, women students are, by and large, young and lacking the sexual experience of older, more demanding women. Thus the student seems "safe," a novice flattered by the attentions of the professor who can introduce her to the mysterious pleasures of adult sexuality. And the harasser can delude himself into believing that he has done no harm and that the student is responding to his sexuality rather than his position.

Even when sexual activity with the student is the end of harassment, it is not the only motivation. Mayer noted that contemporary social scientists, ". . . in contrast to Freud, who said all human actions were shaped by sexual needs . . . now suggest the opposite: that sexual activity is often motivated by other needs. Non-sexual needs."[31] At any point in a man's life cycle, but especially during midlife, one such need may be competition with other males. The college professor at forty is in an unusual position: he is surrounded by physically desirable young women, as well as by young men in their physical prime. If he has been reared in traditional fashion, he knows that beyond all the myths about male friendships, the truth is that males are taught to relate to one another in one way — competition. Fasteau was clear on this point:

> Competition is the principle mode by which men relate to each other — at one level because they don't know how else to make contact, but more basically because it is the way to demonstrate, to themselves, and others, the key masculine qualities of unwavering toughness and the ability to dominate and control. The result is that they inject competition into situations which don't call for it.[32]

The classroom may be one such situation. Male students represent youth, virility, vigor, uncircumscribed futures — everything the man in midlife crisis may feel himself lacking. Added to this may be the professor's doubts about the masculinity of his profession. The males he teaches in the 1980s are interested in careers in high technology, business, engineering, law, and medicine. His own profession is not especially popular — not only because it does not pay well but also because many men do not view it as particularly masculine. A study by David F. Aberle and Kaspar Naegele found, for instance, that middle-class fathers rejected academic careers for their sons because they did "not consider the academic role to exemplify appropriate masculine behavior."[33] The exception was a father who replied that such a role would be appropriate for his son who was shy, bookish, and needed women to care for him.

One way a professor can assert his masculinity in such a situation is to prove to himself and other males that he is attractive to and can control women. Dean Z., a basketball player at a small college in the Midwest, seemed aware of this possibility:

> Sometimes I think my English prof is trying to tell us something when he tries to make it with the girls. I could care less if they like him. He's so over the hill he's not really any competition, but he makes a big deal out of trying to show us that he can get our girls.

The harasser in midlife crisis may also be influenced by curiosity about contemporary youth and their life-styles. The young women who populate the nation's campuses in the 1980s may appear terribly exotic to men who began dating in the 1950s. Alison Lurie's *The War Between the Tates* depicted this condition. Brian Tate, the middle-aged political science professor in the novel, temporarily abandoned his family for Wendy, a seductive student who not only bolstered his ego but also introduced him to a new way of life. Wendy's attraction for Brian resulted in part from her membership in a culture that appeared alien to him:

> Brian had known for some time that he and his colleagues were not living in the America they had grown up in; it was only recently though that he had realized they were also not living in present-day America, but in another country or city state with somewhat different characteristics. The important fact about this state, which can for convenience sake be called "University," is that the great majority of its population is aged eighteen to twenty-two. Naturally the physical appearance, interests, activities, preferences and prejudices of this majority are the norm in University. Cultural and political life is geared to their standards, and any deviation from them is a social handicap.
>
> Brian had started life as a member of the dominant class in America, and for years had taken this position for granted. Now, in University, he finally has the experience of being among a depressed minority.[34]

If some sexual harassment is influenced by adolescent professional, and/or midlife crises, others spring from more disturbing roots that only in-depth analyses of individuals could explain. An undergraduate art student felt that one of her professors was "deeply troubled":

> At first I wasn't so scared of him because I figured his line was just like that of all the other guys I knew, even if he was older. I started to get upset when he started saying crazy things to me — like he would like to smear me with grape jelly and paint me naked. One day he told me that if I was his girlfriend he would tie me up to the bed, and I don't know why but all I could think of was getting the hell out of there. I never went back to his class. And I'm not sorry.

A respondent to the National Advisory Council reported an experience that indicated that harassment is seldom a simple case of "boys will be boys":

> All the incidents with this professor share a pattern: indecent exposure. Although the precise circumstances vary, this faculty member (young, supposedly socially conscious) would initiate the incidents by tucking his shirt in, "fixing his belt," or otherwise rearranging his clothing. He

is also known to verbally sexually abuse students by initiating discussion on penis size, how he has overcome his inferiority complex about his small penis size and following this with a verbal offer to expose his penis to view. This faculty member has also exposed himself in his home to at least one other graduate student in another department.[35]

Obviously, in such cases only individuals skilled in the study of psychology and familiar with the histories of individual subjects should analyze such behaviors. But most sexual harassment follows a more familiar pattern and is easier to understand. Higher education needs to use its resources to learn more about common causes for the behavior and the motivations of those who engage in it. When that happens, people will recognize that sexual harassment is more controllable than most realize.

If the problem is to be understood, there are a number of issues that researchers need to consider. If, for example, the physical appearance of a woman student is relevant in a discussion of sexual harassment, that of her professor is no less important. If the culture and socialization of contemporary women students is worthy of discussion, that of their instructors must also be taken into account. If students' motivations and self-concepts warrant consideration, those of their teachers are equally relevant. If sex stereotyping influences women's behavior, it must also affect men and must be considered in attempts to analyze the behaviors of harassers. There also needs to be more research on the relationships between sexual attitudes and vocational choice and experiences. Are there preestablished sexual attitudes, behaviors, and opportunities within specific occupational groups that attract certain types of men? How do work experiences and relationships affect men's perceptions of the opposite sex?

To an extent, of course, the motivations of professors who harass will always be enigmatic. Like their colleagues, most are products of traditional sex stereotyping; they are schooled in similar attitudes toward women and sexual codes of ethics. Yet harassers act on their impulses and assumptions when others do not. Harassers either cannot or will not subordinate personal drives and desires to professional ethics. Nonharassers can and do.

If responsible college professors have anything to fear as a result of students' and the public's learning about sexual harassment, it is not that women will make unjust or capricious accusations. The real fear should be that students will hold the institution and the faculty accountable for transgressions of which they *are* guilty. Sexual harassment is deviant behavior, and while those within the institution probably cannot alter the personal psychologies of individual academicians, they *can* influence the campus environment. Aberrant organizational activity may be impossible to eliminate, but it can be curtailed if colleagues refuse to tolerate improprieties.

The behaviors of harassers and nonharassers have become much easier to differentiate as awareness has grown. Many professors, often grudgingly, now monitor their behaviors and avoid questionable interactions with students. They hesitate before making certain kinds of statements or engaging in physical gestures; they pause before placing themselves in questionable situations. And none of that really is so bad. It may be annoying, but it is not wrong or oppressive. If men and women had treated one another with greater sensitivity in the first place, sexual harassment would not be such a problem today. If teachers had approached students with greater sensitivity in the past, students would not seem such enigmas.

The harasser lives by an outlaw code. Relying upon colleagues' reluctance to intervene in student-faculty relationships and the romantic notion that eccentricity is tolerable in academe, he has failed to read the signs of change. Higher education may accept idiosyncratic dress, manners, speech, and interests, but sexual harassment is different from these — less superficial and more threatening to the profession. Once professors realize that their own reputations suffer with that of the harasser, male college professors are likely to find the "eccentricity" of the lecherous professor less tolerable and less deserving of defense.

6 : *Women Faculty*

QUEENS ON THE CHESSBOARD

The fact of being separate
enters your livelihood like a piece of furniture
— a chest of seventeenth-century wood
from somewhere in the north.
It has a huge lock shaped like a woman's head
but the key has not been found.

Adrienne Rich,
"When We Dead Awaken"

Sexual harassment by the aberrant few jeopardizes the professional reputations of all male faculty. It casts a similar cloud over women professors. If women faculty actively and collectively confronted sexual harassment, they could create a political energy that would change the character of the campus. But they do not. Ambiguous and complex, the passivity of women faculty mirrors the dilemmas women face in other professions. In *Among Women*, Louise Bernikow uses the predicament of the woman artist to capture the female dilemma:

A woman artist of any kind is a bobbin on the sea, in danger of drowning. She feels herself in danger. She has behind her centuries of civilization in which the known and celebrated artists were male, in which the idea of a female artist was sneered at as often as the idea of a

147

female as an authentic person was sneered at. Misogyny takes its toll. She is in danger of feeling that men are the real artists, that the male mind exists and is good and right and that it is not hers. She bobs in the sea. She holds fast to scraps of evidence of other women who have crossed such seas — the painter Gentileschi in the seventeenth century, the Brontë sisters — whatever evidence happens along, saving notes in the bottle, bouncing by. She is made to worry and often to choose which kind of femaleness she will live out, what she will do about marriage and motherhood, how she will do it or not do it and become, remain, survive as an artist. The waves rise. She nearly drowns. She strikes out again, swimming.[1]

"She" is the real and metaphorical artist, businesswoman, physician, engineer, or college professor — any woman who has chosen a historically male profession. "She feels herself in danger" because she *is* in danger, quite literally. She must succeed as a professional against tradition, against prejudice, against overwhelming odds, but she must also find a way to defuse, define, or deny her own gender, to discover a type of femaleness that will not diminish her chances for professional success. These challenges alone could occupy a lifetime.

But the woman educator has additional professional responsibilities, the most demanding of which is to serve as a role model for women students. Called upon as an advocate in incidents of sexual harassment, the faculty woman is caught in the conflict between being a role model for students and needing peaceful coexistence with her male colleagues. It is, as Huckleberry Finn said, "a close place."[2] The woman professor, like Huck, is forced to choose between her head and her heart, her own welfare and that of others.

As described in chapter two, the status of the woman professor is marginal. Her profession is one in which pay, promotions, and power are unequally distributed between the sexes. Of all the individuals to whom a student might naturally turn for help with a sexual harassment problem, the woman professor risks the most if she assists. Her own status within the institution is so precarious that any kind of advocacy for a sexual harassment victim endangers the good will needed for reappointment, tenure, and professional support. The woman professor depends on men for her continued survival in the institution, the same men she would have to confront about sexual harassment. This dependence can create enormous confusion and ambiguity when the harassment issue arises.

The personal and professional pain of what has been termed the "stag" or "locker room" effect cannot be overlooked in discussions of women faculty's role in combating harassment on campus. Several authors have examined the dilemma of women who enter predominately male fields and are prevented from sharing in the camaraderie of the "old-boys' network." The stag effect denies them professional opportunities and thus seriously inhibits the professional progress of academic women throughout their careers.

In *Sexual Shakedown*, Farley recorded the graduate school experience of a young psychology professor who was admitted to a doctoral program only after great persistence:

> [My adviser] just had too much authority over me. It was absolute. It was even more than the authority that a boss has over you in a job, it has parental aspects to it because this whole graduate experience is an apprenticeship system. You get attached to a guy, they were all guys — there were only two women in the department and neither of them took graduate students — so there was no possibility of getting away from men. There was never the thought that you could go to one of them to help out against another. It was a solid bloc.
>
> It was like gambling, I guess, and it was gambling with something that I wasn't prepared to gamble with. It always seemed at the time that I would rather be sexually exploited than risk my whole career. You see, nobody else really knows that much about what you're doing academically. The whole way they judge you is by what your adviser says to them at coffee and over lunch and so forth. Everything depends on his opinion and I thought if I get him pissed off at a personal level he's going to communicate negativity about me to the others. I knew I couldn't overcome that because I'd seen it happen before, and once you get a reputation for not being a good student they don't ever give you a chance to perform otherwise. I also remember the chairman walking into the common room and banging his fist down on the table and saying, "If I had my way there would never be women in this laboratory, women don't belong in a laboratory." We were marginal there to begin with. We all know we were just being tolerated, that was it.[5]

A chairman of the department of economics observed in I. M. Heyman's *Women Students at Berkeley*:

Research assistantships are assigned by individual faculty members who have the support for this type of appointment. Male faculty members tend to favor male graduate students as research assistants for various and sundry reasons ("because they play squash together") with the result that few women are selected and hence more become teaching assistants by default.[4]

Debra Kaufman's study of academic women, "Associational Ties in Academe: Some Male and Female Differences," described one respondent's disillusionment at being excluded from the mentor system of her college:

Although my research interests are clearly in line with one of the older males in my department, he has never asked me to share my ideas with him or even to read some of his research proposals. I wouldn't feel so badly but I have a male colleague who is my age and whose dissertation was much further removed from this senior professor's area of interest. My young friend has just been asked to help formulate a new research proposal with our older colleague . . . My main contact with my older colleague is that his oldest daughter attends the same university I graduated from and that remains our main topic of conversation.[5]

Even the most independent individuals learn to value the contacts that can make the difference between success and failure in the academic profession. One professor told Kaufman:

Although we don't like to admit it, it's not what you know but who you know in academe. My peers who have "made it" have done so on the coattails of some prominent man. This is true for both men and women. I'm not one of those older women who's going to tell you that it's easier now than it was some twenty years ago. In some ways I think it's harder for young women today than it was then. Discrimination has simply become more subtle. Women have the illusion that they can survive professionally on their own. I watch the young women enter our department out to prove they can make it. They don't form contacts with the older women, they are not accepted by the older men, and they compete directly among themselves and with the younger men. I watch them come and go.[6]

The dilemma of the woman faculty member was most succinctly described by a full professor who observed:

I have been in academia a long time and no matter how many changes occur it is still evident to me that the only colleagues one can feel comfortable with are other women. We may start out believing differently but experience teaches us something else. You can count on your male colleagues to tell you about their personal problems and even share some ideas about departmental politics but when it really counts, when it's time to write the research proposal, when it's time to allocate the merit increases, you can count yourself out if you are a woman. I've seen it happen so many times. University living is male living on male terms. When we try to break barriers we seem to fail.[7]

"University living is male living on male terms," and women discover that one of the easiest ways to violate those terms is to raise troublesome issues that call attention to gender. Women faculty who have been involved in sexual harassment complaints report feeling the need to defend themselves as well as student victims. When a graduate student came to her for advice about a professor who had propositioned and verbally harassed her, Nancy S., an assistant professor at a large school in Illinois, encouraged the student to file a grievance with other women who had suffered similar problems with the man. Nancy S. and the student met several times to discuss their presentation. Shortly before their case was to be presented, a colleague informed her that the alleged harasser had told other faculty that she and the student "spent so much time together" because they were involved in a lesbian relationship and were "out to get" him.

When a female faculty member becomes identified with a sexual harassment case, she opens herself to questions about motivation that would not occur if she were a male. Suddenly there is speculation about her sexual preference, her relationships with men; even her physical appearance becomes a topic. The stereotype of the "plain Jane" bespectacled professor is no accident. Many still treat the roles of woman and college professor as mutually exclusive. Academic women often learn to survive by disguising their femininity. Louise Bernikow captured the stereotype:

Myself again. The late sixties. An Ivy League graduate school, studying literature, which is male, taught, still, by professors who are male, with several exceptions. One is a famous woman scholar, formidable and seen by me through male eyes as "unattractive." I cannot imagine that this woman has a body. Her undergarments must have been as antitactile as my grandmother's. There is no sense of pleasure or amusement about her, no spaces, everything dense and intellectual. She wears sensible shoes and genderless bland clothing. I respect her enormously, but it is hard to learn from her anything about being a woman of intellect, retaining both woman and intellect. This terrible lesson is true, too, in popular films, where career women are ugly bitches. It is clear that women must choose in a way that men need not. There are girl friends for "girl" things and intellectual women for intellectual things.[8]

Whether this stereotype fits most female faculty is less important than the fact that a woman professor's appearance and sexuality often surface as issues if she involves herself in a sexual harassment case. This occurs because higher education is no more comfortable with self-confident, attractive women than it is with those who attempt to conceal their gender. Jessie Bernard recorded one male professor's response to a colleague:

There she stands. A beautiful woman. Above her neck she is talking about the most abstruse subject. From the neck down her body is saying something altogether different. She wears good clothes. They show her body off to good advantage. And yet she acts as though she were completely unconscious of it. She acts as though she were a man, like the dog who thinks he is a human being. Sometimes it strikes me almost as freakish, this split between the way she talks and the way she looks. The two don't go together. Which message am I supposed to be getting?[9]

Lin Farley recounted a discussion at the University of Delaware involving an administrator who suffered because of men's confusion about the relationship between her physical attractiveness and professional abilities:

Here she was a Ph.D. and a woman with all kinds of strengths who also happens to be exceptionally attractive. All her colleagues were men and they just never gave her a chance because they thought she had been brought in to be the playmate of the man who hired her. It wasn't true at all, but she never could establish her credibility as a person. She finally confronted one of the men because, although she was the official channel, they wouldn't come to her about things. He just said they thought she was only there for sex. She said that was completely false and he just said, "Well, you do lead us to that conclusion. You dress real nice and you have a very seductive voice." She eventually got a bad evaluation. The whole thing just kept her from doing her job well, because they wouldn't deal with her, and then she was criticized for not being up on things when there was not any other way to be up on them than to be told. She finally left.[10]

A woman who teaches and does research in higher education is not different from other women; she was a woman before she became a college professor. Reared in the cultural stereotype and then exposed to the women's movement, female college professors — as much or more than their women students — must grapple with the dilemmas created by a society that continues to evaluate a woman on the basis of her appearance and sex.

If a student is propositioned by her geology professor, and his colleague in the German department expresses disapproval of that behavior, the age or physical appearance of the German professor will occur to no one — unless the German professor is a woman. If a woman professor happens to be middle-aged or plain or unmarried, her criticism of the harasser is suspect. Her colleagues will dismiss the sexually harassing behavior and the criticism by analyzing the woman professor's looks, relationships with males, and professional motivations. The complaint will become a vehicle for dissecting the professor's femininity. The incident will be explained away by the assumption that older women, no matter how successful professionally, resent and thus exaggerate males' attention to attractive young females. The credibility of the German professor will be diminished with the interpretation that she is frigid or sexually frustrated and is projecting her own desire to seduce onto her male colleagues, who appear freer to act on their physical instincts. Ultimately, the woman German professor will arouse as much suspicion as the geologist accused of harassment. And both women — student and professor — will be damaged.

When a colleague was accused of harassment by two faculty members and three students, Professor F., a fifty-year-old chemistry professor, refused to serve on the committee hearing the complaint. His position was emphatic:

I don't have time for that crap! These old girls on the faculty wish someone *would* pay attention to them, so they get themselves worked up by identifying with some young beauty. Actually, it's just wishful thinking. What most of them really need is a man.

Academic women find themselves in a Catch-22. They cannot function as responsible professionals and women if they ignore the sexual harassment of students, but they cannot confront it or be advocates without great risk to their own credibility and status within the institution. "Scratch a woman, find a rage,"[11] Marilyn French declared in *The Women's Room*. Sexual harassment is a highly personal, emotion-ridden issue on which even coolly professional women experience confusion, prejudice, and hostilities. An English professor commented:

For the first three years I worked here, ____ would come up behind me, grab me around the waist, and kiss me on the neck. I used to feel physically sick because he's so ugly that he's totally repulsive. I think I subconsciously refused to admit that my response was on such an elemental level because I converted my hostility into verbal conflict. At department meetings, I began to challenge him on everything he said. I told myself I was doing so because I was angry about the male faculty's tolerating the arrogance of such a mediocre pedant. Then I started getting his former students who complained about things he said to women in class, and one of my colleagues asked me to witness a statement from a student to whom he'd made physical advances. Suddenly, I became aware that my aversion wasn't intellectual at all. It was just the normal, and I think healthy, reaction of a woman who had been "hit on" by an unattractive man and who wanted to prevent students from having to endure the same indignity.

"Scratch a woman, find a rage..." But women faculty and administrators are affected by the rage in different ways. It forces academic women into a variety of roles in dealing with the sexual harassment of students. Like the student victims, women faculty deny, ignore, and confront the issue in complex ways. The roles they assume have been previously unnamed, but it is possible to identify patterns of response familiar on most campuses.

The female professor who has endured and attempted to rise above the abuses and injustices inflicted on women in a male-dominated profession is a *survivor*. As a result she is often unsympathetic to harassment victims even though she is aware of their plight. Citing her own strengths and successes, she maintains that other women, however young or unsophisticated, can — and should — act with equal assertiveness. She judges others on the basis of her own abilities and experiences. One such woman, a college dean, declared:

> Okay, there are problems here. What am I supposed to do about that? They aren't mine. I know how to conduct myself, and if these girls expect to live in a world that, like it or not, belongs to men, they have to learn what I learned. It's a long, cold, lonely road, and you can't expect or ask anyone to travel it with you. You make your own success in spite of the obstacles and the grabby men along the way.

Another, a professor of education, was equally adamant about her position:

> No, I don't see I have any responsibility to young women who find themselves in this sort of predicament. I have a job to do. That job is teaching and writing about learning theory. My job description does not include babysitting people who should know how to discourage advances from men.

This kind of woman professor works and struggles against debilitating odds. Some days amid the complaints about grades, the injunctions to publish, the demands to serve on useless committees, the rush to meet bureaucratic deadlines, she feels like Sisyphus at the very bottom of the hill. She does not need another weight added to the already overwhelming mass of the rock. The price she has paid, the energy she has expended are too great to risk on the helplessness of a twenty-year-old who will come and go and leave her pushing a rock grown heavier under the weight of another's burden. Such women are realists and loners; they recognize the truth about the situation on the campus but often can't find a way to change it.

Woman professors who are concerned about maintaining their status as colleagues often deceive themselves about campus harassment. They see it, hear about it, and are sometimes victims of sexual harassment themselves, but they are always able to explain it away. A young political science instructor asked:

> Come on, what's the big deal? These kids know the score better than we

ever did. There's not a freshman in my class who hasn't been hit on by some kid her own age, so why should I get excited if one of my male colleagues gets a little adventurous once in a while?

This kind of woman professor copes by being an amiable member of the group. Grateful for its solidarity, she avoids confrontation over disturbing issues like sexual harassment. When the group is predominately male, controversies that involve gender-related topics mean pain for the females in its midst. Shelley B., the only woman in a philosophy department, declared:

> It's a continual dilemma. We can all be sitting around in the coffee room just talking, but if somebody comments on a woman's issue, they refer to women as "them," as if I have nothing to do with "them." And there's always that moment when they turn to look at me to see if I agree. I could make myself an outcast, but I'd rather be part of the group.

Such women act out of self-preservation. But the cost women usually pay for being "one of the boys" may eventually force them to turn against or away from "the girls."

There is a third group of women professors who assume roles which are much less ambiguous than those previously described. These are the *innocents*, the women who manage to see and hear no evil from their colleagues. Since sexual harassment is seldom overt, its existence is easy to ignore. Even the most public kind of harassment, sexist language, is carried out within the sanctity of the individual classroom. The woman professor who denies knowledge of sexual harassment can rely on circumstantial evidence to support her position. The offending colleague probably has been careful about his behavior before other faculty members, so she can maintain that she has not observed any inappropriate behavior. Confronted with an accusation against a colleague, she is likely to insist that the complainant has distorted or confused the professor's behavior. Sooner or later, she will offer the penultimate defense: "I've worked with ____ for years, and no one ever complained to me about him."

A professor of mathematics, for decades the only woman in her department, expressed astonishment at a former student's story:

> A student who had graduated several years ago dropped by my office to

chat about discrimination in her field — physics — both in the job market and in graduate school. We had a very pleasant conversation, very interesting. I suggested she might want to talk to some younger women faculty who were more recently on the job market.

And then I was very surprised. As she was leaving, she recounted an episode that had disturbed her for two years. The student was working after 5:00 at the computer terminal in the common room, and one of our faculty came up and made a pass. The student said she just left and avoided working there after that. She didn't think anyone would be empathetic, so she didn't say anything, but apparently it's still bothering her.

I was absolutely shocked at who it was — a nice, young family man. I guess anyone would have shocked me — I'm so stupid and naive about these things. But especially him. He's no longer with us . . . Went on to another job. It must have really bothered the student. She was still upset two years later.

This "naive" professor has been a leader in campus politics and faculty governance for years. Greatly respected by both faculty and administration for her intelligence and political acumen, she did not recognize that the former student might have come to talk particularly about that episode. The revelation seemed to her an afterthought, despite the young woman's obvious distress and her two-year hesitancy in reporting the incident. The professor's final perception of the experience was that younger faculty women are more likely and better able to help victims because, despite her sympathy, she belongs to "a different generation on the campus."

Although refusal to confront sexual harassment is disturbing, the extreme anger and concern that some women faculty demonstrate can also cause difficulties for both students and their advocates. More and more academic women, reflecting the mood of contemporary society, are angry about the real and imagined abuses they have suffered at the hands of their male colleagues. To be a woman in a male-dominated profession is especially difficult when that profession deceives itself and others about its liberality. Until recently, aspiring women were wary of one another. This too was a survival mechanism. Bernikow commented:

Myself in graduate school in the company of many other women like myself and not knowing them. We stayed away from each other. We tried, in the privacy of our student apartments, to be smarter on the subject of John Donne or the Victorian Novel, than anyone else, but especially smarter than other women — because there was room for only some of us, because the struggle to be taken seriously by our male professors was relentless . . . Our culture had taught us to deny what we had in common, to put out the fire of our identification and empathy with each other.[12]

Once "the fire of identification and empathy" is lit, however, the angry professor may identify too strongly with the harassed student. Viewing herself as a *militant* in the struggle for a better life for women, this educator may use the student as a means of venting her own hostilities and redressing wrongs that she has endured. Thus the student victim suffers another blow at the hands of higher education; once again her welfare is subordinated to the will of a faculty member. Emphasis shifts from remediation of the student's grievance to the advancement of a cause. The truth is that most college students are more concerned with their private lives than they are with movements and moral crusades. The typical student who is being harassed simply wants it to end. She is usually not comfortable having her personal life moved into the public forum — not even at the urging of the best-intentioned professor.

Such women professors can be as threatening to students as those who deny and disengage themselves from sexual harassment. They may also damage their own careers. College professors like to think that objectivity and rationality characterize their individual and collective actions. Deviation from those sacred principles is often punished more severely than are the transgressions of sexual harassers. Anger, even righteous anger, threatens the calm that prevails in the Garden of Academe, and it is met with disapproval. Thus the militant professor often accomplishes little of value for herself or a sexual harassment victim.

There are, however, women faculty who refuse to deny the obvious, who act independently and unselfishly and accept responsibility for students victimized by harassment. In a sense, they are *risk takers*. They confront enormous obstacles when they attempt to deal with sexual harassment. They face disdain from colleagues of both sexes because the sexual harassment issue seems to threaten the principle of professional autonomy that faculty so cherish. They risk disapproval from men who, whether they admit it or not, may suffer something akin to castration anxiety at the prospect of female colleagues and students "ganging up" on a male colleague. They may have to endure hostility from other women who hesitate to disturb the male status quo or who do not want to be asked to share in the responsibility.

Such women who become involved with victims of harassment often do so with limited counseling expertise and limited knowledge of the academic procedures governing the issue. Higher education offers no training for this task, and lack of support systems and demands for confidentiality pose additional burdens. Perhaps most discouraging to women who want to help is knowing that the risk and effort may be doomed to defeat from the beginning. Their own experiences have taught them such painful truths. An assistant to the provost in an Eastern university stated unequivocally that, on the basis of personal experience, she would hesitate to advise a student to file a sexual harassment grievance. The cost to the woman is "just too high," she maintained. She described her own professional evolution on the issue:

> The first few times women came to me with problems they were having with sexual harassment, I was naively confident that there was truly an opportunity to help. I was carefully professional and cool, questioning the women for details and consistency. One was a terrified freshman woman who had been grabbed and lunged at by a fiftyish professor. She had run from his office, spent a hysterical night in the dorm while her roommate answered phone calls from the professor (he was apparently attempting to cover his tracks), and had sought administrative help at the urging of her dorm advisor. The student's concern was that she'd get a bad grade from the professor. The assistant dean and I assured her that she would get the grade she had earned, that we could monitor that.
>
> She calmed down, and we advised her of the full range of options, from doing nothing to filing an official complaint to criminal charges. It was a good counseling session, I think. The student really did understand that she had several choices, that we really did care, that she had sympathy and protection. She went home for the break and talked things over with her parents. Although I didn't have any direct role in the grievance procedure, eventually I learned that she had decided to file a complaint. I knew the professor had a long, long history of sexual harassment and other abusive treatment of students, and I stupidly thought that something might happen.

Much later I learned that it took months to set up a hearing, the male dean was afraid to take any independent action, the faculty member enlisted other students in a public opinion campaign so the woman was ostracized and harassed by other students in her classes and by phone, and the concern for "objectivity" eliminated all sympathetic behaviors by university administrators.

When the hearing finally occurred — by an all-male faculty committee — the student was bullied and cross-examined about her grades, motivation, even her sex life. There was no confidentiality for her at all. The faculty grapevine was buzzing with titillating gossip about some "sexy undergraduate" who was trying to get a tenured faculty member fired. The committee decided it couldn't rule on the facts of the case because there were no eyewitnesses and there should be no action.

The faculty member continues to harass students, sexually and otherwise. The student transferred to another college, not really understanding what had happened. But I did, and so did the assistant dean. It was a hard lesson: the "good guys" have no control, no way to ensure fairness or sensitivity.

Those who are traditionally considered "good guys" or friendly *helpers* to sexual harassment victims are student services personnel. Depending on the size and climate of the institution, there are any number of individuals who might serve this function. In small schools, the dean of students is probably the most logical resource. In large universities, there are affirmative action officials, student affairs staff, and ombudsmen (troubleshooters, mediators who work outside formal administrative structures). On the surface, the situation appears promising. For the cost of tuition and room and board, parents can send their daughter to college with the reassuring knowledge that, even if she should find herself at the mercy of some lecherous professor, there are individuals specially charged with protecting her.

But appearances deceive. One dean of students stated the situation quite simply: "You can call us 'helpers,' but the truth is we're really more like a bunch of dwarfs." Frequently, such individuals *are* "dwarfed" within the system of higher education. This may be particularly true in large universities where sheer size decreases their influence and power. There are, however, even more obvious explanations for the powerlessness of student services staff.

The first is that they are not, in proper academic terms, "colleagues." They are not faculty. Even when the student affairs staff, the affirmative action officer, or the ombudsman possess academic training and credentials, they are perceived as part of the academic support system, as administrators and service personnel. They are employed, not tenured. They advise and counsel; they do not teach or do research. Since the faculty does not regard them as equals, they do not have the prestige or power necessary to affect any but the most blatant sexual harassment cases.

Another reason for the powerlessness of student services is the fact that this is the area where females are concentrated in higher education. The tasks of protecting, nurturing, and healing the hurts of students fall predictably to women. In the case of sexual harassment, however, this task presents difficulties. The campus is not comfortable with harassment; when demands for change come from the traditional "woman's" area, it diminishes the importance of the demands from the start. It is easier to regard sexual harassment as a manufactured problem, a figment of the imaginations of staff and students. "[The faculty] don't think we do anything worthwhile in the first place," an ombudsman commented. "I feel absolutely helpless when I try to find ways to get them to confront [sexual harassment]."

Many women are courageous about the problem of sexual harassment and lead the way to change, but there are not enough of them. "Misogyny takes its toll . . . The waves rise. [A woman] nearly drowns."[13] And it is not easy to save others when one can barely stay afloat herself. "It's the pits. I'd like to help, but what can I do? I can barely survive myself," a sociologist comments. That has been the most frequent response of the women in academe. Like the men, they advocate individual responsibility and commitment to the welfare of others. Also like the men, many have adopted a "live and let live" attitude toward harassment.

For the students to whom they are role models, such a posture is, at the very least, discouraging. It conveys a sense of hopelessness not simply about life on campus, but about the roles of women in all of society. Disengagement and pseudoinnocence on the part of women with power only increase the distress of students for whom faculty claim concern.

Being a female in higher education may not be easy, but it does not relieve one of responsibility. The women of academe have, over the years, been disconcerted and frustrated by sexual harassment of students and its potential impact upon their own status in the academic community. Their attempts to cope have been varied, fragmented, and, more often than not, lonely. If it is time for male professors to act together to combat the problem, their female colleagues face an identical — perhaps greater — challenge.

7 : The Future of Academe

We, however, are not prisoners . . . We have no reason to mistrust our world, for it is not against us. Has it terrors, they are our *terrors; has it abysses, those abysses belong to us . . . and if only we arrange our life according to that principle which counsels us that we must always hold to the difficult, then that which now still seems to us the most alien will become what we most trust and find most faithful.*

Rainer Maria Rilke,
Letter

No one in higher education means for sexual harassment of students to exist. And no one approves of it. There is consensus on campus that sexual harassment is bad behavior and should be stopped. And what more appropriate place for reform to begin than the academic community.

The notoriety of *Alexander* v. *Yale University* in 1977 startled campus communities across the country into realizing that they needed to deal with the sexual harassment issue. In the wake of the decision, some individuals achieved visibility by making strong statements on their own campuses. A statement by President Edward J. Bloustein of Rutgers, for instance, was widely circulated as an example of administrative leadership (see Appendix). In 1979, when the American Council on Education held a series of national seminars on sexual harassment policy, the institutions with models available for study were the University of Washington, the University of Louisville, and Tulane University. Since then, articles and reports on the procedures of other institutions have appeared in both the academic and popular press. There is value, especially for administrators, in analyzing the models of other colleges and universities.

But the policies and procedures of one college or university cannot adequately reflect the needs of all. Campus environments and circumstances vary so much that it is inadvisable to propose one procedure for dealing with sexual harassment. Organized attempts to curtail the problem are still so new that no institution can claim to have developed a model system. Most journal articles on the sexual harassment policies of specific institutions are descriptive rather than evaluative. Until there is reliable feedback from students, faculty, and administrators influenced by the procedures on various campuses, there is no way of determining their value to others.

Guidance for individuals and institutions affected by sexual harassment is limited, but some general rules can be identified. The following sections offer practical advice to students, parents, administrators, faculty, deans and department heads. They should aid these groups in better understanding the issue and in recognizing their rights and responsibilities in dealing with it.

STUDENTS

Women students must interpret and assess how faculty behave towards them; they must also eventually react. What they do or do not do has significant impact on the professor and the institution. Women must make the effort to understand the dynamics of sexual harassment and to develop strategies for dealing with it.

The following suggestions can help students understand and constructively confront sexual harassment if it occurs.

- The student must learn about sexual harassment and become acquainted with the deans, ombudsman and the student affairs, affirmative action, and other campus officials assigned responsibility for this issue. Reading the campus policy and procedures for sexual harassment complaints is essential.
- Attending residence hall programs, workshops, and public lectures intended to give a better understanding of harassment and learning the formal and informal support systems within the college or university is most important.

- The student should talk to friends and check the campus "grapcvine," as well as be alert to warnings about faculty who pursue inappropriate relations with women students.
- If a student begins to feel that a professor's behavior toward her is questionable, if he seems to confuse her role as a student and as a woman, objective examination of the situation is the next step. This means assessing his behavior against established definitions of sexual harassment. She needs to consider specific events, appropriate faculty-student relations, and the unexpected assumptions the professor may be making about her behavior. In making a judgment, the student must review her thoughts with someone she trusts.
- The student should remember that she is a student. There are conventional ways that faculty treat students. No professor needs to use unusual or extraordinary techniques to gain access to a student. Are meetings taking place in social settings? Are conversations leading to intimacies that are better avoided? Are academic issues deferred for personal ones?
- The student should not assume that offensive behavior will go away by ignoring it. Sexual harassment frequently increases when students attempt to disregard it. The student should find ways to show her discomfort, for example, by changing the subject when the professor asks personal questions unrelated to the course work, refusing social invitations even if the stated purpose is academic, picking up assignments or grades only during times specified for the entire class, avoiding one-on-one meetings in offices with closed doors, and bringing a third party to meetings with the professor.
- If a professor does not respond to these indirect demonstrations of distress and rejection, the student should be more direct by telling him that his language, jokes, or special treatment make her uncomfortable and that she wishes he would stop.
- If verbal requests do not work or seem too confrontive, a request in writing should be made. In a 1981 article in the *Harvard Business Review*, Mary P. Rowe, special assistant to the president of Massachusetts Institute of Technology, recommended that victims of harassment write the offender a three-part letter.[1] Rowe, who served as mediator in numerous cases from universities and corporations, suggested beginning with what may be an extensive first section that details the facts as the writer sees them. She then recommended a second part in which the writer describes her feelings about the alleged harassment and any perceived or actual damages inflicted on her. Rowe recommended that the letter conclude with a section explaining what the victim would like to have happen next. This process would give the offending professor a

chance to assess his behaviors and to amend them or to defend himself if he is wrongly accused. In addition to providing him with fair warning, it would help the student to assess the strength of her case and to prove that she has actively sought to curtail the harassment.

- Before removing herself from the situation, the student should not assume that this is the only solution. If it means going to school an extra quarter, changing her major, or quitting her job to reschedule the class, the cost may be too high.

- If harassing behavior continues or escalates, the student should repeat her request that the professor discontinue his activity and add that she will inform the department head, the dean, or some other authority if the request is ignored.

- It is important for the student to keep dated records of specific offenses and attempts to communicate her discomfort to the professor.

- If possible, the student should find other women with similar complaints or other students who have witnessed the offensive behavior. This will add the security of numbers.

- Because her role as student is less powerful than that of the faculty member, the student needs to be prepared to augment her power. Corroborating evidence from other victims or witnesses and the influence of her parents, husband, or other supportive "outside" forces are possibilities. A similar technique is used by harassers, who often defend themselves with testimonies from their wives and colleagues, portraying them as dedicated husbands, fathers, and teachers.

- If the student decides to report the problem to the professor's superior, she should get advice from campus support personnel before doing so. They are familiar with campus policy, grievance mechanisms, and the experiences of other complainants.

- The student should not be surprised to find that the institution generally attempts informal resolutions to sexual harassment problems. It considers these easier on both the student and the professor because they limit the number of people involved.

- If the informal method does not work and/or the offensive behavior becomes so serious that the student considers a formal grievance, she should make her decision carefully. Formal grievances are never easy, they can involve risk for the student, and they don't always result in prompt or "right" solutions. Nevertheless a formal grievance process may be the only way to stop the sexual harassment for her and unknown others.

- In addition to institutional grievance procedures, the other standard avenues of recourse are appeal to federal enforcement agencies or, if the situation is serious enough, a lawsuit alleging prohibited discrimination. The student may simultaneously pursue several areas of recourse (see Appendices). The federal agency to which appeals should be directed is the Office for Civil Rights in the Department of Education. There are very specific rules governing the filing, acknowledgment, and investigation of a sexual harassment complaint. The Office for Civil Rights will investigate at no cost to the student and its investigation will be taken seriously by the college. Court litigation is a lengthy, complex process and the student should get reliable professional advice before proceeding.

- If a student is having a personal relationship with a professor and is sure that sexual harassment has nothing to do with her situation, she should think again. One type of sexual harasser has a pattern of making a student believe she is intellectually or physically gifted, "special" somehow. Because he recognizes her good qualities or traits that others may not see, she is attracted to that recognition. A student should never overestimate her control over the male-female boundaries in a relationship with a faculty member or her ability to handle an affair with him. The student role *always* has less power than the professor's. If his interest in the student becomes manipulative, coercive, or exploitive, the intrinsic role inequities can make her feel vulnerable and confused. She may tolerate behavior from him that she would not accept from a peer because she feels reluctant or impotent to challenge him.

- If the student is simply an observer of instances of harassment, she should not assume that she is free of responsibility. Harassment flourishes on the campus because it is regarded as the problem only of victims. Individual students need to consider seriously their responsibility to peers who are harassment victims. This may mean simply listening to their problem, but some may have to weigh the costs of offering active support to peers in grievance cases. Student groups can also have an impact. They may contribute simply by offering programs that raise consciousness about the problem. Some organizations may deal with it more actively. Women Organized Against Sexual Harassment greatly influenced the outcome of the Hermassi case at Berkeley, and other groups like the Committee Against Sexual Harassment at Washington University in Missouri have been active in conducting surveys to alert the campus to the problem. The student media can be extremely influential. *Women's Forum Quarterly*, a publication of Seattle Central Community College in Washington, publishes the winner of the "Sexist Remark of the Quarter Award"; the purpose is to increase awareness of sexist humor and bias in the classroom. The *Harvard Crimson's* investigative reporting was one of the most important factors in exposing the Kilson case to the Harvard University community.

PARENTS

Parents also can have an active role in ending sexual harassment on campus. Parents, after all, pay most of higher education's bills through taxes and tuition. Their influence on the student and the institution can be direct and effective.

Parents with daughters in college should consider these suggestions:

- Overestimating their daughter's knowledge or her college's concern about sexual harassment is a mistake. Parents should see that she is basically informed about the issue, and let the institution know that they are aware of the possible problem.
- Parents should neither dismiss nor overreact to their daughter's concern about a professor's behavior. Parents sometimes assume that professors can do no wrong and that their daughter is misinterpreting a situation. Some parents even increase their daughter's confusion by accusing her of encouraging a professor's behavior. College professors *do* sexually harass, and parents who deny the problem need to question their assumptions. Parents should not jump to conclusions. They should help their daughter understand the problem, by asking for specific details, and they should work with her to assess objectively the professor's behavior and her response to it.
- If parents believe their daughter is being sexually harassed, they should encourage her to attempt to resolve the problem herself. They should give her emotional support and explain that confronting and coping with such situations is a difficult but necessary part of growing up. They should make sure that their daughter knows the official college policy and procedures and that she understands the campus administrative structure and the available support services.
- Parents may eventually choose or need to become directly involved if their daughter cannot get adequate information and help, if the campus system seems unresponsive or too slow, if she seeks their active support, or if the situation is severe enough that they want to add parental weight from the outset.
- If parents do take an active role, they should use the organizational chain of command. This means going first to the dean of the college or the student affairs office or both. Deans have authority over their faculty and can resolve problems; they are also accountable to others in the heirarchy. Student affairs personnel are trained to mediate problems and advocate for students; they also are accountable to others. Both the dean and the student affairs offices may have historical information about past complaints and would benefit from hearing from students

and parents. Student-faculty problems are most often resolved at lower levels. While a phone call to the president may create a stir and consternation, the most likely action from the president will be to refer the problem to another office. If parents contact the president's office to inquire about the appropriate chain of command, that office will be acquainted with the situation and will be interested in the follow-up. If parents later complain about unresponsiveness at lower levels, they will have added impact and the credibility of having tried to use the organization's system. They will, in effect, be calling the system to account.

- The practical ways to make parental support and concern felt on campus are simple. If their daughter requests it, the parents' presence at discussions with the dean or department head will give her support. It will also increase the pressure for clarity, decisive resolution, and deadlines for actions. The presence of a parent will discourage the administrator's inclination to let the problem fade away. If parents can't be present, they should encourage their daughter to take an advocate with her to such meetings. If she wants to pursue the issue herself, parents should send a letter informing the college that they are monitoring the process by creating a "paper trail" to the next administrative level and by using the telephone to clarify the process their daughter is following.
- Parents should be supportive of their daughter's efforts to be independent and care for herself. Their involvement in a sexual harassment complaint should not take the form of undermining that self-confidence.
- If parents are ultimately dissatisfied with the institution's response, they can use an attorney. Lawyers add pressure and are familiar with bureaucracies and their problems. The involvement of an attorney adds to the seriousness of a complaint. It also implies that public attention might eventually be turned on the problem. An attorney's assessment of the options for remedy can benefit parent and daughter. If the family's emotional reaction to a situation is high, an intermediary can provide relief. Finally, an attorney can advise additional remedies from outside agencies or processes.

ADMINISTRATORS

Because of recent media attention to sexual harassment, the legal liabilities of institutions, and the increased litigiousness of students and employees, higher education must police itself. If it does not, it risks being policed by other institutions and forces with less sensitivity and understanding of the academic environment and mission. Administrators responsible for making campus policy will need to consider steps involved in establishing prevention, grievance, and sanction procedures.

Prevention

- A clear policy statement on sexual harassment is essential. It is required by law of employers to limit institutional liability, but the need goes beyond legal compliance. The administrative officers of the college or university must lend their authority to an unequivocal condemnation of sexual harassment. This "message from the top" conveys to the diffuse authorities within the organization the mandate to act. If those with greatest power and visibility on campus state that sexual harassment will not be tolerated, victims feel their complaints will be heard and harassers will worry about being caught. In 1980, the ombudsman at the University of Washington reported that after the president made a strong statement against sexual harassment, the number of harassment complaints decreased from one per week to one per month. When M.I.T. adopted a strong policy to monitor harassment for the 1978–1979 school year, complaints increased three to four times over the preceding years. The increase probably reflected women's willingness to come forward once the institution took a stand.
- A critical part of the prevention process is creation of a written statement that defines sexual harassment and describes for students and faculty specific examples of the behavior. This will help the community evaluate the basis for subsequent complaints. It will have greater credibility if the president appoints a committee of representatives from all campus constituencies to write it and if it is ultimately reviewed and approved by campus governance groups. Students as well as faculty and administrators should assist in giving examples of the "do's" and "don't's" of faculty-student relations.
- Prevention also requires written grievance procedures like those required for other institutional issues. Students need to know the recourses available to them when a faculty member violates campus policy. Some institutions use their standard grievance mechanisms to deal with harassment complaints. These usually dictate that the student first address the professor. If there is no resolution, she approaches the department head, then the dean, and eventually, in a formal complaint, a committee. When the source of discomfort is a midterm grade, this system makes sense. When the problem is a professor asking a freshman to sleep with him and she must complain to the male department head and male dean who are his colleagues, the normal system seems

prejudiced and threatening. The solution for campuses using established grievance procedures is to allow some steps in the process to be waived in harassment cases. In 1982, Miami University in Ohio, for example, altered its policy so that the first step in a sexual harassment grievance no longer required students to confront professors with their complaints. The aid of an intermediary, such as an ombudsman, can also relieve some of the pressure on the student.

Some campuses feel that special grievance procedures are necessary to accommodate the distinctive aspects of harassment. Yale and Stanford, for instance, have special systems to deal with the problem. The need for confidentiality, the delicacy of most complaints, and the threat of a predominately male environment bring most grievance procedures into question. Specifically designed procedures can, however, raise complicated discussions about due process, peer review, and capricious complaints. Flexibility and sensitivity are essential so that the grievance process itself does not become a source of discouragement to women.

• Well-informed, visible support offices are essential to preventing sexual harassment on campus. The role can be filled by a variety of offices, such as those of ombudsman, affirmative action, human resources, women's center, dean of students, or student affairs. On large campuses, a number of these resources are available to students. The dean of the college or the dean of students usually handles problems on smaller campuses. What matters are not the titles but visibility; students and faculty must recognize there are people interested in complaints who have the authority to provide more than tea and sympathy to complainants. Students must know that support offices have the power to act on complaints or to transmit them directly to an office that can.

Not surprisingly, sexual harassment, like racism and sexism, is often "ghettoized." As an issue, sexual harassment is usually referred to an office staffed by women. It frequently lacks the staff or budget to have real political power. It is appropriate to think that female administrators are more comfortable resources for harassment victims and perhaps to assume that they have more nurturing styles in helping to resolve difficulties. A problem occurs, however, when sexual harassment is viewed as simply a "women's issue." The more it is removed from the campus attention and the center of power, the easier it is for the institution to overlook and deceive iteself about sexual harassment. When a college "ghettoizes" the issue, it gives the appearance of concern when, in fact, it relegates sexual harassment to a powerless office so that the "real" business of the campus is not affected.

• The success of sexual harassment prevention depends on publicity and education. Bernice Sandler, director of the Women's Project of the Association of American Colleges, and others maintain that most harassers would stop if people were adequately informed about the issue. Sexual harassment will not be curtailed by policy statements circulated to the deans or grievance procedures known only to the committees that wrote them. The ways to inform the campus are well-established. Handbooks, residence hall programs, public lectures, information on bulletin boards, special classes, panel discussions, and articles in the student newspaper are standard ways to inform the campus. Circulation of policy statements must be campus-wide. Some college students are unsophisticated in recognizing the verbal subtleties of a harasser. A few are so dazzled by professors' authority that they accept as appropriate any behaviors short of being grappled to the floor of the chemistry lab. Although most women are not so naive, all benefit from official language about sexual harassment and advice about what to do when it occurs.

- Administrators need to be aware that research demonstrates that sex difference and sex-role beliefs affect the ways in which individuals respond to sexual harassment. In their article "Attributions and Assignment of Responsibility in Sexual Harassment," Inger W. Jensen and Barbara A. Gutek demonstrated that "men are more likely than women to blame women for being sexually harassed . . . [and] that sex-role beliefs will dictate how a woman who has been sexually harassed is going to feel about the incident. If she has incorporated the traditional sex-role beliefs, she will be highly likely to blame other women, as well as herself, for incidents of sexual harassment. Such an attribution process, in return, will affect whether she reports the incident to someone in authority or talks to co-workers or friends about it."[2]

  The implications of sex-role beliefs for higher education are clear. Prevention of sexual harassment requires more than superficial familiarity with the issue and the institutional procedures for combating it. Faculty, administrators, and students will deal more effectively and objectively with the problem if they are consistently encouraged to reevaluate sex-role stereotypes. Until the campus community becomes educated enough to move beyond sex-stereotyping, grievance committees and campus officials may respond with bias to victims and victims may continue to engage in self-blame.

- Workshops or guest lectures that address the specialized concerns of deans, department heads, and faculty can be useful preventive devices. These may deal directly with the problem of sexual harassment, or they may approach it as part of the larger issue of the "chilly classroom climate"[3] to which women students in higher education are subjected. Faculty, for example, benefit from workshops that teach them to identify the ways in which they treat men and women students differently; heads of units need to investigate techniques for insuring equitable campus climates for both sexes.

The effectiveness of such presentations depends not only upon selecting well-informed leaders and speakers but also upon fitting the program to the needs and political climate of the particular institution. Information sessions often work best if a male and female team makes the presentation. The American Council on Education's leadership seminars on sexual harassment policy development employed teams of men and women to work with the approximately 600 faculty and administrators who attended. In some cases, discussion groups might work well; in others, they might increase tension. The best approach is for the administrator to use information from periodic faculty surveys and student evaluations to assess the political climate and educational needs of his or her campus.

Grievance

When the student's own efforts cannot control harassing behavior, she has the right to support from the institution. This can come in the form of informal mediation or a formal grievance. Certain points about students' responses to sexual harassment cannot be repeated too frequently. Students are reluctant to pursue formal grievances because they perceive — often correctly — great personal risk. Women are very seldom casual, arbitrary, or vindictive about sexual harassment. Except in extreme circumstances, most simply want the behavior to stop and request that "nothing really bad" happen to the professor.

A formal grievance process is an ordeal for everyone, but sympathy often centers on the professor. *His* career, *his* reputation, *his* family, *his* future are in jeopardy. Yet the same concerns apply to the student. She stakes *her* career, *her* reputation, *her* future on the very risky process of telling a panel of professors that their colleague has abused her. Concern about protecting male faculty from "witch hunts" is well-established. But institutional regard for due process, confidentiality, and protection from arbitrary use of authority must be directed toward all involved. Students almost always indicate concern for professors' personal lives when they discuss their own situations. Statements like "I don't want to make trouble" or "I don't want his wife to know" are common. Professors should have similar concern for students. Everyone involved in a sexual harassment situation has personal and professional issues at risk. Again and again, lawyers and administrators state that in an harassment case, "No matter who wins, everyone loses."

The traditional first step in a campus complaint is to attempt informal mediation between the individuals involved. This may mean encouraging a one-on-one confrontation between the student and the professor or using an intermediary to affect resolution. The following are issues concerning informal mediation which the institution should consider:

- The student in a sexual harassment case will be understandably reluctant to confront the professor. One-on-one discussion may be the situation that created the problem in the first place. Her reluctance should not be taken as evidence that her charges are without credibility.
- Whenever the student can, without undue stress, confront the professor, she should be encouraged to do so. The presence of a student advocate may lend her support. One-on-one mediation promotes individual responsibility and establishes that direct communication is a desirable norm on the campus.
- The distinction between acceptable and unacceptable behavior by a faculty member may on rare occasions be difficult to recognize. The intention underlying some kinds of touching, eye contact, and verbal statements may be open to dispute. Determination of whether certain words or actions constitute sexual harassment should be based on consideration of individual rights and facts of the case. Professors possess academic freedom and First Amendment protections, but these do not permit them to encroach upon the rights of students. In determining whether a behavior is appropriate, the institution should apply to the facts of the case the standard of behavior of a reasonable person in similar circumstances. When a behavior appears genuinely ambiguous, several points can be considered:
  a. The professor's response to complaints about his behavior can be critical. If a student or an agent of the institution informs a professor that a particular behavior is offensive and he refuses to alter it, he may justifiably be considered suspect. Another professor might not realize the discomfort created by his words or actions. His good intentions will be clearer if he can prove that upon being made aware of the unintended effect of his behavior, he sought to explain it and/ or to change it so that the student would no longer feel uncomfortable.
  b. Additional complaints of sexual harassment against a professor must be considered. If a number of individuals perceive that a behavior is offensive, it becomes less difficult to judge. Investigations

of complaints often result in evidence that consists solely of one person's word against another's. Thus any corroborating evidence is useful. Even when several students allege they have experienced similar treatment from a professor, there may be a problem if there were no witnesses to each incident.

c. There are often tangible effects that lend support to complaints of sexual harassment. For example, a student may allege that a professor offered her an "A" in exchange for sexual favors and she refused. If she can prove that she subsequently received a "C" grade for a paper of "A" quality, this would help corroborate her claim. There are other types of evidence that might demonstrate that some form of retaliation followed a sexual harassment incident. A student may be given inappropriate academic assignments, poor office or desk space, less access to faculty assistance, or poor recommendations. Other typical reprisals are denying students warranted honors, appointments, job referrals, or financial aid.

- Informal mediation should always be attempted. It saves time, energy, and money and helps to avoid the greater anxiety and embarrassment of formal grievances. The informal system is also consistent with the academic concept of progressive discipline, which allows an individual the opportunity to correct his own behavior before invoking peer inquiry and disciplinary actions. For instance, in 1979, the University of Florida adopted an informal grievance procedure that resulted in an increase in the number of students willing to report instances of harassment.

  Although informal mediation is the most frequent way of addressing sexual harassment problems, its limitations cannot be overlooked. Ironically, successful informal mediation deceives the campus community into not knowing or acknowledging that there are harassment problems. Files are not kept, public knowledge is minimal, and sanctions for an offender are limited. Without some form of record keeping, the same professor can abuse individual students one at a time and be given the same "second chance" over and over again. Without an attempt to document the frequency of problems on a campus, the institution can deceive itself into believing that sexual harassment is only a minor issue.

- Formal grievances involving supervisors, deans, and committee hearings are far more complex and ennervating. There are, however, situations in which they are the only recourse. If a professor's behavior is systematically abusive or damaging (propositions, threats, assaults) or if informal mediation has failed to change his inappropriate conduct, the formal grievance becomes the last on-campus resort. Institutions cannot overlook their own liability when repeated complaints about an individual have occurred. One of the crucial messages in current legal guidelines is that a college or university can be held responsible for what it knows or can reasonably be expected to know about sexual harassment.

By the time a complaint reaches this stage, administrators must be concerned about several points:

a. The institution must be able to demonstrate that a policy statement on sexual harassment and grievance procedures has been established and articulated to all campus constituencies. It should also be prepared to prove that its grievance process provides students with reasonable and prompt access to resources that will advise them and hear complaints.

b. Once a formal complaint is made, the institution should act immediately to investigate the charges and to seek a fair resolution. This will demonstrate, if necessary later, that it recognizes its legal responsibilities and has attempted to resolve the complaint.

c. A campus official with institutional credibility and authority should be authorized to interview the complainant to learn specific information about the situation, to evaluate whether informal mediation has been attempted, and to mediate an informal resolution if it is still possible.

d. At some point, students must be willing to be identified and to put their complaint in writing. Without signed statements, the institution's investigatory powers are limited. It cannot, without legal risk, act on anonymous complaints. Written statements establish the grievant's credibility and provide the institution with specific legal grounds for carrying on the investigations.

Having a student sign a complaint does not have to mean that her confidentiality will be violated. An institution cannot keep a complaint anonymous, but it can maintain reasonable confidentiality by informing only those officials and individuals with a *need to know* in order to respond to the case. Yale, for example, has a "limited identification" process that in certain circumstances allows the student to protect her identity from the professor named in a complaint. Institutions must remember that sexual harassment is a hidden issue because students fear the consequences of identification and so refuse to come forward. Unlike courtrooms, where face-to-face confrontation is mandatory, colleges and universities can adopt procedures that do not require this kind of encounter.

e. Allowing individuals to file grievances after graduation is another way to combat reluctance about reporting sexual harassment. Graduates who hesitate to become involved in formal grievances may write letters to offending professors and send copies to their department heads. Such information should not be used in formal proceedings, but it can assist administrators in better understanding the institutional climate.

f. The professor should be informed of all oral and written complaints against him. Although anonymous complaints cannot be placed in his records, he has the right to know that they have occurred and to be told what records are kept. Time deadlines for response must be clear, reasonable, and rigorously observed. The professor must have the opportunity to prepare a case and must be informed of the appeal process if he disagrees with the findings of the grievance committee.

g. The details of the handling of a complaint should be documented by date and hour. Interviews, conferences, and even unsuccessfully completed telephone calls and notes from meetings act as safeguards to prove the institution's good faith in acting to solve the problem.

h. There must be institutional commitment to confidentiality about a complaint. This serves the student and the faculty member, as well as the adjudication process. When public discussion occurs, when details are treated as campus gossip, all are damaged and the possibility of remedy is greatly diminished. There can be no guarantee that a professor or student will not choose to talk about the situation. But the administration and faculty can make it a policy that they will not and that they will treat violations of such policy as actionable offenses. When this is clearly articulated to all parties, there is at least a campus norm set.

i. Administrative leaders must be aware of the complex legal issues surrounding sexual harassment. Title IX has limited enforcement history, and there have been very few court cases. Complicated legal questions about degree of proof required in sexual harassment cases, indirectly affected parties, the concept of the poisoned environment, and relief for tangible harm have yet to be answered. The burden on college and university legal experts is to anticipate the evolution of this issue in the courts and to protect institutional liability.

Sanctions

Even model prevention and grievance policies will fail if an institution refuses to punish harassment.

- A grievance that finds fault with faculty behavior should never end in token sanctions or meaningless slaps on the wrist. Compromise and vacillation defeat all of a college's good intentions by implying to victims and offenders that no one is really committed to stopping sexual harassment.

An administrator at an Illinois college expressed this point: "By the time a case goes to grievance and an individual is determined guilty beyond a shadow of a doubt — and that's not always as hard to do as some would have us believe — it's time for the college to 'put up or shut up.' Either we're serious about ending this thing, or we're not. If we *are* serious, then the point where we take our stand has to be our firmness in dealing with people who cause the problem."

- The one advantage the campus has over the courts is great latitude in fitting the punishment to the offense. An institution is best advised to adopt a system of progressive discipline for cause. This allows it to respond to inappropriate behaviors in a variety of ways that can be suited to specific offenses and records of offenders. The system works especially well where offenses differ so greatly that blanket sanctions or detailed series of punishments are impossible. This does not mean that first-reported offenses should, as a matter of course, receive minimum penalties. The sanction must always be determined by the seriousness of the offenses.

  This point became clear in a recent case in which a professor at a Midwestern university was accused of propositioning and sexually assaulting a student. Two of her classmates witnessed his behavior and initially supported her complaint. Later they withdrew their support and urged the student to drop her grievance. As the time for the formal hearing approached, the two revealed to the complainant that the professor had asked them to lie about what they knew and to serve as character witnesses for him. During the hearing the faculty member argued that this was "a first offense" and should be treated with leniency. But in cases like this where single episodes reveal serious abuses of students, penalties should be equally serious.

- When a complaint against a faculty member is validated and he has a previous history of sexual harassment, that record must be considered in determining punishment. This course is morally advisable because it sends a message to the campus. The legal implications, however, are equally important. As sexual harassment law becomes better understood, it is increasingly apparent that the courts expect institutions/employers to keep records and to review the full context of grievances. The history of complaints against an individual becomes very important. "What do you know?" and "When did you know it?" are critical questions for institutions when sexual harassment cases are examined by agencies or the courts. An organization that ignores its own memory makes itself vulnerable.

- The institution has a right and responsibility to deal discreetly with grievances, but it cannot allow self-interest and concern for the guilty to become disproportionate. If it confuses discretion with compromise, the result is a permissive moral atmosphere in which proven offenders feel freer than ever and students become even more frightened to protest.

PROFESSORS

Feelings of vulnerability extend to male professors as well as to women students and institutions. Those who do not sexually harass, clearly the majority, perceive themselves to be in precarious positions. They have been taught strange things about the opposite sex, the behavior of "masculine" men, academic freedom, and collegiality. Suddenly they are being asked to interfere in colleagues' relationships with students and to decide whether peers' notions of masculinity have diminished their professionalism. They also worry that they can somehow be confused with sexual harassers. What should their positions be?

- First, they must acknowledge that sexual harassment does exist and that it does not imply guilt by association. Denial of a problem does not make it go away. Admission that some members of a group behave aberrantly does not mean that all are guilty. The fact is that the distinctions between harassers and their peers are very definite. There are few closet harassers. Most have long, although undocumented, records — sometimes years — of clearly questionable behavior. In most academic departments, there are too many shared students, too close an environment, too much discussion, too small a space for complete invisibility or confusion about who is a genuine offender.
- Faculty must identify the real culprits in this dilemma facing their profession. The culprit is not women voicing frustration about an abuse that has for years been suffered in silence. It is an aberrant few college professors whose activities embarrass the profession and do great harm to students. Faculty's first responsibility is to students, not to the people who share their offices. There is nothing admirable in the "my colleague, right or wrong" mentality.
- Faculty should recognize that attempts to portray sexual harassment as a threat to academic freedom are unfounded. Sexual harassment has nothing to do with academic freedom; there are tested, defined procedures to protect those whose academic freedoms may have been violated. The angst associated with separating these two issues is largely academic theatrics and filibuster. Faculty must not be swayed by contentions that sexual harassers act because of "extenuating

circumstances" or ignorance. There are crises in every life; they do not justify abuse of innocent victims. The contention that an offender "didn't know" his behaviors were offensive is even more curious. The irony of faculty defending someone on the basis of ignorance — an excuse they would never tolerate in the classroom — is ludicrous. College professors are not fond of being called stupid, but the cost of this defense strategy may be just that. In the 1980s, educated men and women recognize that they must reevalute their assumptions about and behaviors toward one another. The relationships in academe are no exception. Such reevaluation is not painful — it is ordinary business.

- If faculty fear that increased attention to sexual harassment makes them somehow suspect, there are simple procedures they can follow:

  a. References to female students' physical appearances are unnecessary. Male faculty members do not compliment male students on their bodies or clothing, and there is really no reason they must do so with women.

  b. Comments about students' races and religions are not considered "teaching techniques," and those about sex are no different. It is possible to make a point, to provide an example, or to add humor without offending or embarrassing students.

  c. Physical contact with students is acceptable when it is appropriate. Students do not scurry to register grievances against a professor who at the end of class pats someone on the shoulder because she is upset over a grade. They *do* express fear and hostility when intimacy is forced on them. Most people learn very early that where, when, and how they touch a member of the opposite sex can have serious implications. A person able to earn a Ph.D. is surely bright enough to insure that his intentions are clear, the circumstances proper, and his gestures appropriate when he touches a student.

  d. Contacts outside class deserve thought. Student-teacher conferences should be held in appropriate settings. Any digressions from normal faculty settings must be weighed against the possibility of misinterpretations. College professors must be able to make educated judgments about the intentions and emotional stability of students. If a situation is potentially threatening, a colleague can always be asked to sit in on student-teacher conferences.

  e. Most faculty internalize early in their career, usually when they are apprentice graduate students, the standards for acceptable teacher behavior. Some academic departments, recognizing the need to instruct graduate assistants who may be teaching undergraduate courses, give orientation sessions. These can provide advice about appropriate relationships as well as about keeping records, reporting attendance problems, and detecting plagiarism. Advice on self-protection is regularly shared and usually well learned by the time an individual is hired as an assistant professor.

DEANS AND DEPARTMENT HEADS

Despite their roles as campus leaders, some deans and department heads convince themselves that they do not have the authority or responsibility for intervening in sexual harassment problems. The administrator who is confused or uneasy about the issue finds powerlessness the most comfortable posture, the easy way out. Nowhere in his or her job description is there a charge to talk with faculty about their sexual behaviors or about student rumors. Nowhere is a dean told how to respond when irate parents demand that someone "do something" about a professor who has propositioned their daughter.

There are traditional assumptions about the roles of deans and department heads: they organize the academic chores, appoint committees, run meetings, evaluate faculty for promotion and tenure, and collect data on performance. On campuses where faculty are unionized, there may be specific language in the collective bargaining contract about deans' and department heads' obligations and limitations. But there is a whole set of activities that are unaddressed in any formal way. Campuses with painstakingly detailed civil service rules and requirements for clerks and custodians may have no carefully worded job descriptions for administrators. The common assumption has been that the nature of the job is self-evident, that leadership is hard to define.

Some embrace this absence of specificity as an excuse for inaction in cases of sexual harassment. But in other controversial areas such as departmental feuds, political battles, or student disruptions, administrators use it to claim their rights and even obligations to take active roles. Too often sexual harassment issues elicit the opposite response. The hesitancy is understandable. Sexual harassment is, in a sense, a "new" concern. There are few models or precedents to guide deans and department heads.

But none of this is sufficient to justify deans' and department heads' inactivity. They can and must play direct roles in resolving questions of sexual harassment within their domains. One of the most frequent questions raised by academic departments in sexual harassment workshops is, "How can I talk to a professor without judging the truth or falsity of a student's complaint?" Following are some possible approaches:

- The adminsitrator can and should, in a positive tone, alert the faculty member to any complaints made against him. A dean or department head can make a nonjudgmental observation: "I want you to know that there has been a complaint about your behavior toward women students, a perception of inappropriate comments or action. You might want to think about how that perception can be avoided." There is no blaming, no assertion of guilt in such a statement. No action is threatened or taken; the faculty member is simply alerted and can respond or not. Intrusions and threats are distinguishable from positive interventions and expressions of professional concern. The administrator needs to have confidence that his or her faculty can tell the difference.

- If a student's complaint is very serious or is part of a history of such charges, the approach must be more direct. The faculty member should be informed about disciplinary actions that may be taken. The illegality and inappropriateness of such behavior should be clearly mentioned. The conversation can be deliberate without being determinant: "Have you considered the professional consequences if this student files a formal grievance? Are you aware that it could result in . . . ?"

- The dean or department head should rely on his or her own professionalism. Other judgments of a faculty member need not be "tainted" if a sexual harassment complaint is addressed. The minds of deans and department heads are filled with all sorts of impressions — a drunken scene at a faculty party, a pass at the dean's wife, financial problems, medical difficulties, late grades, a student grievance over a grade. Administrators know the difference between their personal reactions or suspicions and what they should include in their official judgments of professional competence. Sexual harassment charges are no different. They can be treated with the same objectivity, discretion, and judiciousness that characterize other administrative perceptions.

- Attention should be given to the possibility that members of racial, religious, or national minorities tend to be suspect in organizations. While nothing excuses harassing behavior, it is worthwhile to remember that some individuals are more vulnerable to scrutiny than others.

- The administrator should recognize that both the student and the faculty member deserve support, professional treatment, objective assessment of the problem, and decisive judgment. Administrators who accept responsibility for the actions of their faculty and the well-being of their students do not wait for gossip to erupt into formal grievances and adverse publicity. That is not what leadership, impartiality, or professional propriety are about. What they *do* imply is that those in authority must be willing to act and lead.

CONCLUSION

The resolution of sexual harassment will come when it is made the concern and responsibility of everyone who is associated with the institution. If the climate on campus is to change, the men and women who work there must lead the way.

In *The Leaning Ivory Tower*, Warren Bennis' observations about higher education are correct:

> Our inability to transcend the dangerous notion that we don't wash our dirty linen in public verges on the schizophrenic. It implies not only that dissent is bad but that our public institutions are made up not of men but of saints, who never engage in vulgar and offensive activities... In fact, organizations are vulgar, sweaty, plebeian; if they are to be viable, they must create an institutional environment where a fool can be called a fool and all actions and motivations are duly and closely scrutinized for the inevitable human flaws and failures. In a democracy, meanness, dullness, and corruption are always amply represented. They are not entitled to protection from the same rude challenges that such qualities must face in the "real" world. When banal politeness is assigned a higher value than accountability or truthfulness, the result is an Orwellian world where the symbols of speech are manipulated to create false realities.[4]

"Banal politeness" and "false realities" cannot disguise the truth about most administrators and faculty members. At base, they are adept "people-watchers," a highly self-conscious lot, politically and professionally sensitive to others. This explains the unwritten codes governing their behaviors. There is, for example, no formal supervision in the typical college classroom. Yet the faculty member who intends to keep his job meets classes regularly, evaluates students objectively, prepares class presentations, refrains from denigrating colleagues, avoids appearing bigoted or racist. It is time to add to that list "refrains from sexist behaviors."

Higher education needs what Margaret Mead termed "new taboos" in her 1978 article "A Proposal: We Need Taboos on Sex at Work":

What should we — what can we — do about sexual harassment on the job? . . . As I see it, it isn't more laws that we need now, but new taboos . . .

When we examine how any society works, it becomes clear that it is precisely the basic taboos — the deeply and intensely felt prohibitions against "unthinkable" behavior — that keep the social system in balance . . .

The complaints, the legal remedies and the support institutions developed by women are all part of the response to the new conception of women's rights. But I believe we need something much more pervasive, a climate of opinion that includes men as well as women, and that will affect not only adult relations and behavior on the job but also the expectations about the adult world that guide our children's progress into that world.

What we need, in fact, are new taboos, that are appropriate to the new society we are struggling to create — taboos that will operate within the work setting as once they operated within the household. Neither men nor women should expect that sex can be used either to victimize women who need to keep their jobs or to keep women from advancement or to help men advance their own careers. A taboo enjoins.[5]

Taboos enjoin. They make demands. They establish that some forms of behavior are "unthinkable." Creating a taboo on the campus means that male professors must establish new male norms. Male faculty will have to let each other know that the campus is not a locker room, that sexual harassment does not prove virility, that abusing professional authority to exact sexual favors makes a man not more but less masculine. Women faculty who have accepted or ignored harassment of their students must cease being passive and accommodating in their male-dominated campus world.

College professors must be willing to say directly to sexual harassers what they already say behind their backs. If there is such a thing as collegiality, faculty should feel free, even obligated, to deal personally with the issue. The notion that academic protocol prohibits someone from warning another of threats to his reputation is distorted. A colleague feels concern for a co-worker, or he does not. If he suspects that the individual is unjustly accused, then he must alert him for his own protection. A teacher either feels concern for students and the reputation of the institution, or not. If there is the suspicion that a charge against a colleague is accurate, the responsibility is to inform the colleague so that he may alter his behavior.

Because so many academicians — both male and female — have allowed harassment to become a private rather than a professional consideration, they have been inarticulate and naive in their discussions. Sexual harassment has been a titillating closet issue because professionals have confused their personal conflicts about male-female relationships with an institutional concern. When academics learn to recognize sexual harassment as abusive behavior — an aberrant manifestation of a need for power, prestige, recognition, or acceptance — they can discuss it rationally, as they would any other problem in their institutions.

The taboo has implications for students as well. Like faculty, they do not like to assume personal responsibility for the campus environment. But the people most affected by the problem must take the lead in remedying it. If students were to take a more aggressive stand, sexual harassers would be far less likely to act and to go unpunished. Women who have experienced harassment and yet allow a handful of peers to complain for an entire group take the easy way out. Student newspapers that do in-depth reporting on campus athletics and editorializing on federal economic programs shirk their responsibilities if they ignore sexual harassment on their own campuses. The roles that individual students and their organizations can and should assume are at present controversial. But one point is clear — when they have involved themselves, students have made a difference. For groups without power, there is always safety and visibility in numbers.

The unique characteristic of higher education, which sets it apart from and, to many, above other institutions in society is its ability to analyze and understand complexity. The pursuit of knowledge — whether in scientific, social, technological, or humanistic realms — is undertaken with exquisite concern for detail, innuendo, subtlety, and implication. Sophisticated inquiry is what higher education does better than any other institution, not because of its ivory-tower purity but because of the intrinsic pride academics have in acquiring understanding and communicating it to others.

But forced to deal with sexual harassment, higher education has behaved as if it is incapable of sophisticated inquiry and must rely instead on second-grade approaches to determine what is knowable and believable. Confronted with cases of harassment, the same minds that move gracefully through dazzling theoretical issues revert to an eighteenth-century dunking-stool standard of truth. This lapse cannot be explained as inability to apply complex rationality to the housekeeping issues of higher education. The explanation, instead, is that cultural patterns of society hold firmer sway than intellectual method, that sexism and stereotyping overcome sophisticated rationality.

It is possible to apply academe's own rigorous standards of inquiry to understanding sexual harassment. The very act of analyzing the problem should lead naturally to an intellectual and psychological breakthrough for institutions, administrators, faculty, and students. To learn is not to wallow in self-recrimination over past failures and negligence. Genuine education means change; it involves understanding the past in order to design a better future.

In the late 1960s the image of the campus as a sanctuary where fresh-faced youngsters strolled tree-lined paths between the chapel and library vanished forever. With the dissolution of the myth went the fiction of the benign, fatherly professor. Neither was a great loss. Fantasies about real places and real people are never as compelling as the truth. The truth about higher education is that it is struggling to discover as well as to preserve an identity in a world which it did not anticipate and for which it is, in many ways, ill prepared. The campus is not inhabited by omniscient deities; it never was. Its people are no more or less flawed than the rest of us.

The campus is a mirror held up to our society, and in it all are reflected. If it succeeds in curing itself of sexual harassment, higher education will prove that human beings and the institutions they create, while far from perfect, are nevertheless capable of coping with their limitations. If it should fail, no amount of rationalization will restore its lost myth or compensate for its harsh reality.

APPENDIXES

I : Title VII Guidelines on Sexual Harassment

These federal guidelines, enacted in 1980, are still in effect.

EQUAL EMPLOYMENT OPPORTUNITY COMMISSION

Discrimination Because of Sex Under Title VII of the Civil Rights Act of 1964, as Amended; Adoption of Final Interpretive Guidelines

AGENCY: Equal Employment Opportunity Commission.

ACTION: Final Amendment to Guidelines on Discrimination Because of Sex.

SUMMARY: On April 11, 1980, the Equal Employment Opportunity Commission published the Interim Guidelines on sexual harassment as an amendment to the Guidelines on Discrimination Because of Sex, 29 CFR part 1604.11, 45 FR 25024. This amendment will re-affirm that sexual harassment is an unlawful employment practice. The EEOC received public comments for 60 days subsequent to the date of publication of the Interim Guidelines. As a result of the comments and the analysis of them, these Final Guidelines were drafted.

EFFECTIVE DATE: November 10, 1980.

PART 1604 — GUIDELINES ON DISCRIMINATION BECAUSE OF SEX

§ 1604.11 Sexual harassment.

(a) Harassment on the basis of sex is a violation of Sec. 703 of Title VII.[1] Unwelcome sexual advances, requests for sexual favors, and other verbal or physical conduct of a sexual nature constitute sexual harassment when (1)

189

submission to such conduct is made either explicitly or implicitly a term or condition of an individual's employment (2) submission to or rejection of such conduct by an individual is used as the basis for employment decisions affecting such individual, or (3) such conduct has the purpose or effect of unreasonably interfering with an individual's work performance or creating an intimidating, hostile, or offensive working environment.

(b) In determining whether alleged conduct constitutes sexual harassment, the Commission will look at the record as a whole and at the totality of the circumstances, such as the nature of the sexual advances and the context in which the alleged incidents occurred. The determination of the legality of a particular action will be made from the facts, on a case by case basis.

(c) Applying general Title VII principles, an employer, employment agency, joint apprenticeship committee or labor organization (hereinafter collectively referred to as "employer") is responsible for its acts and those of its agents and supervisory employees with respect to sexual harassment regardless of whether the specific acts complained of were authorized or even forbidden by the employer and regardless of whether the employer knew or should have known of their occurence. The Commission will examine the circumstances of the particular employment relationship and the job functions performed by the individual in determining whether an individual acts in either a supervisory or agency capacity.

(d) With respect to conduct between fellow employees, an employer is responsible for acts of sexual harassment in the workplace where the employer (or its agents or supervisory employees) knows or should have known of the conduct, unless it can show that it took immediate and appropriate corrective action.

(e) An employer may also be responsible for the acts of non-employees, with respect to sexual harassment of employees in the workplace, where the employer (or its agents or supervisory employees) knows or should have known of the conduct and fails to take immediate and appropriate corrective action. In reviewing these cases the Commission will consider the extent of the employer's control and any other legal responsibility which the employer may have with respect to the conduct of such non-employees.

(f) Prevention is the best tool for the elimination of sexual harassment. An employer should take all steps necessary to prevent sexual harassment from occurring, such as affirmatively raising the subject, expressing strong disapproval, developing appropriate sanctions, informing employees of their right to raise and how to raise the issue of harassment under Title VII, and developing methods to sensitize all concerned.

(g) Other related practices: Where employment opportunities or benefits are granted because of an individual's submission to the employer's sexual advances or requests for sexual favors, the employer may be held liable for unlawful sex discrimination against other persons who were qualified for but denied that employment opportunity or benefit.

[1]The principles involved here continue to apply to race, color, religion or other origin.

Reprinted from:
Federal Register / Vol. 45, No. 219 / Monday, November 10, 1980 / Rules and Regulations 74676-74677

II : A Student's Guide to Legal

This guide was published by the National Advisory Council on Women's Educational Programs in 1980.

Remedy	Description	Types of Benefit/Sanction
Title IX, 1972 Education Amendments	Federal law prohibiting sex discrimination in education; complaints may be filed with any Federal agency which grants assistance to the school, or private suit may be initiated.	Agencies can require school to correct problem or face cut-off of Federal funds; suit may result in injunctive relief; some possibility of damages through litigation; successful plaintiffs eligible for attorneys' fees awards under Attorneys Fees Act.
Civil Lawsuits	Tort lawsuits; breach of contract.	Financial compensation for any losses or physical/emotional/mental injury; injunctions.
Rape and other criminal statutes	Varies by State; usually includes sexual assault, assault, and battery claims; prosecution at discretion of police authorities, public prosecutor.	Fines imprisonment.
State Civil Rights Laws	Prohibit sex-based discrimination; usually enforced by Human Rights Commissions; great variance from State to State.	Varies; in some States can include cease and desist orders, jury trial award of damages.

Reprinted from the Report on Sexual Harassment on Campus, National Advisory Council on Women's Educational Programs.

Remedies for Sexual Harassment

Duration

With some exceptions, agencies are required to resolve complaints within 195 days of receipt of complaint; if school does not come into compliance, enforcement can take several years; litigation may provide quick short-term relief, but suits will take a year or more to complete.

Drawbacks

Only the Education Department, Department of Energy and Department of Agriculture have final regulations; other agencies may not accept complaints; only the Education Department has full-scale enforcement program; no hard policy from any agency on coverage of harassment issues, so complaints may languish while agencies work out policy problems; no real judicial history to provide precedent; risky.

Varies; 2-3 years likely where damages are sought.

Expensive (fees come out of, and may exceed the amount of any damages); slow.

1 year.

Compensation for victim possible but unlikely; prosecution unlikely in "minor" crimes without witnesses and/ or strong corroboration; great emotional strain; convicted offenders from upper socio-economic classes likely to receive only suspended sentences or court ordered therapy even where rape is involved.

Great variation; 6 months to 3 years.

Differ from State to State; may be difficult to secure agreement that sexual harassment of students is covered.

III : Statement on Sexual Harassment, American Council on Education

This letter and the statement that follows it were sent from the office of the president, Robert H. Atwell, to members of the American Council on Education in April 1989.

In December 1986, ACE published a statement on sexual harassment in the workplace. At that time, the United States Supreme Court had recently decided the case of *Meritor Savings Bank, FSB,* v. *Vinson,*[1] an important decision that firmly established a remedy under Title VII of the Civil Rights Act of 1964 for individuals exposed to a hostile or offensive work environment, even though such an environment did not result in the tangible loss of a job or other employment benefit. Our statement stressed the importance of developing an effective campus program addressing sexual harassment, and suggested specific elements to be included in a sexual harassment program.

Since the Supreme Court decision in the *Meritor* case, there has been substantial litigation in the area of "hostile environment" sexual harassment, and definitions and standards for determining liability have been more clearly defined. Recently, the Equal Employment Opportunity Commission issued guidelines to its field office personnel for use in evaluating sexual harassment claims under Title VII [. . .].

---

1. 477 U.S. 57 (1986).

194

The frequency of litigation involving sexual harassment claims and the EEOC's recent policy guidelines accentuate the importance of continued attention to the issue of sexual harassment by every ACE member institution. Now is a propitious time to review the key points made in the December 1986 statement. It stresses that your institution should take the steps necessary to establish and maintain an effective sexual harassment policy that incorporates a definition of sexual harassment, a strong policy statement against sexual harassment in any form, an effective communication and educational program and an accessible grievance procedure. A copy of the 1986 statement is included in this document for your information.

The principles emphasized in 1986 are still viable. ACE has made no substantial changes in the recommendations except for some additions and changes in the resource materials section of this document. The EEOC's recent policy guidelines and litigation do clarify institutional obligations with regard to avoiding and dealing with claims of sexual harassment on campus. Reviewing some of the areas where the law has been clarified may assist you in focusing review of your current sexual harassment program.

The most important developments in the sexual harassment cases concern the circumstances under which an employer will be held responsible for sexual harassment committed by supervisors or co-employees. In order to properly analyze this area, it is necessary to divide harassment claims into two categories: (1) "quid pro quo" cases, or cases where a supervisor has made or threatened to make a decision affecting the victim's employment based on whether the victim submits to sexual demands, and (2) "hostile environment" cases, as recognized in *Meritor,* which include the creation of a hostile or offensive work environment based upon sex. In the former situation, the courts and the EEOC generally conclude that an employer is almost always responsible for acts of a supervisor, because the supervisor is making decisions that directly affect a specific condition of the victim's employment.

In the area of "hostile environment" sexual harassment, an employer is much more in control of its own destiny, and the courts and the EEOC have made clear since 1986 that the suggestions contained in our December 1986 statement concerning the importance of developing a campus program on sexual harassment, including an accessible grievance procedure, are now more critical than ever. The general test for employer liability in "hostile environment" cases is whether the employer knew or should have known of the alleged sexual harassment and failed to take immediate and appropriate corrective action.[2] Of course, if an employer has direct knowledge of the existence of a hostile working environment, and takes no action to correct it, the employer would be liable for that hostile environment. Moreover, the EEOC's recent guidelines state that the EEOC will impute to the employer the responsibility for a supervisor's actions in creating a hostile work environment where the employer failed to establish an explicit policy against sexual harassment and did not have a reasonably available avenue that victims could use to complain as well as to get someone in authority to investigate and remedy the problem. Significantly, the EEOC's guidelines, in conformity with judicial opinion since *Meritor*, will generally not seek to impose liability on an employer who maintains "a strong, widely disseminated, and consistently enforced employer policy against sexual harassment," backed by an "effective complaint procedure." It is therefore critical that your policies and procedures are clear and unequivocable in their condemnation of sexual harassment and their creation of accessible grievance procedure. If your program does not meet these tests, *you risk liability for hostile environment sexual harassment, despite the fact that you may have had no actual knowledge of its existence.*[3]

During the years since we issued our sexual harassment statement, the courts and the EEOC have also defined more clearly just what it is that comprises an illegal "hostile environment" under Title VII. In *Meritor*, the Supreme Court explained that in order for hostile environment sexual harassment to violate Title VII, it must be "sufficiently severe or pervasive 'to alter the conditions of [the victim's] employment and create an abusive working environment.' "[4] Since *Meritor*, the courts have developed a list of factors to be considered in determining whether an allegedly hostile working environment meets this general standard articulated by the Supreme Court. One court has suggested that four factors be considered in determining whether a hostile work environment exists:

1. Unwelcome sexual acts or words. Unwelcome physical touching, generally, is more offensive than unwelcome verbal abuse. However,

---

2. *Jones* v. *Flagship International*, 793 F.2d 714 (5th Cir. 1986).
3. *See* e.g., *Yates* v. *AVCO Corp.* 819 F.2d 630 (6th Cir. 1987). (Employer was held liable for sexual harassment where its policy against sexual harassment was vague and its grievance procedure required the employee to report sexual harassment incidents to immediate supervisors, in this case, the harasser.)
4. *Meritor*, 477 U.S. at 56.

in specific situations the type of language used may be more offensive than a type of physical touching.

2. The frequency of the offensive encounters. It is considered less likely that a hostile work environment exists when the offensive encounters occur only occasionally, than if the encounters occur on a regular basis.
3. The total number of days over which all of the offensive meetings occur.
4. The context in which the sexually harassing conduct occurred.[5]

The nonexistence of one of these factors does not, in and of itself, prevent a Title VII action.

It is clear that developments since the *Meritor* case, including the EEOC's recent guidelines, have placed increasing emphasis on the problem of sexual harassment. Our status as institutions of higher education presents ethical and moral considerations that require a special emphasis on the eradication of sexual harassment on our campuses. These considerations, along with the practical need to reduce the chance of exposure to liability for sexual harassment, strongly counsel in favor of establishing and enforcing a campus policy on sexual harassment.

As we suggested in 1986, your policy against sexual harassment should be clearly and regularly communicated to all supervisory and non-supervisory employees. Your strong disapproval of sexual harassment should be emphasized, and the sanctions for harassment should be explained. Your grievance procedure for victims of alleged sexual harassment should be designed to encourage victims of harassment to come forward, and should not require an alleged victim to complain first to an offending supervisor. The details of a good campus program on sexual harassment are contained in the attached statement. If you create, communicate, and enforce a viable program on sexual harassment, you will fulfill the dual goal of reducing the occurrence of sexual harassment on campus, as well as minimizing your liability for sexual harassment if and when it occurs.

I urge you to give this issue your full attention and to make clear that sexual harassment of any type will not be tolerated, and to address these issues as a top administrative priority.

Our work in this area is being coordinated by [the] director of

---

5. *See Ross* v. *Double Diamond, Inc.*, 45 FEP Cas. 313, 216 (N.D. Tex. 1987). *See also Scott* v. *Sears, Roebuck & Co.*, 798 F.2d 210, 213 (7th Cir. 1986).

ACE's Office of Women in Higher Education and our general counsel. If you have any questions, please call them.

SEXUAL HARASSMENT ON CAMPUS: SUGGESTIONS FOR REVIEWING CAMPUS POLICY AND EDUCATIONAL PROGRAMS

Since the civil rights movement of the '60s, our consciousness has been raised about the issue of sexual harassment. It is easy to assume that the problem is under control. Wrong. In a recent study done at Harvard University, for example, substantial numbers of women across the academic spectrum reported that they had experienced sexual harassment. Thirty-two percent of tenured female professors, 49 percent of those without tenure, 41 percent of female graduate students, and 34 percent of undergraduate women reported encountering sexual harassment in some form from a person in authority at least once while at the university. These figures correspond with a number of other students that report that between 20 and 30 percent of undergraduate women and 30 to 40 percent of graduate women experience some form of sexual harassment.

INTRODUCTION
This statement is designed to provide guidance to colleges and universities in reviewing or establishing policies, procedures, and programs on sexual harassment.

The recent Supreme Court decision on *Meritor Savings Bank, FSB* v. *Vinson* is reviewed and general guidelines for establishing effective campus programs on sexual harassment are presented.

THE *MERITOR SAVINGS BANK, FSB* V. *VINSON,* DECISION
In *Meritor Savings Bank, FSB* v. *Vinson* (June 1986), the Supreme Court unanimously ruled that sexual harassment in the workplace which causes a hostile or offensive job environment is actionable under Title VII of the Civil Rights Act of 1964, even if it does not result in job or promotion loss.

The Court declared that an employee need not suffer any tangible economic loss to bring such a claim. The ruling enunciates the conditions under which sexual harassment may violate federal civil rights laws, and serves as an important reminder of the need to establish policies that clearly prohibit sexual harassment. Further, the ruling suggests procedures for limiting an employer's liability for sexual harassment claims.

The decision in *Vinson* concluded that a hostile work environment, created by the unwelcome sexual advances of a supervisor, amounts to illegal employment discrimination. The case also makes clear that whether or not sex-related conduct is "voluntary" in the sense that an individual is not forced against his or her will to participate, it will not serve as a defense to a sexual harassment suit brought under Title VII where the conduct is unwelcome. However, the Court declined to issue definitive guidelines regarding the scope of employer liability. The Court further stated that employers could not use ignorance of the harassment experience as a complete shield from liability. The existence of a general or a harassment-specific grievance policy also would not necessarily provide an adequate shield.

Although the *Vinson* decision applies specifically to employment, it is prudent to examine the case and its implications for the campus setting. This provides an opportunity to renew institutional commitment to eliminating sexual harassment, or to develop an institution-wide program to address the problem.

THE IMPORTANCE OF DEVELOPING A CAMPUS PROGRAM ON SEXUAL HARASSMENT

The educational mission of a college or university is to foster an open learning and working environment. The ethical obligation to provide an environment that is free from sexual harassment and from the fear that it may occur is implicit. The entire collegiate community suffers when sexual harassment is allowed to pervade the academic atmosphere through neglect, the lack of a policy prohibiting it, or the lack of educational programs designed to clarify appropriate professional behavior on campus and to promote understanding of what constitutes sexual harassment. Each institution has the obligation, for moral as well as legal reasons, to develop policies, procedures, and programs that protect students and employees from sexual harassment and to establish an environment in which such unacceptable behavior will not be tolerated.

Taking preventative steps can help shield the institution from potential liability as well as address legitimate constituent concerns.

KEY COMPONENTS OF EFFECTIVE CAMPUS PROGRAMS

An effective campus program on sexual harassment has several key elements affecting both policy and procedure. These elements can also be found in successful business and government programs. They are:

1. *A basic definition:* What constitutes sexual harassment?
2. *A strong policy statement:* Sexual harassment will not be tolerated.
3. *Effective communication:* Channels exist for informing students, faculty, staff, and administrators about the campus policy against sexual harassment.
4. *Education:* Educational programs are designed to help all members of the community recognize and discourage sexual harassment.
5. *An accessible grievance procedure:* Alternative methods of initiating complaints and a procedure to ensure the rights of all parties are protected as much as possible should be provided. Complaints are investigated and resolved promptly.

Common Elements of Sexual Harassment
The task of developing a basic statement of what constitutes sexual harassment is an important part of the educative process for the campus. This paper does not attempt to give a model definition suitable to all campuses, but instead presents some of the elements to consider in developing a basic statement.

Sexual harassment is a form of sex discrimination which is illegal under Title VII of the Civil Rights Act of 1964 for employees and under Title IX of the Elementary/Secondary Education Act of 1972 for students. Some states' laws and/or regulations also render it illegal.

Sexual harassment can be verbal, visual, or physical. It can be overt, as in the suggestion that a person could get an "A" if a particular sexual favor is granted. Or, it can consist of persistent, unwanted attempts to change a professional relationship to a personal one. Sexual harassment can range from inappropriate put-downs of individual persons, unwelcome sexual flirtations, or classes of people to serious physical abuses such as rape. It is coersive and threatening; it creates an atmosphere that is not conducive to teaching, learning, and working.

The University of Wisconsin has taken these elements and turned them into a working policy statement, which here serves as an example. This policy definition is contained in a document that includes additional descriptions of what constitutes sexual harassment and how the policy will be implemented.

For general policy purposes, sexual harassment may be described as unwelcome sexual advances, requests for sexual favors, and other physical and expressive behavior of a sexual nature where: (1) Submission to such conduct is made either explicitly or implicitly a term or condition of an individual's employment or education; (2) Submission to or rejection of such conduct by an individual is used as the basis for academic or employment decisions affecting the individual; or (3) Such conduct has the purpose or effect of substantially interfering with an individual's academic or professional performance or creating an intimidating, hostile or demeaning employment or educational environment.

University of Wisconsin, May 7, 1981

Grievance Procedures

If a general grievance procedure is not already in place, a complaint and reporting system should be created. It should allow students and employees to report harassment free from threats of reprisals and should adequately protect the anonymity of all parties involved. The design of the grievance procedure should include a provision that allows the complaining party to avoid her or his immediate supervisor or department head, who frequently, as in *Vinson*, may be the source of the problem.

In some situations it may be impossible to determine whether the sexually harassing conduct did or did not occur. Therefore, substantial sensitivity and confidentiality should be accorded in investigation.

GUIDELINES FOR DEVELOPING A CAMPUS PROGRAM ON SEXUAL HARASSMENT

The following guidelines may be helpful in improving a current sexual harassment policy/program, or designing a new one:

1. Develop a strong policy prohibiting sexual harassment. A formal policy should be in place that defines sexual harassment and includes a statement as to why it is important for your institution to prevent sexual harassment. The policy may be more effective if it is endorsed by the faculty governing body and monitored by a committee of that body.
2. Develop a grievance procedure that encourages the reporting of incidents of sexual harassment, that allows first for informal resolution and then, if the process fails, for formal resolution.
3. Disseminate the policy to all faculty, staff, administrators, and students as well as to those who contract to do business on

campus including those agencies, businesses, education groups, etc., that provide students with internships. The policy and supporting materials could be included in the student handbook; course catalog; course timetable; employee handbook; administrative, faculty, and staff handbooks; pamphlets; institutional campus contracts; and could be incorporated into the academic governance code.

4. Develop a method for informing new staff, faculty, students, and administrators about the policy and for including them in all education programs. Orientation programs and other in-house workshops and seminars may serve as appropriate forums.

5. Create and keep current a campus-wide educational program designed to help all members of the campus community to understand, prevent, and combat sexual harassment. Brochures describing what kinds of behavior constitute sexual harassment and what the person who is being harassed should do about it have been used very successfully on a number of campuses. (See campus resource listing below.)

6. Provide additional training to supervisory personnel, especially deans, department heads, and administrative and student affairs staff, through workshops and seminars. Student and collegiate governance structures may be appropriate outlets for ongoing training and discussion.

7. Appoint a coordinator to handle reports of harassment. The ombudsperson, affirmative action officer, a student affairs staff member, or a combination of people in these positions, could serve in such capacity. This person or persons should be known to students, faculty, staff, and administrators, and be highly respected by the entire campus community.

8. Adopt, publicize, and enforce penalties for violations of the policy.

9. Investigate and resolve complaints promptly.

10. Keep written records, but take precautions to protect the privacy of all parties involved.

11. Take action to resolve claims even if a discrimination charge has been filed with EEOC or a state EEO agency.

12. Publish the results of resolved complaints on a periodic basis, making certain that all information to be used protects the privacy of parties involved.

IV : Presidential Statement and Policy on Sexual Harassment, University of Minnesota

The following letter to the University of Minnesota community from President Nils Hasselmo, dated January 20, 1989, is an example of executive leadership and support for sexual harassment concerns. The letter was distributed with the University Policies and Procedures on Sexual Harassment, reprinted here. The policy statement is an example of a comprehensive institutional statement on sexual harassment and includes commentary on consensual relationships.

The enclosed brochure deals with an important and troubling issue in our society and in our University: sexual harassment. There are few of us who would disagree that sexual harassment is offensive and inappropriate, that it is quite properly illegal in our society, and that the University had good reason first in 1981 and then again in 1984 to adopt strong policies proscribing such behavior.

The difficulty is that while most of us would agree to these statements in the abstract, sexual harassment remains a complicated subject. It is complicated because the harassment takes many forms and too often has been accepted or excused or explained as part of our ordinary experience or behavior. It is complicated because the term suggests an easily identifiable, aggressive, conscious act and oftentimes it is considerably more subtle than that.

The enclosed brochure is intended to illuminate some of these issues, to explain the University's definition of sexual harassment and the policies toward it, and to provide through discussion and examples a better understanding of the problem.

I invite your particular attention to the section on consenting relationships. Because terms like "sexual harassment" and "power differential" suggest conscious and threatening circumstances, the sense in which consensual relationships can fall under the category of sexual harassment is sometimes misunderstood or lost. Our policy states that ". . . it will be exceedingly difficult to prove immunity (from a charge of sexual harassment) on grounds of mutual consent." The interpretation we place on that statement is that mutual consent implies a consent free from conscious or unconscious negative psychological or material factors, some of which are almost always inherent in a relationship, for example, between faculty member and student. It implies further that a faculty member or another person practicing as a professional within the institution should be expected to be very sensitive to such issues and, therefore, should bear a large fraction of the responsibility for the negative outcomes of a relationship that appears, superficially, to be consenting.

There are other important points in the policy that warrant your careful study. Let me emphasize that sexual harassment is a real problem at the University. Each year we deal with a number of cases that affect people's lives and careers and destroy some part of our fragile academic environment. I hope that if you have questions or suggestions as to how we could improve the brochure or how we might better inform the community about this problem, you will contact [. . .] our Office of Equal Opportunity and Affirmative Action.

UNIVERSITY POLICIES AND PROCEDURES

In some cases, union contracts modify policies and procedures printed below. For additional information about these situations, consult the appropriate office listed in the resource section of this brochure.

POLICY STATEMENT ON SEXUAL HARASSMENT*
Sexual harassment in any situation is reprehensible. It subverts the mission of the University, and threatens the careers of students,

---

* As approved by the University Senate, May 17, 1984

faculty, and staff. It is viewed as a violation of Title VII of the 1964 Civil Rights Act. Sexual harassment will not be tolerated in this University. For purposes of this policy, sexual harassment is defined as follows:

> Unwelcome sexual advances, requests for sexual favors, and other verbal or physical conduct of a sexual nature constitutes sexual harassment when (1) submission to such conduct is made either explicitly or implicitly a term or condition of an individual's employment or academic advancement, (2) submission to or rejection of such conduct by an individual is used as the basis for employment decisions or academic decisions affecting such individual, (3) such conduct has the purpose or effect of unreasonably interfering with an individual's work or academic performance or creating an intimidating, hostile, or offensive working or academic environment.

As defined above, sexual harassment is a specific form of discrimination in which power inherent in a faculty member's or supervisor's relationship to his or her students or subordinates is unfairly exploited. While sexual harassment most often takes place in a situation of power differential between persons involved, this policy recognizes also that sexual harassment may occur between persons of the same University status, i.e., student-student, faculty-faculty, staff-staff.

It is the responsibility of the administration of this University to uphold the requirements of Title VII, and with regard to sexual harassment specifically, to insure that this University's working environment be kept free of it. For that purpose, these Senate procedures and guidelines are promulgated to avoid misunderstandings by faculty, students, and staff on (1) the definitions of sexual harassment, and (2) procedures specifically defined to file and resolve complaints of sexual harassment.

Justice requires that the rights and concerns of both complainant and respondent be fully assured. The University shall make every effort to assure and protect these rights, and shall undertake no action that threatens or compromises them.

In determining whether alleged conduct constitutes sexual harassment, those entrusted with carrying out this policy will look at the record as a whole and at the totality of the circumstances, such as the nature of the sexual advances and the context in which the alleged incidents occurred. The determination of the suitability of a particular action will be made from the facts, on a case-by-case basis.

Consensual Relationships

Consenting romantic and sexual relationships between faculty and student or between supervisor and employee, while not expressly forbidden, are generally deemed very unwise. Codes of ethics for most professional associations forbid professional-client sexual relationships. In the view of the Senate, the professor-student relationship is one of professional and client. The respect and trust accorded a professor by a student, as well as the power exercised by the professor in giving praise or blame, grades, recommendations for further study and future employment, etc., greatly diminish the student's actual freedom of choice should sexual favors be included among the professor's other legitimate demands. Therefore, faculty are warned against the possible costs of even an apparently consenting relationship, in regard to the academic efforts of both faculty member and student. A faculty member who enters into a sexual relationship with a student (or supervisor with an employee) where a professional power differential exists must realize that if a charge of sexual harassment is subsequently lodged, it will be exceedingly difficult to prove immunity on grounds of mutual consent.

The administration and the Sexual Harassment Board involved with a charge of sexual harassment shall be expected, in general, to be unsympathetic to a defense based upon consent when the facts establish that a professional faculty-student or supervisor-employee power differential existed within the relationship.

This policy on sexual harassment applies to the entire University and to the conduct of students, civil service persons, and academic staff alike. The responsibility for administering the policy, however, varies with the status of the respondent. If the respondent is a student, the procedures for dealing with complaints will be found in the current regents' policy concerning "A Statement of Standards of Student Conduct Enforceable by University Agencies." If the respondent is a civil service employee, the procedures are outlined in the current "Civil Service Rules."

If the respondent is a member of the academic staff, the procedures are set forth in the document entitled "Procedures for Handling Complaints of Sexual Harassment Against Academic Staff." If the respondent is a student appointed as a graduate assistant (teaching assistant, research assistant, etc.) and was acting in that capacity when the alleged offense occurred, the same procedures will be followed as are required for academic staff, except in regard to appeals.

PROCEDURES FOR HANDLING COMPLAINTS OF
SEXUAL HARASSMENT AGAINST ACADEMIC STAFF*
Scope: These procedures are applicable to complaints by students, civil service persons, and academic staff against academic staff and apply to the conduct of academic staff in their capacity as members of the academic staff of the University of Minnesota. In all proceedings regarding allegations of sexual harassment, the provisions of the Regulations Concerning Faculty Tenure shall be faithfully observed.

I. An Entry-Level Office.
   A. The administration will provide and appropriately publicize an entry-level office. This office shall have resources made available to it (1) for handling sexual harassment complaints, (2) for disseminating adequate information on the University policies and procedures for dealing with sexual harassment, and (3) for securing resource personnel who have either legal training, counseling skills, or other such skills as are necessary for the effective operation of the office in resolving complaints and assisting those who may have been victimized by sexual harassment. It is expected that in cases involving academic staff, this office will maintain close liaison with the Office of the Vice President for Academic Affairs.
   B. Complaints of sexual harassment may be brought by students, civil service persons, and academic staff. It shall be a duty of this office to design forms and to maintain fair and adequate procedures to process a complaint if a complainant wishes to formalize it.
   C. It will be a function of this office to discuss specific incidents in an informal fashion and to draw on other support and counseling services to assist complainants. Advice shall also be given concerning the details of formalizing a complaint,

---

* As approved by the University Senate, May 17, 1984

the safeguards of due process, and the possible sanctions and modes of relief. Counseling and informal discussion shall be an integral part of the functioning of this office.

D. As part of the process, this office will also apprise appropriate line officers of units from which complaints arise of the nature of charges raised, and assist them in resolving the problem at the lowest appropriate level. The intent of this section is to insure that all line officers of the administration be aware of their responsibilities toward securing an academic atmosphere within their province that properly deters sexual harassment. A record of line officer involvement with each complaint will be kept by this office.

E. If the complaint cannot be resolved informally, this office shall ask the complainant to submit a formal written complaint, including a statement of the alleged incident and the remedy desired. This office shall ask the respondent to reply to the written complaint within 10 days of the receipt of the complaint. The filing of such response shall be mandatory and the person responding shall be required to indicate denial in whole or in part, or agreement with the assertions in whole or in part. Failure to respond shall be deemed a breach of academic responsibility requiring notice of such failure to respond to be given to the academic vice president by this office.

F. Upon receipt of the response, this office may further investigate the complaint and may schedule a meeting of the parties. Each party may have an adviser present at this meeting. This office shall settle the formal written complaint in one of the following three ways:

1. It may dismiss the complaint as being without merit.

2. It may arrange for the parties to sign a written statement of agreement in which the parties resolve the differences between them according to terms set out in writing.

3. It may find reason to suspect that the respondent acted in violation of the University Policy Statement on Sexual Harassment; in this case, this office shall describe the nature of the alleged violation, the evidence that supports its judgment, and the sanction, if any, that it recommends that the vice president for academic affairs apply. The possibility of violation and any recommendation of sanction by this office will be forwarded to the vice president for academic affairs. Only the aca-

demic vice president can officially find a respondent in violation of the University Policy on Sexual Harassment and issue a sanction. Both parties shall be notified immediately in writing of the action of the office.

G. If this office dismisses the complaint and the complainant does not appeal the dismissal or if the parties sign a written statement of agreement, the file shall be closed. The material retained in the file shall include a copy of the formal written complaint, a copy of the respondent's reply, a statement of the action of this office, and a copy of any agreements. This file shall be kept in a secure place. The information in the file will be forwarded to the appropriate line officers.

H. If the complainant wishes to appeal the dismissal of the complaint he or she may do so by filing a notice of appeal with the Sexual Harassment Board within 10 days of written notification of the action of this office. In the case of appeal, all materials shall be retained in the files and the files shall be forwarded to the board.

I. If this office finds reason to suspect that the respondent may have acted in violation of the University Policy on Sexual Harassment, the vice president may direct the Sexual Harassment Board to conduct a hearing. Any hearing shall be conducted in accordance with basic and traditional principles of fairness and in accordance with procedures that guarantee due process to complainant and respondent.

J. Responsibility for reviewing the activities of the entry-level office shall be assumed by the Sexual Harassment Board. This board shall receive summaries of all dispositions of cases and shall see that the University Policy on Sexual Harassment is administered properly and fairly by this office. It is also the responsibility of this board to report periodically to the University Senate through the Senate Committee on Faculty Affairs.

II. The Sexual Harassment Board

A. The main body for reporting on the entry-level office to the Senate and for hearing appeals of the actions of the entry-level office is a nine-person board to be appointed by the president. In order to achieve continuity, the board members shall be appointed initially for staggered terms of service varying in length from one to three years, and thereafter for terms of three years. The membership of the board shall consist of five faculty members, one academic professional-administrative person, one civil service person, and two students.

B. A board member of any class (faculty, academic professional-administrative, civil service, or student) may participate in any hearing or appeal without regard to the class to which the respondent or complainant belongs.

C. The Office of the University Attorney shall serve to advise the board on substantive or procedural issues that arise under the University Policy on Sexual Harassment.

D. A primary function of the board is to hear appeals and conduct hearings. The board shall hear appeals from complainants whose complaints have been dismissed by the entry-level office, and shall conduct hearings when directed to do so by the academic vice president. The board shall also review the findings and recommendations of the office when the office has found reason to believe that a respondent acted in violation of the Policy on Sexual Harassment. It will also hear appeals by student respondents against whom complaints have been filed regarding their actions in an instructional capacity (as teaching assistants, research assistants, etc.), if administrative action has already been taken.

E. In carrying out its appeal and hearing function, the board shall adopt hearing procedures that accord due process to every party and are consistent with the Procedures of Committees of the Senate.

F. Standard of Proof. A violation of this policy on sexual harassment shall be found by the board only where there is a preponderance of evidence that a violation occurred.

G. In hearing appeals made by a complainant, in hearing cases referred to it by the vice president for academic affairs, or in reviewing an action by the vice president, the board may make up to three determinations. It may determine the truth or falsity of the evidence considered. It may decide whether the factual allegation constitutes a violation of the University Policy on Sexual Harassment. Lastly, the board may decide what if any sanction is appropriate.

H. The board will conduct a continuous review of the Sexual Harassment Policy and Procedures, as described in I.J. above.

III. Appeals
   A. The complainant may appeal the action of the office to dismiss his or her complaint to the Sexual Harassment Board.
   B. Respondents may appeal a ruling by the vice president for academic affairs that they have acted in violation of the University Policy on Sexual Harassment or may appeal any sanction imposed in this regard by the vice president for academic affairs as follows:
      1. Faculty may appeal to the Senate Judicial Committee.
      2. Academic professional/administrative staff may appeal to the Appeals Committee of the Academic Staff Advisory Committee.
      3. Students may appeal to the Student Behavior Committee.
IV. Sanctions
   A. Violations of the University Policy on Sexual Harassment may be met with a variety of sanctions. These could include such sanctions as a reprimand, denial of merit pay, reassignment of teaching responsibilities, or suspension without compensation for a specified period. Acts of sexual harassment of a very serious nature may warrant a recommendation of removal for cause, or may warrant criminal action.

PROCEDURES TO BE FOLLOWED IN SEXUAL HARASSMENT COMPLAINTS INVOLVING CIVIL SERVICE AND ACADEMIC STAFF PERSONNEL

Two different procedures in regard to sexual harassment complaints exist at the University, depending upon whether the respondent is a member of the civil service or academic personnel system. Except as specified below, complaints alleging violations of the sexual harassment policy by civil service personnel will follow civil service procedures, and complaints made against academic personnel will follow the procedures approved by the University Senate on May 17, 1984.

1. Whenever an academic employee, because of a supervisory relationship, is charged by a civil service employee with sexual harassment, the academic employees must abide by civil service procedures for such complaints.
2. The Office of the Vice President for Academic Affairs will be represented at any formal hearings of sexual harassment com-

plaints brought by a civil service employee against an academic employee.

3. The Office of Equal Opportunity and Affirmative Action will be represented at any formal hearings against academic employees under the Senate Sexual Harassment Procedures.

4. So that sanctions will be evenly applied across the University in cases of findings of sexual harassment, recommendations of sanctions against employees in both personnel systems will be reviewed by the following ad hoc committee: [the] associate vice president for health sciences, [the] associate vice president for academic affairs, [the] associate vice president for finance and operations, [the] director, Office of Equal Opportunity and Affirmative Action, and [the] University equal opportunity officer.

V : Institutional Committee Statement and Policy on Sexual Harassment, Gettysburg College

This letter and the statement that follows it were sent by the assistant director of career services, the associate dean of student life, the psychological counselor, and the associate dean of Gettysburg College to employees and students on February 24, 1986.

This letter is to describe what constitutes sexual harassment of students by employees and to set out the procedures we have at Gettysburg College to deal with such harassment if it occurs. We want any student who has a complaint or any employee who hears a complaint to understand the procedures the College has for dealing with the problem. There is a formal procedure outlined in the *Student Handbook* [. . .] and the *Faculty Handbook* [. . .] for handling such complaints. When an individual is unwilling to pursue a formal complaint, there are also informal means of dealing with the problem.

Two different types of behavior can constitute sexual harassment of a student by an employee. The first is unwelcome sexual advances, requests for sexual favors, and other verbal or physical conduct of a sexual nature (e.g., comments about physical appearance, joking of a sexual nature, or offensive touching, etc.) which can lead the student to believe that submissions to such conduct or failure to submit to it can affect his or her academic, co-curricular, or residential status at the College. The second type of sexual harassment occurs when verbal or physical conduct of a sexual nature has the effect of unreasonably interfering with the student's performance or participation in the academic, co-curricular, or residential program of the College. This type of harassment does not necessarily involve behavior aimed at an individual student; it can arise in a group setting through the oppressive use of sexist humor, comments that disparage the ability or attributes of students of one sex, etc.

Persons with a complaint that seems to fall under the category of sexual harassment should realize the following:

1. We have been named by the College as persons who can receive and deal with such complaints under the College's Grievance Procedure for Sexual Harassment which is contained in the *Student Handbook* and *Faculty Handbook* as indicated above.

2. Not only can complaints be brought to us, but we are available to offer informal advice and support to students who do not wish to lodge a formal complaint.

3. It is the policy of Gettysburg College to solve problems, whenever possible, at the lowest possible level. If a student is willing to write a letter directly to the employee involved, this often is an informal, successful way to stop the behavior that is the subject of the complaint. We are, of course, willing to help students frame such a letter.

4. If the student is unwilling to write a letter directly to the employee, we can initiate a process whereby an informal letter can be sent by a College official to the employee. Such a letter will not become part of the employee's employment file.

5. We can assist those students who wish to pursue the complaint through the steps in the College's sexual harassment grievance procedure. The informal steps indicated above are not meant to discourage use of our published grievance procedure for those students who prefer to make a formal complaint.

We urge employees who receive a complaint from a student about behavior that might be sexual harassment to at least let one of us know that such a complaint has been made in a situation where the student does not wish to pursue either informal or formal procedures to remedy the problem. We urge this so we can at least gather information that tells us how prevalent the problem of sexual harassment may be on our campus. Thus, we have instituted the informal procedures indicated above to supplement our formal procedures. We want to be sure that we have procedures that give us a good estimate of the prevalence of this problem at Gettysburg and then encourage steps to deal positively with the problem. Please cooperate with us in this effort.

GRIEVANCE PROCEDURES CONCERNING SEXUAL DISCRIMINATION, DISCRIMINATION ON THE BASIS OF HANDICAP, SEXUAL HARASSMENT, AND SOME COMPLAINTS ABOUT TERMS AND CONDITIONS OF EMPLOYMENT

I. WHO MAY USE THESE GRIEVANCE PROCEDURES
    The grievance procedures below are for all employees and students at Gettysburg College who have a complaint about actions of an employee of the College. These procedures do not apply to applicants for admission or employment at the College. The person presenting a grievance is called "the grievant" below. The person whose actions are the basis of the grievance is called "the respondent." The term "days" in this document means calendar days.

II. WHAT CATEGORIES OF GRIEVANCES ARE NOT COVERED BY THESE PROCEDURES
    Gettysburg College has additional grievance procedures for the following situations. Grievants with a complaint that falls under these other procedures should refer to them.
    A. Dismissal of a Faculty Member for Cause (*Faculty Handbook*).
    B. Non-Reappointment of a Non-Tenured Faculty Member (*Faculty Handbook*).
    C. Rights of Students Under the Rights and Responsibilities of Students (*Student Handbook*).

III. WHAT CAN BE THE SUBJECT OF A GRIEVANCE UNDER THESE PROCEDURES
    The procedures below apply to grievances concerning:
    A. Alleged Sex Discrimination Under Title IX of the Education Amendments of 1972
    B. Alleged Discrimination on the Basis of Personal Handicap Under Section 504 of the Rehabilitation Act of 1973.
    C. Complaints of Sexual Harassment Committed by an Employee of the College.

D. Complaints Reasonably Related to Terms and Conditions of Employment of an Employee of the College (except for complaints covered under the Grievance Procedures listed in II. above).

Grievances concerning salary or promotion or termination of employment which might fall under the provisions of these Grievance Procedures are only covered when it is reasonably alleged that the action complained of was a result of discrimination based on race, color, sex, national origin, personal handicap, or age.

A grievance does not include dissatisfaction with a College policy of general application challenged on the ground that the policy is unfair or inadvisable.

Under these grievance procedures a student may be the grievant but not the respondent. Complaints about the actions of students fall under the jurisdiction of the Dean of Student Life.

IV. INFORMAL RESOLUTION OF COMPLAINTS

If possible, grievances should be resolved informally between or among the parties involved. If the grievance cannot be informally resolved by these persons, the grievant shall next (within 30 days of the incident that is the basis of the grievance) seek assistance in obtaining an informal resolution by contacting an appropriate person listed below:

A. The Affirmative Action Officer of the College for Grievances Concerning Sexual Discrimination Under Title IX, Racial Discrimination, or Discrimination on the Basis of Personal Handicap Under Section 504 of the Rehabilitation Act of 1973.

B. The Affirmative Action Officer of the College and Others Designated by the President for Complaints of Sexual Harassment by an Employee of the College. The list of persons so designated shall include representatives of the faculty, administration, and support staff. The list of such persons will be widely published on campus and will be available from the Affirmative Action Office, the Office of Student Life, and the Counseling Services Office.

C. The College Grievance Officer for All Other Complaints Under These Grievance Procedures. The College Grievance Officer is an employee of the College to whom the President assigns the additional duties of Grievance Officer on a yearly basis.

The person contacted under this section will work informally with the grievant and the respondent in order to reach a solution satisfactory to all parties. The grievant must submit a written statement to the person contacted that outlines the action or actions that are complained of and the facts that substantiate the complaint. No formal written grievance can be filed under Section V. below until ten days have expired from the date on which one of the persons listed above is contacted to assist in the informal resolution of the grievance. If the grievance cannot be informally resolved within ten days to the satisfaction of the grievant and the respondent, the person contacted will provide within seven days (after the end of the ten-day period) to the grievant and respondent a written statement that efforts to resolve the grievance informally were unsuccessful. The ten-day period during which informal resolution is attempted may be extended upon the mutual agreement of the grievant and the respondent.

All proceedings to resolve and formulate a complaint shall be confidential with the understanding that the Affirmative Action Officer will be apprised of such proceedings and that testimony about the informal resolution of these complaints may be heard as part of the hearing process outlined in section V., below.

V.   A FORMAL RESOLUTION OF GRIEVANCES

A grievant who has received a written statement that the informal grievance resolution efforts were unsuccessful may seek a formal resolution of the grievance. To do this, he or she must file in writing with the College Grievance Officer (within 15 days of the date of the statement that informal resolution efforts were unsuccessful) a formal grievance. This formal grievance shall specify the action or actions that are complained of, the facts that constitute such action, the evidence that will be presented to establish such facts, and the names of witnesses who may testify to present such evidence.

The College Grievance Officer will immediately forward this formal grievance to the respondent and to the Chairperson of the College Grievance Committee. The College Grievance Committee is a committee of four faculty members selected by the Executive Committee, four administrators appointed by the President, and four staff employees appointed by the College Business Manager. It shall select its own chairperson.

When a formal grievance is filed, the Chairperson of the College Grievance Committee shall select a hearing panel of five persons from the Committee to conduct a formal hearing on the grievance. The hearing panel shall have at least two persons from the employee groups (faculty, administration, staff) of each party to the grievance who is an employee of the College. If a student is a party to the grievance, the student may request to the Chairperson of the College Grievance Committee that the hearing panel include one student appointed by the President of the Student Senate. Such student shall be one of the five persons on the hearing panel.

The hearing panel will meet before scheduling a hearing to review the formal grievance and these grievance procedures. The hearing panel may decide on the basis of the written grievance presented to it that the action alleged does not fall within the definition of a grievance under these procedures or that it is of such minimal consequence that a grievance hearing is not merited. In such cases, the panel shall forward this determination within 15 days of the filing of the grievance in writing to the President.

The hearing panel will schedule a hearing within 20 days of the date of the filing of the grievance with the understanding that complaints filed within 20 days of the end of a semester may be heard in the following semester. At this hearing, the burden of proof will be on the grievant to establish the allegations of the grievance by a preponderance of the evidence. The hearing panel shall select its chairperson. The hearing will not be an open meeting; only the grievant, respondent, and the hearing panel will be present. Witnesses will be present only when their testimony is being taken. There will not be attorneys present for the parties. The hearing panel will not be bound by strict rules of legal evidence. The panel may receive any evidence of probative value in determining the issues involved. Every possible effort will be made to obtain the most reliable evidence available. All questions relating to the admissibility of evidence or other legal matters will be decided by the chairperson of the panel. The parties to the grievance will have the right to present evidence and call witnesses and respond to evidence presented at the hearing. The hearing panel may receive written or oral evidence. It may request an account of the informal efforts to resolve the grievance from the person listed in section IV. above who assisted in this process. It may call persons to testify before it. It shall compile a summary of the substance of oral and written testimony presented to it. A tape recording of the hearing shall be made and retained for two years, and a transcript shall be prepared free of charge upon the request of the grievant or the respondent.

The hearing panel shall make written findings concerning the allegations of the complaint. A majority vote of the hearing committee shall be required for each finding and recommendation of the group. These findings plus recommendations for resolution of the complaint shall be forwarded within ten days of the hearing to the grievant, the respondent, and to one of the following persons: the Provost, if the respondent is a faculty member; the President, if the respondent is an administrator; or the Business Manager, if the respondent is a staff employee. If the grievant is a student, the Dean of Student Life will also receive a copy of the findings plus recommendations. If the named administrator to whom the findings and recommendations are to be forwarded is a grievant or respondent under the grievance, the findings and recommendations shall be forwarded to the President. The panel has no restrictions upon it as to what it can recommend, from a finding that the grievance is not established, to a reprimand, to further proceedings for dismissal of the employee.

The person to whom the report of the hearing panel is forwarded (other than the Dean of Student Life) shall act on the recommendations of the hearing panel within ten days of the receipt of findings and recommendations. These findings and recommendations are not binding upon him or her. His or her decision on the actions to be taken shall be made in writing and submitted to the parties. This person has the power to institute any penalty or determine any resolution of the grievance within the authority of his or her position.

The grievant or the respondent may appeal this decision to the President (or ask for reconsideration of the decision by the President, if it was made by him or her) only on the grounds that there was a substantial and prejudicial departure from these procedures in the consideration and the resolution of the grievance or that there is demonstrated new evidence not available to the person making the appeal (appellant) at the time of the hearing and which might have reasonably affected the decision of the hearing panel had it been available. The appellant shall specify the act or acts that constitute such a departure. The President may request that a new hearing panel be constituted to hear the grievance again. In such a case, the grievance procedure will begin again at the formal hearing stage unless the grievant and respondent both agree that informal resolution attempts should first be made. The President's decision on the appeal shall be final.

All proceedings to resolve formally a grievance shall remain confidential among the persons involved and the Affirmative Action Officer of the College.

VI. GRIEVANCE WHERE THE PRESIDENT IS RESPONDENT

In a case where the President is the respondent in a grievance, the role of the President under these procedures shall be filled by another person chosen by mutual agreement of the President and the grievant.

VII. REPORT TO THE COLLEGE COMMUNITY

The Affirmative Action Officer should consult with the persons listed in section IV., B. and C. at least yearly and make a report to the College community concerning the number of grievance cases, both formal and informal, that were brought and resolved within the preceding year.

VI : Sexual Harassment Survey, University of Illinois at Urbana-Champaign

The following survey, developed in 1987 by Deborah Allen of the University of Illinois Counseling Center, is an example of a research instrument that treats a comprehensive range of sexual harassment issues, some of which have seldom been addressed.

COUNSELING CENTER SURVEY

YOUR EXPERIENCE AS A STUDENT

1. Unwanted Sexual Statements
   a) While you've been a student at the University of Illinois, how many times, if ever, have U. of I. faculty or staff members directed *unwanted sexual statements* toward you *personally?* (Unwanted sexual statements are defined as unwanted jokes, remarks, or questions directed to you which have sexual implications or sexual content.)

Reprinted from *Sexual Harassment Survey*, University of Illinois, 1987, by Deborah Allen and Judith L. Bessai.

Never (Skip to Item 2) 1
Once 2
Several (2-5) times.............. 3
Many (more than 5) times....... 4

b) Approximately how many different U. of I. faculty or staff members have directed unwanted sexual statements toward you *personally?*

One 1
Several (2-5).................... 2
Many (more than 5)............. 3

c) What was the sex of the faculty or staff member(s) involved?

Male only...................... 1
Female only 2
Both male and female.......... 3

2. Unwanted Personal Attention

a) While you've been a student at the University of Illinois, how many times, if ever, have U. of I. faculty or staff members directed *unwanted personal attention* toward you? (Unwanted personal attention is defined as unwanted letters, calls, visits, pressure for meetings, dates, etc., where personal [romatic] interest in you is implied, but no sexual expectations are stated.)

Never (Skip to Item 3) 1
Once 2
Several (2-5) times.............. 3
Many (more than 5) times....... 4

b) Approximately how many different U. of I. faculty or staff members have directed unwanted personal attention toward you?

One 1
Several (2-5).................... 2
Many (more than 5)............. 3

c) What was the sex of the faculty or staff member(s) involved?

Male only...................... 1
Female only 2
Both male and female.......... 3

3. Unwanted Sexual Propositions

a) While you've been a student at the University of Illinois, how many times, if ever, have U. of I. faculty or staff members directed *unwanted sexual propositions* toward you *personally?* (Unwanted sexual propositions are defined as unwanted demands or invitations for sexual favors.)

Never (Skip to Item 4) 1
Once 2
Several (2-5) times.............. 3
Many (more than 5) times....... 4

b) Approximately how many different U. of I. faculty or staff members have directed unwanted sexual propositions toward you *personally?*

One 1
Several (2-5).................... 2
Many (more than 5)............. 3

c) What was the sex of the faculty or staff member(s) involved?

Male only....................... 1
Female only 2
Both male and female........... 3

4. Unwanted Physical or Sexual Advances

a) While you've been a student at the University of Illinois, how many times, if ever, have U. of I. faculty or staff members directed *unwanted physical or sexual advances* toward you *personally?* (Unwanted physical or sexual advances are defined as unwanted touching, hugging, kissing, fondling, sexual intercourse, or other sexual activity.)

Never (Skip to Item 5) 1
Once 2
Several (2-5) times.............. 3
Many (more than 5) times....... 4

b) Approximately how many different U. of I. faculty or staff members have directed unwanted physical or sexual advances toward you *personally?*

One 1
Several (2-5).................... 2
Many (more than 5)............. 3

c) What was the sex of the faculty or staff member(s) involved?

Male only........................ 1
Female only 2
Both male and female........... 3

5. Have you ever avoided taking a class from or working with a U. of I. faculty or staff member because of the person's reputation for engaging in any of the previously mentioned behaviors?

Yes 1
No 2

ONE INCIDENT IN DETAIL

In order to learn from your experiences we would like to ask you to provide detailed information about one specific incident.

a) If you *have* experienced any of the previously mentioned behaviors, please go on to Item 6.
b) If you have *not* experienced any of the previously mentioned behaviors, please skip to Item 20.

6. From your experience, please think about the incident that was most personally distressing to you. What was the sex of the faculty or staff member involved?

Male............................... 1
Female 2

7. In what college or unit was the faculty or staff member?

Agriculture............... 01
Applied Life Studies 02
Aviation 03
BMS & Clinical
   Medicine 04
Commerce & Business
   Adm. 05
Communications.......... 06
Education 07
Engineering 08
Fine & Applied Arts 09

Law 11
Liberal Arts & Sciences .. 12
Library & Info. Science .. 13
Nursing 14
Social Work 15
Veterinary Medicine...... 16
Other administrators/
   academic professionals/
   university employees
   (please specify) 17
_____

8. In what department was the faculty or staff member? _____

9. What was the primary relationship of the faculty or staff member to you at the time of the incident?

Your graduate teaching or research assistant 1
Your professor/instructor................................. 2
Your academic advisor 3
Your department chairperson or dean..................... 4
Supervisor of your university employment................. 5
Other administrator/academic professional/university
    employee (please specify relationship to you)............. 6

10. What type of behavior was involved?

Unwanted sexual statements 1
Unwanted personal attention 2
Unwanted sexual propositions 3
Unwanted physical or sexual advances..................... 4

11. In what year did this incident occur? .... 19____

12. Where did the incident occur?

Faculty or staff member's office..... 1
Classroom or lab.................... 2
Place of campus employment 3
Other (please specify) 4

13. In order to help us learn how to prevent such incidents in the future, we would like to know more about the incident you experienced. Please write as much or as little as you feel comfortable with in order to describe the incident. (Use the back of this page if you need more room.)

14. Did you experience any of the following effects as a result of the incident?

	Yes	No
Strong emotions (e.g., anger, anxiety, depression)	1	2
Physical problems or symptoms....................	1	2
Negative feelings about yourself..................	1	2
Impaired academic performance	1	2
Altered academic or career plans (e.g., dropping certain courses, changing major)	1	2
Avoidance of the person or situations involving the person	1	2

15. Please describe the effects of the incident in your own words. (Use the back of this page if you need more room.)

16. a) Did you express your objections about the behavior to the person involved?

    Yes 1
    No (Skip to Item 17)............ 2

    b) Following your objections, did the behavior stop?

    Yes 1
    No............................. 2

17. Did you talk to any of the following people about the incident?

	Yes	No
Friends..	1	2
Parents or other family members.................	1	2
RA or other residence hall staff..................	1	2
Faculty member...................................	1	2
Counselor...	1	2
Other (please specify)............................	1	2

18. a) Did you make a complaint to any university official or office?

    Yes (please specify to whom) _____ 1
    No (Skip to Item 19).................................. 2

b) How was the complaint handled?

c) Were you satisfied with the outcome?

Yes 1
No............................. 2

Please skip to Item 20.

19. Were any of the following factors in your decision not to make a complaint?

	Yes	No
Felt I handled the situation adequately	1	2
Didn't think of it as a problem the university could/would help me with	1	2
Concern about not being believed	1	2
Concern that no action would be taken	1	2
Concern about retaliation	1	2
Embarrassment at being involved in the incident	1	2
Concern that I was somehow responsible	1	2
Unwillingness to talk to a person of the opposite sex about the incident	1	2
Concern about anonymity	1	2
Lack of knowledge about where to complain	1	2
Concern about what actions would be taken	1	2
Other (please specify)	1	2

VISIBILITY OF CAMPUS POLICY

20. Prior to responding to this survey were you aware that sexual harassment is prohibited by campus policy?

Yes 1
No 2

21. Prior to responding to this survey were you aware that sexual harassment is illegal under federal and state laws?

Yes 1
No 2

22. Please list below any university office that you are aware of that is officially designated to answer your questions about sexual harassment, take your reports, and give you advice on informal complaints and formal grievance procedures.

YOUR SUGGESTIONS

23. The following factors would make me more likely to report an incident of sexual harassment to a university office or official:

	Strongly agree	Agree	Undecided	Disagree	Strongly disagree
Assurance of confidentiality............	1	2	3	4	5
Assurance that my complaint will be taken seriously and thoroughly investigated...........................	1	2	3	4	5
Having only one person designated by the campus to handle initial complaints...........................	1	2	3	4	5
Having the person responsible for hearing the complaint be of the same sex.............................	1	2	3	4	5
Knowing that the person I report the incident to has the authority to take action...............................	1	2	3	4	5
Having an investigation team which is independent of the department of the person involved	1	2	3	4	5
Clear and uniform consequences for specific behaviors, with severity of the punishment increasing with the severity of the incident..............	1	2	3	4	5
Protection from retaliation.............	1	2	3	4	5
Other (please specify)...................	1	2	3	4	5

24. If you were to experience any of the previously listed behaviors, would an anonymous hotline that provided telephone counseling and information about informal complaint and formal grievance procedures be useful to you?

Yes 1
No 2

25. If you were to experience any of the previously listed behaviors, what other kinds of services would you find useful in helping you cope with your feelings about the incident, the process of reporting the incident to the university, or any other aspects of the incident? Please be as specific as possible.

BACKGROUND INFORMATION

Please give us some background information about yourself:

26. What is your sex?

    Male.............................. 1
    Female 2

27. What is your age?

28. What is your marital status?

    Single 1
    Married 2
    Separated/divorced................ 3
    Other (please specify) 4

29. Are you a U.S. citizen?

    Yes 1
    No 2

30. What is your racial/ethnic group?

    White 1
    Black............................. 2
    Hispanic.......................... 3
    Asian or Pacific Islander........... 4
    American Indian or Alaskan native . 5
    Other (please specify) 6

31. What is your class?

Freshman 1
Sophomore........................ 2
Junior 3
Senior........................... 4
Masters.......................... 5
Doctoral.......................... 6
Professional 7
Other (please specify) 8

32. What is your college?

Agriculture....................... 01
Applied Life Studies 02
Aviation 03
BMS & Clinical Medicine 04
Commerce & Business Adm. 05
Communications 06
Education 07
Engineering 08
Fine & Applied Arts 09
Graduate College 10
Law 11
Liberal Arts & Sciences........... 12
Library & Info. Science........... 13
Nursing 14
Social Work 15
Veterinary Medicine 16
Other (please specify) 17

Thank you for your cooperation!

Please return your completed questionnaire in the enclosed return envelope.

Notes

1 : Harassment on Campus

1. Frank J. Till, *Sexual Harassment: A Report on the Sexual Harassment of Students,* Report of the National Advisory Council on Women's Educational Programs (Washington, D.C., 1980), p. 9.
2. Joan Roberts, "Women's Right to Choose, or Men's Right to Dominate," *Women in Higher Education,* ed. W. Todd Furniss and Patricia Graham (Washington, D.C.: American Council on Education, 1974), p. 51.
3. Till, p. 39.
4. Arlene Metha and Joanne Nigg, "Sexual Harassment on Campus: An Institutional Response," *Journal of the National Association for Women Deans, Administrators, and Counselors* 46 (Winter 1983): 9.
5. Suzanne Perry, "Sexual Harassment on the Campuses: Deciding Where to Draw the Line," *The Chronicle of Higher Education,* March 23, 1983, p. 21.
6. Bernice Lott, Mary Ellen Reilly, and Dale R. Howard, "Sexual Assault and Harassment: A Campus Community Case Study," *Signs* 8 (Winter 1982): 296-319.
7. Nancy Maihoff and Linda Forrest, "Sexual Harassment in Higher Education: An Assessment Study," *Journal of the National Association for Women Deans, Administrators, and Counselors* 46 (Winter 1983): 3-8.
8. Phyllis M. Meek and Ann Q. Lynch, "Establishing an Informal Grievance Procedure for Cases of Sexual Harassment of Students," *Journal of the National Association for Women Deans, Administrators, and Counselors* 46 (Winter 1983): 31.
9. Maihoff and Forrest, p. 4.

10. "Sexual Harassment," Report by the Office of Women's Services and Programs, University of Cincinnati (Cincinnati, Ohio, 1980).
11. Maihoff and Forrest, p. 4.
12. K. S. Pope, H. Levenson, and L. R. Schover, "Sexual Intimacy in Psychology Training: Results and Implications of a National Survey," *American Psychologist* 34 (1979): 682-89.
13. National Center for Educational Statistics, "Fall Enrollment at Public and Private Institutions," *The Chronicle of Higher Education*, November 24, 1982, p. 7.
14. Till, p. 20.
15. Lin Farley, *Sexual Shakedown: The Sexual Harassment of Women on the Job* (New York: McGraw-Hill, 1978), p. 102.
16. Lin Farley and Catharine MacKinnon, *Sexual Harassment of Working Women: A Case of Sex Discrimination* (New Haven: Yale University Press, 1979).
17. Antonio J. Califa, Memorandum to Regional Civil Rights Directors, Regions I-X, Office for Civil Rights, United States Department of Education (Washington, D.C., August 31, 1981).
18. *Alexander* v. *Yale University*, 459 F. Supp. 1 (D. Conn.) (1977), and *Alexander* v. *Yale University*, 631 Fed2d. 178, and Cir. (D. Conn.) (1980).
19. Till, pp. 11, 7.
20. Phyllis Franklin et al., *Sexual and Gender Harassment in the Academy*, Report of the Commission on the Status of Women in the Profession (New York: The Modern Language Association of America, 1981), p. 4.
21. "Sexual Harassment: A Hidden Issue," *On Campus With Women*, Project on the Status and Education of Women (Washington, D.C.: Association of American Colleges, 1978), p. 2.
22. This information was gathered from the following newspaper reports: "SJS Prof Asked to Quit After Charges of Sexual Harassment," *San Jose News*, June 23, 1979; "Prof Faces SJS Hearing in 'Attempted Seduction' Case," *San Jose News*, October 19, 1979; "Professor's Hearing Is Closed to Public," *San Jose News*, October 23, 1979; "SJS Prof Wins Closed Hearing," *San Jose News*, October 27, 1979; "Probe into Professor's Alleged Misconduct Ended," *San Jose News*, November 7, 1979; "Prof Accused of Immoral Conduct Is Fired at SJS," *San Jose News*, January 8, 1980; "Professor Fired for Sexual Harassment of Students," *Los Angeles Times*, p. 20, January 9, 1980; "2 Universities Act on Sex Charges," *San Francisco Chronicle*, January 9, 1980; "Judge Upholds SJS in Firing of Professor in Morals Case," *San Jose News*, April 10, 1981.

23. This information was gathered from the following newspaper reports: "Sex Charges Stir UC Campus, Anonymous Accusers Could Cost Professor's Job," *Los Angeles Times*, p. 20, April 14, 1979; "Professor Suspended in Sex Case," *Oakland Tribune*, January 8, 1980; "Professor Docked in Salary Over Sex Charges," *Berkeley Independent Gazette*, January 8, 1980; "Bowker Suspends Professor for Sexual Misconduct," *California Monthly*, February 1980.

24. This information was gathered from the following newspaper reports: "Harvard Professor Reprimanded," *Boston Globe*, p. 26, December 14, 1979; "Fighting Back," *Boston Globe*, p. 21, March 5, 1980.

25. This information was gathered from the following newspaper reports: "Poet Admonished by Harvard Dean," *Boston Globe*, p. 31, June 9, 1982; *The Harvard Crimson*, 1982 Commencement Issue, p. 35; "Ad Board Gives Grade Change in Sex Harassment Complaint," *The Harvard Crimson*, October 20, 1982.

26. This information was gathered from the following newspaper reports: "Ethics Panel Ends Probe of Garner," *Tampa Tribune*, p. 1B, September 18, 1982; "Ethics Board Urged to Fire HCC's Garner," *Tampa Tribune*, p. 1A, September 20, 1982; "Panel: Suspend Garner without Pay," *Tampa Tribune*, p. 1A, October 29, 1982.

27. Press release, Clark University.

2 : Inside the Ivy Walls

1. Michael Cohen and James March, *Leadership and Ambiguity: The American College President* (New York: McGraw-Hill, 1974), p. 33.

2. J. Victor Baldridge, *Policy Making and Effective Leadership* (San Francisco: Jossey-Bass, 1978), p. 25.

3. Jacques Barzun, *The American University* (New York: Harper & Row, 1968), p. 2.

4. Harry Zehner, "Love and Lust on Faculty Row," *Cosmopolitan*, April 1982, p. 269.

5. Frank J. Till, *Sexual Harassment: A Report on the Sexual Harassment of Students*, Report of the National Advisory Council on Women's Educational Programs (Washington, D.C., 1980), p. 10.

6. Till, p. 11.

7. Hazard Adams, *The Academic Tribes* (1976; Urbana: University of Illinois Press, 1988), p. 4.

8. J. Victor Baldridge, *Power and Conflict in the University* (New York: Wiley, 1971), p. 167.

9. Mary McCarthy, *The Groves of Academe* (New York: Harcourt, Brace & World, 1963), p. 60.
10. John Knowles, *The Paragon* (New York: Random House, 1971), pp. 1-2.
11. Samuel Beckett, *Waiting for Godot* (New York: Grove Press, 1966), p. 27.
12. Alexander W. Astin, "The American Freshman: National Norms for Fall, 1982," published by the American Council on Education and the University of California at Los Angeles, as reported in *The Chronicle of Higher Education Fact File,* January 26, 1983, pp. 11-12.
13. College and University Personnel Association, "Median Salaries of Administrators for 1982-83," *The Chronicle of Higher Education Fact File,* March 2, 1983, p. 21.

3 : Contemporary College Women

1. Adrienne Munich, "Seduction in Academe," *Psychology Today,* February 1978, p. 82.
2. Bernard Malamud, *Dubin's Lives* (New York: Farrar, Straus & Giroux, 1977), pp. 24, 27.
3. Shane Adler, "Dressing Up," *Becoming Female: Perspectives on Development,* ed. Claire B. Kopp (New York: Plenum Press, 1979), p. 393.
4. Jessie Bernard, *The Female World* (New York: The Free Press, 1981), pp. 476, 478, 479.
5. Susan Jacoby, *The Possible She* (New York: Farrar, Straus & Giroux, 1973), pp. 66-67.
6. Gail Zekman et al., "Misreading the Signals," *Psychology Today,* October 1980, p. 28.
7. A. Abbey, "Sex Differences in Attributions for Friendly Behavior: Do Males Misperceive Females' Friendliness?" *Journal of Personality and Social Psychology* 42 (1982): 830-38.
8. Malamud, pp. 35, 36-37, 47.
9. Malamud, p. 31.
10. Malamud, p. 227.
11. Morton Hunt, *Sexual Behavior in the 1970s* (Chicago: Playboy Press, 1974), pp. 34, 38.
12. Alexander W. Astin, "The American Freshman: National Norms for Fall, 1982," published by the American Council on Education and University of California at Los Angeles, as reported in *The Chronicle of Higher Education Fact File,* January 26, 1983, pp. 11-12.

13. Astin, p. 11.
14. Astin, p. 11.
15. Astin, p. 11.
16. Herbert Livesey, *The Professors* (New York: Charterhouse, 1975), pp. 153-54.
17. Howard Moss and Jerome Kagan, *Birth to Maturity* (New York: John Wiley, 1962).
18. Elizabeth Douvan and Joseph Adelson, *The Adolescent Experience* (New York: John Wiley, 1966).
19. David Bradford, Alice Sargent, and Melinda Sprague, "The Executive Man and Woman: The Issue of Sexuality," *Bringing Women into Management*, eds. Francine Gordon and Myra Strober (New York: McGraw-Hill, 1975), p. 18.
20. Malamud, p. 143-44.
21. Eleanor Maccoby and Carol Nagy Jacklin, *The Psychology of Sex Differences* (Palo Alto: Stanford University Press, 1974), p. 359.
22. Eileen Shapiro, "Some Thoughts on Counseling Women Who Perceive Themselves to Be Victims of Non-Actionable Sex Discrimination: A Survival Guide," in "Sexual Harassment: A Hidden Issue," *On Campus with Women*, Project on the Status and Education of Women (Washington, D.C.: American Association of Colleges, 1978), p. 3.
23. Frank J. Till, *Sexual Harassment: A Report on the Sexual Harassment of Students*, Report of the National Advisory Council on Women's Educational Programs (Washington, D.C., 1980), pp. 26-27.

4 : Voices of Women

1. Florence King, *HE: An Irreverent Look at the American Male* (New York: Stein and Day, 1978), p. 148.
2. Frank J. Till, *Sexual Harassment: A Report on the Sexual Harassment of Students*, Report of the National Advisory Council on Women's Educational Programs (Washington, D.C., 1980), p. 20.
3. Till, p. 18.
4. Till, p. 24.
5. Till, p. 27.

5 : The Lecherous Professor

1. Harry Zehner, "Love and Lust on Faculty Row," *Cosmopolitan*, April 1982, pp. 271-72.
2. Anna Sequoia, *The Official J.A.P. Handbook* (New York: New American Library, 1982), pp. 114-15.

3. John Barth, *The End of the Road* (New York: Doubleday, 1958), p. 98.
4. Marilyn B. Brewer, "Further Beyond Nine to Five: An Integration and Future Directions," *Journal of Social Issues* 38 (1982): 155.
5. Rollo May, *Power and Innocence* (New York: Dell, 1972), p. 102.
6. Herb Goldberg, *The Hazards of Being Male* (New York: New American Library, 1976), p. 175.
7. Erik Erikson, *Identity, Youth and Crisis* (New York: Norton, 1968).
8. Ralph Keyes, *Is There Life After High School?* (Boston: Little, Brown, 1976), pp. 94-95.
9. James S. Coleman, *The Adolescent Society* (New York: The Free Press, 1961).
10. Quoted in Nancy G. Clinch, *The Kennedy Neurosis* (New York: Grosset & Dunlap, 1973), p. 266.
11. Mark Feigen Fasteau, *The Male Machine* (New York: McGraw-Hill, 1974), p. 105.
12. Burt Avedon, *Ah, Men* (New York: A & W Publishers, 1980), p. 72.
13. Avedon, p. 45.
14. Ellen Berscheid, Elaine Walster, and George Behrnstedt, "Body Image," *Psychology Today*, November 1973, p. 250.
15. Keyes, p. 10.
16. Keyes, pp. 97, 98.
17. Erica Jong, *Fear of Flying* (New York: Holt, Rinehart and Winston, 1974), p. 188.
18. The data on college professors are derived from James Coleman's *The Adolescent Society* and Lloyd Temme's *"Adolescent Society" Follow-up Study* (Washington, D.C.: Bureau of Social Science, 1976). Temme and his associate Jere Cohen made this previously unreported information available for use in *The Lecherous Professor*. This particular question was selected for analysis to demonstrate that college professors were not among Coleman's athletic "elite." It should be noted that the responses of the total sample were similar to those of men who became professors; 92 percent of the total gave negative responses to this query.
19. Keyes, p. 56.
20. Keyes, p. 57.
21. Mopsy Strange Kennedy, " 'A' for Affairs with the Professor: What Happens When a Student Falls in Love with Her Teacher?" *Glamour*, August 1980, p. 237.
22. Kennedy, p. 241.
23. Avedon, p. 72.

24. American Association of University Professors, "9-Month Salaries for 1982-83," *The Chronicle of Higher Education Fact File*, June 22, 1983, p. 20.
25. Walter F. Abbot, "Commentary: When Will Academicians Enter the Ranks of the Working Poor?" *Academe* 66 (October 1980): 349.
26. Nancy Mayer, *The Male Mid-Life Crisis* (New York: New American Library, 1978), p. 164.
27. David Bradford, Alice Sargent, and Melinda Sprague, "The Executive Man and Woman: The Issue of Sexuality," *Bringing Women into Management*, eds. Francine Gordon and Myra Strober (New York: McGraw-Hill, 1975), pp. 18-19.
28. Zehner, p. 273.
29. Mayer, pp. 107, 111-13.
30. Mayer, p. 103.
31. Mayer, p. 107.
32. Fasteau, p. 11.
33. David F. Aberle and Kaspar Naegele, "Middle-Class Fathers' Occupational Role and Attitudes toward Children," *American Journal of Orthopsychiatry* 22 (1952): 366.
34. Alison Lurie, *The War between the Tates* (New York: Warner Books, 1975), p. 40.
35. Frank J. Till, *Sexual Harassment: A Report on the Sexual Harassment of Students*, Report of the National Advisory Council on Women's Education Programs (Washington, D.C., 1980), p. 23.

6 : Women Faculty

1. Louise Bernikow, *Among Women* (New York: Harper Colophon Books, 1980), p. 134.
2. Mark Twain, *The Adventures of Huckleberry Finn, The Portable Mark Twain*, ed. Bernard De Voto (New York: Viking Press, 1946), p. 451.
3. Lin Farley, *Sexual Shakedown: The Sexual Harassment of Women on the Job* (New York: McGraw-Hill, 1978), p. 110.
4. I. M. Heyman, "Women Students at Berkeley: Views and Data on Possible Sex Discrimination in Academic Programs," as quoted in Roberta Hall, "The Classroom Climate: A Chilly One for Women?" *On Campus with Women*, Project on the Status and Education of Women (Washington, D.C.: Association of American Colleges, 1983).
5. Debra Kaufman, "Associational Ties in Academe: Some Male and Female Differences," *Sex Roles* 4 (1978): 16.

6. Kaufman, p. 20.
7. Kaufman, p. 20.
8. Bernikow, p. 150.
9. Jessie Bernard, *Academic Women* (New York: Viking, 1964), p. 198.
10. Farley, pp. 106-7.
11. Marilyn French, *The Women's Room* (New York: Summit Books, 1977), p. 462.
12. Bernikow, p. 152.
13. Bernikow, p. 134.

7 : The Future of Academe

1. Mary P. Rowe, "Dealing with Sexual Harassment," *Harvard Business Review* 59 (1981): 42-46.
2. Inger W. Jensen and Barbara A. Gutek, "Attributions and Assignment of Responsibility in Sexual Harassment," *Journal of Social Issues* 38 (1982): 133-34.
3. Roberta M. Hall, "The Classroom Climate: A Chilly One for Women?" *On Campus With Women,* Project on the Status and Education of Women, Association of American Colleges (Washington, D.C., 1983).
4. Warren Bennis, *The Leaning Ivory Tower* (San Francisco: Jossey-Bass, 1973), pp. 108-9.
5. Margaret Mead, "A Proposal: We Need Taboos on Sex at Work," *Sexuality in Organizations,* eds. Dail Ann Newgarten and Jay Shafritz (Oak Park, Ill.: Moore Publishing Co., 1980), p. 56.

Selected Bibliography

This selected bibliography focuses on research, theoretical analyses, and documents concerning sexual harassment on campus. It is intended as a guide for individuals conducting research or designing educational programs in this area. In addition, many organizations and campuses have produced informative reports and educational materials helpful to further study and understanding. The Project on the Status and Education of Women, American Association of Colleges, and its newsletter, On Campus with Women, *continue to be valuable sources of news and resource information about sexual harassment on campus.*

Adams, Jean W., Janet L. Kottke, and Janet S. Padgitt. "Sexual Harassment of University Students." *Journal of College Student Personnel* 24 (November 1983): 484-90.

Alexander et al. v. *Yale University,* 459 F. Supp. 1 (D. Conn. 1977), affirmed 631 F.2d 178 (2d Cir. 1980).

Allen, Deborah, and Judy Bessai Okawa. "A Counseling Center Looks at Sexual Harassment." *Journal of the National Association for Women Deans, Administrators, and Counselors* 51 (Fall 1987): 9-16.

American Association of University Professors. "Sexual Harassment: Suggested Policy and Procedures for Handling Complaints." *Academe* 69 (March/April 1983): 15a-16a.

———. "Resolution on Sexual Harassment." *Academe* 66 (November 1980): 390-91.

Arond, Miriam, Madeline Hutcheson, and Ann O'Reilly, "Power Play: Sexual Politics on Campus." *CV: The College Magazine* 1 (April 1989): 32-37.

Backhouse, Constance, and Leah Cohen. *Sexual Harassment on the Job.* Englewood Cliffs, N.J.: Prentice-Hall, 1981.

Barnett, Edith. "Sexual Harrassment: A Continuing Source of Litigation in the Workplace." *Trial* 25 (June 1989): 35-38.

Benson, Donna J., and G. E. Thompson. "Sexual Harassment on a University Campus: The Confluence of Authority Relations, Sexual Interest, and Gender Stratification." *Social Problems* 29 (February 1982): 236-52.

Blanshan, Sue A. "Activism, Research, and Policy: Sexual Harassment." *Journal of the National Association for Women Deans, Administrators, and Counselors* 46 (Winter 1983): 16-22.

Bogart, Karen. "Sexual Harassment in Academe: A New Assessment." Paper presented at the annual meeting of the National Association for Women Deans, Administrators, and Counselors, April 1984. Mimeo.

Brandenburg, Judith Berman. "Sexual Harassment in the University: Guidelines for Establishing a Grievance Procedure." *Signs* 8 (Winter 1982): 320-36.

Brewer, Marilyn B. "Further Beyond Nine to Five: An Integration and Future Directions." *Journal of Social Issues* 38 (1982): 149-57.

Buek, Alexandra. *Sexual Harassment: Fact of Life or Violation of Law? University Liability under Title IX.* Washington, D.C.: National Advisory Council on Women's Educational Programs, 1978.

Cnudde, Charles F., and Betty A. Nesvold. "Administrative Risk and Sexual Harassment: Legal and Ethical Responsibilities on Campus." *PS* 18 (Fall 1985): 780-88.

Collins, Eliza G. C., and Timothy B. Blodgett. "Sexual Harassment, Some See It . . . Some Won't." *Harvard Business Review* 59 (March/April 1981): 76-95.

Crocker, Phyllis L. "An Analysis of University Definitions of Sexual Harassment." *Signs* 8 (Summer 1983): 696-707.

———. "Annotated Bibliography on Sexual Harassment in Education." *Women's Rights Law Reporter* 7 (Winter 1982): 91-106.

Crocker, Phyllis, and Anne E. Simon. "Sexual Harassment in Education." *Capitol University Law Review* 10 (1981): 541-84.

Crosthwaite, Jan, and Christine Swanton. "On the Nature of Sexual Harassment." *Australasian Journal of Philosophy.* Supplement to vol. 64 (June 1986): 91-106.

Deane, Nancy H., and D. L. Tillar. *Sexual Harassment: An Employment Issue.* Washington, D.C: College and University Personnel Association, 1981.

"Discrimination because of Sex under Title VII of the Civil Rights Act of 1964, as Amended: Adoption of Final Guidelines." *Federal Register,* 10 November 1980, 74676-74677.

Equal Employment Opportunity Commission. "Sexual Harassment Guidelines." Code of Federal Regulations, vol. 29. sec. 1604.11.

Farley, Lin. *Sexual Shakedown: The Sexual Harassment of Women on the Job.* New York: McGraw-Hill, 1978.

Fishbein, Estelle A. "Sexual Harassment: Practical Guidance for Handling a New Issue on Campus." Office of the General Counsel, The Johns Hopkins University, 1982.

Franklin, Phyllis, Helen Moglen, Phyllis Zatlin-Boring, and Ruth Angress. *Sexual and Gender Harassment in the Academy.* New York: The Modern Language Association of America, 1981.

Gartland, P. A., and W. Bevliacqu. "Sexual Harassment: Recent Research and Useful Resources." *Journal of the National Association for Women Deans, Administrators, and Counselors* 46 (Winter 1983): 47-49.

Gibbs, A., and R. B. Balthrope. "Sexual Harassment in the Workplace and Its Ramifications for Academia." *Journal of College Student Personnel* 23 (1982): 158-62.

Glaser, Robert D., and Joseph S. Thorpe. "Unethical Intimacy: A Survey of Sexual Contact and Advances between Psychology Educators and Female Graduate Students." *American Psychologist* 41 (January 1986): 43-51.

Goldberg, Alan. "Sexual Harassment and Title VII: The Foundation for the Elimination of Sexual Cooperation as an Employment Condition." *Michigan Law Review* 76 (May 1978): 1007-35.

Gray, Phyllis. "Sexual Harassment in the Classroom and on the Job." *The Woman Engineer* (Spring 1985): 31-34.

Gutek, Barbara A., and C. Y. Nakamura. "Gender Roles and Sexuality in the World of Work." In *Gender Roles and Sexual Behavior: Changing Boundaries.* E. Allgeier and N. McCormick, eds. Palo Alto, Calif.: Mayfield, 1982.

Hall, Roberta M., and Bernice R. Sandler. *The Classroom Climate: A Chilly One for Women?* Project on the Status and Education of Women. Washington, D.C.: Association of American Colleges, 1982.

Hoffman, Frances. "Sexual Harassment in Academia: Feminist Theory and Institutional Practice." *Harvard Educational Review* 56 (May 1986): 105-21.

Hughes, Jean O'Gorman, and Bernice R. Sandler. *Peer Harassment: Hassles for Women on Campus.* Project on the Status and Education of Women. Washington, D.C.: Association of American Colleges, 1988.

————. *In Case of Sexual Harassment: A Guide for Women Students.* Project on the Status and Education of Women. Washington, D.C.: Association of American Colleges, 1986.

Institute of Labor and Industrial Relations Program on Women and Work, University of Michigan/Wayne State University. *Sexual Harassment in the Workplace: A Bibliography*. Ann Arbor: Library Extension Service, 1979.

Jensen, Inger W., and Barbara A. Gutek. "Attributions and Assignments of Responsibility in Sexual Harassment." *Journal of Social Issues* 38 (1982): 121-36.

Kanter, Rosabeth Moss. "Some Effects of Proportions on Group Life, Skewed Sex Ratios and Responses to Token Women." *American Journal of Sociology* 82 (1977): 965-90.

Kaufman, Susan, and Mary Lou Wylie. "One-Session Workshop on Sexual Harassment." *Journal of the National Association for Women Deans, Administrators, and Counselors* 46 (Winter 1983): 39-42.

Keller, Elisabeth A. "Consensual Relationships and Institutional Policy." *Academe* 76 (January-February 1990): 29-32.

———. "Consensual Amorous Relationships between Faculty and Students: The Constitutional Right to Privacy." *Journal of College and University Law* 15 (1988): 21-42.

Kenig, Sylvia, and John Ryan. "Sex Differences in Levels of Tolerance and Attribution of Blame for Sexual Harassment on a University Campus." *Sex Roles* 15 (November 1986): 535-49.

Kraus, Linda. "A Situational Analysis of Sexual Harassment in Academia." Master's thesis, East Carolina University, 1981.

Langevin, Judith Bevis. "Sexual Harassment—Vinson Is Just the Beginning." *Trial* 22 (December 1986): 34-38.

Langevin, Judith Bevis, and Thomas C. Kayser. "Sexual Harassment in Educational Institutions: A Problem Seeking Legal Solutions." *Trial* 24 (June 1988): 29-33.

Largen, Mary Ann. *What to Do If You're Sexually Harassed*. Arlington, Va.: New Responses, 1980.

Largen, Mary Ann., and A. McAdem. *The Sexually Harassed Woman: A Counselor's Guide*. Arlington, Va.: New Responses, 1980.

Lebrato, Mary T., ed. *Help Yourself: A Manual for Dealing with Sexual Harassment*. Sacramento: California State Commission on the Status of Women. 1986.

Livingston, Joy A. "Responses to Sexual Harassment on the Job: Legal, Organizational, and Individual Actions." *Journal of Social Issues* 38 (1982): 5-22.

Lorimer, Linda Koch. "Sexual Harassment: Overview of the Law."

Office of Leadership Seminars, American Council on Education, Washington, D.C., June 1981.

Lott, Bernice, Mary Ellen Reilly, and Dale R. Howard. "Sexual Assault and Harassment: A Campus Community Case Study." *Signs* 8 (Winter 1982): 296-319.

McCormack, Arlene. "The Sexual Harassment of Students by Teachers: The Case of Students in Science." *Sex Roles* 13 (July 1985): 21-32.

MacKinnon, Catherine. *Feminism Unmodified: Discourse of Life and Law.* Cambridge: Harvard University Press, 1987.

———. *Sexual Harassment of Working Women: A Case of Sex Discrimination.* New Haven: Yale University Press, 1979.

Maihoff, Nancy, and Linda Forrest. "Sexual Harassment in Higher Education: An Assessment Study." *Journal of the National Association for Women Deans, Administrators, and Counselors* 46 (Winter 1983): 3-8.

Meek, Phyllis, and Ann Q. Lynch. "Establishing an Informal Grievance Procedure for Cases of Sexual Harassment of Students." *Journal of the National Association for Women Deans, Administrators, and Counselors* 46 (Winter 1983): 30-33.

Metha, Arlene, and Joanne Nigg. "Sexual Harassment on Campus: An Institutional Response." *Journal of the National Association for Women Deans, Administrators, and Counselors* 46 (Winter 1983): 9-15.

Minnich, Elizabeth, Jean O'Barr, and Rachel Rosenfeld, eds. *Reconstructing the Academy: Women's Education and Women's Studies.* Chicago: University of Chicago Press, 1988.

Moss, Debra Cassens. "S-E-X, SEC, & L-A-W S-U-I-T." *ABA Journal* 74 (August 1, 1988): 21.

National Association of College and University Attorneys. *Sexual Harassment on Campus: A Legal Compendium.* Washington, D.C.: National Association of College and University Attorneys, 1988.

Northwest Women's Law Center. *Sexual Harassment in the Schools: A Statewide Project for Secondary and Vocational Schools.* Seattle: Northwest Women's Law Center, 1986.

Padgitt, Steven C., and Janet S. Padgitt. "Cognitive Structure of Sexual Harassment: Implications for University Policy." *Journal of College Student Personnel* 27 (January 1986): 34-39.

Pearson, Carol S., Donna L. Shavlik, and Judith G. Touchton. *Educating the Majority.* New York: American Council on Education/Macmillan, 1989.

Pope, K. S., H. Levenson, and L. R. Schover. "Sexual Intimacy in

Psychology Training: Results and Implications of a National Survey."
American Psychologist 34 (1979): 682-89.

Project on the Status and Education of Women. *Harvard Issues Statement about Sexual Harassment and Related Issues.* Washington, D.C.: Association of American Colleges, 1984.

———. *Title VII Sexual Harassment Guidelines and Educational Employment.* Washington, D.C.: Association of American Colleges, 1980.

———. *What to Do If Sexually Harassed.* Washington, D.C.: Association of American Colleges, 1979.

———. *Sexual Harassment: A Hidden Issue.* Washington, D.C.: Association of American Colleges, 1978.

Pryor, John B., and Jeanne D. Day. "Interpretation of Sexual Harassment: An Attributional Analysis." *Sex Roles* 18 (April 1988): 405-17.

Rearman, Marilyn I., and Mary T. Labrato. *Sexual Harassment in Employment: Investigator's Guidebook.* Sacramento: California State Commission on the Status of Women, 1984.

Reilly, Timothy, Sandra Carpenter, Valerie Dull, and Kim Bartlett. "The Factorial Survey: An Approach to Defining Sexual Harassment on Campus." *Journal of Social Issues* 38 (1982): 99-109.

"Report of the Dean's Advisory Committee on Grievance Procedures." Yale University, New Haven, 1979.

Richardson, L. *Dynamics of Sex and Gender.* Boston: Houghton Mifflin, 1981.

Robertson, Claire, Constance E. Dyer, and D'Ann Campbell. "Campus Harassment: Sexual Harassment Policies and Procedures at Institutions of Higher Learning." *Signs* 13 (Summer 1988): 792-812.

Rowe, Mary P. "Dealing with Sexual Harassment." *Harvard Business Review* 59 (May/June 1981): 42-46.

Safran, Claire. "Sexual Harassment: The View from the Top" and "The Joint *Redbook–Harvard Business Review* Report on Sexual Harassment: A Survey of 2,000 Executives." *Redbook*, March 1981.

———. "What Men Do to Women on the Job: A Shocking Look at Sexual Harassment." *Redbook*, November 1976, pp. 217-24.

Sandler, Bernice R. *Writing a Letter to the Sexual Harasser: Another Way of Dealing with the Problem.* Project on the Status and Education of Women. Washington, D.C.: Association of American Colleges, 1983.

Sandler, Bernice R., et al. "Sexual Harassment: A Hidden Problem." *Educational Record* 62 (1981): 52-57.

Schneider, Beth E. "Graduate Women, Sexual Harassment, and University Policy." *Journal of Higher Education* 58 (January/February 1987): 46-65.

————. "Consciousness about Sexual Harassment among Heterosexual and Lesbian Women Workers." *Journal of Social Issues* 38 (1982): 75-98.

Simon, Lou Anna K., and Linda Forrest. "Implementing a Sexual Harassment Policy at a Large University." *Journal of the National Association for Women Deans, Administrators, and Counselors* 46 (Winter 1983): 23-29.

Simeone, Angela. *Academic Women: Working toward Equality.* South Hadley, Mass.: Bergin & Garvey, 1987.

Somers, Amy. "Sexual Harassment and Employment: Why College Counselors Should Be Concerned." *Journal of the National Association for Women Deans, Administrators, and Counselors* 46 (Winter 1983): 43-46.

————. "Sexual Harassment in Academe: Legal Issues and Definitions." *Journal of Social Issues* 38 (1982): 23-32.

————. "Sexual Harassment: A Call for Responsible Action in the Profession." Paper presented to the Midwest College Placement Association, September 1981. Mimeo.

Stokes, Jean. "Effective Training Programs: One Institutional Response to Sexual Harassment." *Journal of the National Association for Women Deans, Administrators, and Counselors* 46 (Winter 1983): 34-38.

Strauss, Susan. "Sexual Harassment in the School: Legal Implications for Principals." *NASSP Bulletin* 72 (March 1988): 93-97.

Sullivan, Mary, and Deborah I. Bybee. "Female Students and Sexual Harassment: What Factors Predict Reporting Behavior?" *Journal of the National Association for Women Deans, Administrators, and Counselors* 50 (Winter 1987): 11-16.

Terpstra, David R. "Organizational Costs of Sexual Harassment." *Journal of Employment Counseling* 23 (September 1986): 112-19.

Till, Frank J. *Sexual Harassment: A Report on the Sexual Harassment of Students.* Washington, D.C.: National Advisory Council on Women's Educational Programs, 1980.

Tillar, Darrel Long. *Sexual Harassment in Employment: Legal Perspectives for University Administrators.* Occasional Paper Series, No. 8. Charlottesville: Center for the Study of Higher Education, Curry Memorial School of Education, University of Virginia, 1980.

Title IX: The Half Full, Half Empty Glass. Washington, D.C.: National Advisory Council on Women's Educational Programs, 1981.

Tong, Rosemarie. "Sexual Harassment." In *Women and Values: Readings in Recent Feminist Philosophy.* Marilyn Pearsall, ed. Belmont, Calif.: Wadsworth, 1986.

Tuana, Nancy. "Sexual Harassment in Academe: Issues of Power and Coercion." *College Teaching* 33 (1985): 53-63.

United States Merit System Protection Board, Office of Merit Systems Review and Studies. *Sexual Harassment in the Federal Workplace: Is It a Problem?* Washington, D.C.: Government Printing Office, 1981.

Van Tol, Joan, ed. *Sexual Harassment on Campus: A Legal Compendium.* Washington, D.C.: National Association of College and University Attorneys, 1988.

Welzenbach, Lanora, et al., eds. *Sexual Harassment: Issues and Answers. A Guide for Education, Business, Industry.* Washington, D.C.: College and University Personnel Association, 1986.

Wilson, Kenneth R., and Linda A. Kraus. "Sexual Harassment in the University." *Journal of College Student Personnel* 24 (May 1983): 219-24.

Women's Legal Defense Fund. *Legal Remedies for Sexual Harassment.* Washington, D.C.: Women's Legal Defense Fund, 1980.

Working Women United Institute. *Sexual Harassment on the Job: Questions and Answers.* New York: Working Women United Institute, 1975.

Index

247